ASP Web Development with Macromedia Dreamweaver MX 2004

RACHEL ANDREW AND ROB TURNBULL
WITH
ALAN FOLEY AND DREW MCLELLAN

Apress™

ASP Web Development with Macromedia Dreamweaver MX 2004
Copyright © 2004 by Rachel Andrew and Rob Turnbull with Alan Foley and Drew McLellan

ISBN (pbk): 1-59059-349-9

Printed and bound in the United States of America 12345678910

Technical Reviewer: Matt Machell

Editorial Board: Steve Anglin, Dan Appleman, Gary Cornell, James Cox, Tony Davis, John Franklin, Chris Mills, Steven Rycroft, Dominic Shakeshaft, Julian Skinner, Jim Sumser, Karen Watterson, Gavin Wray, John Zukowski

Assistant Publisher: Grace Wong

Project Manager: Sofia Marchant

Copy Editor: Nancy Depper

Production Manager: Kari Brooks

Production Editor: Noemi Hollander

Proofreader: Linda Seifert

Compositor: Diana Van Winkle, Van Winkle Design Group

Indexer: Carol Burbo

Cover Designer: Kurt Krames

Manufacturing Manager: Tom Debolski

Distributed to the book trade in the United States by Springer-Verlag New York, Inc., 175 Fifth Avenue, New York, NY, 10010 and outside the United States by Springer-Verlag GmbH & Co. KG, Tiergartenstr. 17, 69112 Heidelberg, Germany.

In the United States: phone 1-800-SPRINGER, email orders@springer-ny.com, or visit http://www.springer-ny.com. Outside the United States: fax +49 6221 345229, email orders@springer.de, or visit http://www.springer.de.

For information on translations, please contact Apress directly at 2560 Ninth Street, Suite 219, Berkeley, CA 94710. Phone 510-549-5930, fax 510-549-5939, email info@apress.com, or visit http://www.apress.com.

Contents at a Glance

Contents

About the Authors

Rachel Andrew is a director of edgeofmyseat.com, a UK-based web solutions company, and is an experienced web developer. Rachel is a member of the Web Standards Project on the Dreamweaver Task Force, and she hopes to encourage best practices in the support and use of W3C Standards in Dreamweaver. In addition to coauthoring several books, Rachel writes for various magazines and resource sites, both online and offline.

When not writing code or writing about writing code, Rachel spends time with her daughter, tries to encourage people to use Debian GNU/Linux, studies with the Open University, and enjoys a nice pint of beer.

Rob Turnbull is the senior developer for Lighthouse, an established new media design and marketing company based in Shrewsbury, England. Clients across Europe, from small businesses to blue-chip companies, provide an increasing workload, which includes the development of SQL Server database-driven web sites, multimedia presentations, interactive CD-ROMs, promotional videos and DVDs, and 3D artwork in both animated and still form.

Rob's personal web site, `www.robgt.com`, is primarily focused on offering help and guidance to fellow Dreamweaver users, including tutorials and links to helpful resources and some useful extensions.

Alan Foley is an assistant professor of instructional technology at North Carolina State University in Raleigh, North Carolina, where he teaches graduate classes in the College of Education. Alan holds a Ph.D. in educational technology from the University of Wisconsin—Madison. His current research interests include web accessibility and pedagogy, and accessible multimedia production.

Prior to completing his Ph.D., Alan was a high school English teacher. While teaching, he was introduced to the world of instructional technology and web design. He has taught web design in a variety of educational and corporate settings, and consults for schools and universities on accessibility and usability issues.

Drew McLellan is an experienced and knowledgeable web developer with over 7 years' experience designing and developing for the web. Among his strengths he counts a good awareness of design, team leadership, and the ability to communicate technical issues and concepts to nontechnical people. Drew is the author of *Dreamweaver MX Web Development* (New Riders, 2002).

Drew fights for standards in browsers and development tools with the Web Standards Project (`www.webstandards.org`), and he can often be found working on the sharp edge of his industry's technologies, always seeking to push the boundaries. He is an advocate of modular design and reusable code. Drew recently served a 4-year term as a Team Macromedia representative, and he has written a number of technical articles for `www.macromedia.com` and other online publications.

About the Technical Reviewer

A man of many talents, **Matt Machell** has been a web developer, technical editor, author, market researcher, and jewelry picker. He is currently freelancing and lurks on more web design–related discussion lists than is healthy. His personal web site is www.eclecticdreams.com. He lives in Birmingham, England, with his girlfriend, Frances, and lots of books.

Acknowledgments

THANKS MUST GO TO the Apress team, to all those whose brains I have picked on mailing lists and Usenet over the years, to Drew for his constant love and support, and to my daughter Bethany.

Thank you,
Rachel Andrew

CHAPTER 1

Introducing
Dreamweaver MX 2004

THIS NEW RELEASE of Macromedia's industry-leading web-development software brings several new and exciting features to the table. The biggest change is the interface. If you used Dreamweaver MX, you know you could choose the floating panel layout that was familiar to Dreamweaver users from its previous incarnations, or the new MDI (Multiple Document Interface) panel layout that gave the software a much more application-like feel to it. The MDI is standardized in this new release. The old style floating panels are no longer an option.

To help combat the always-present threat of piracy, when you install Dreamweaver, you are now required to activate it, which is a quick and easy process using an online system. You can also activate over the phone or by mail.

The new start page that is displayed when you first run Dreamweaver MX 2004 offers shortcuts to create many different types of documents or a new site. You can also take a guided tour or run the tutorials. Once you have used the program to create or edit documents, a list of the ten most recently opened files is available so you can quickly re-open them, as shown in Figure 1-1.

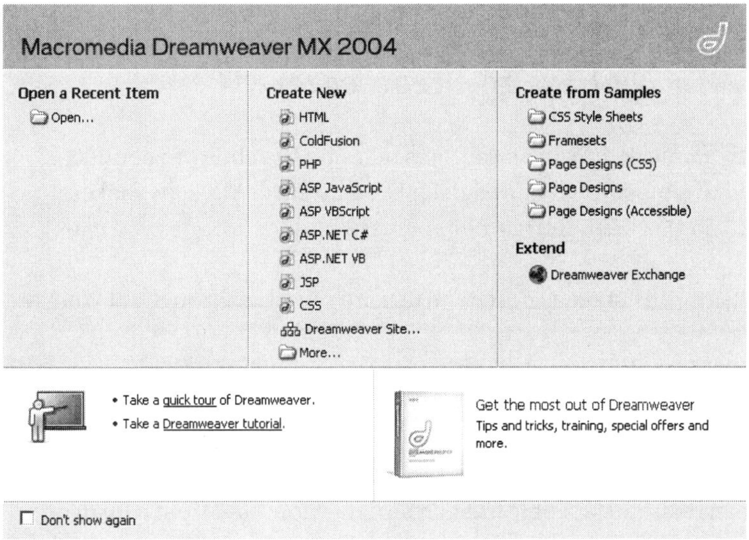

Figure 1-1. Start page

Static to Dynamic

Older versions of Dreamweaver were great for producing static HTML pages. With the release of Dreamweaver MX, though, everything went dynamic! Dynamic web site production is possibly the largest area of web development today, and as more and more web sites are hooked up to databases for their content, the need for a tool to create this new breed of dynamic web application grows.

There are a growing number of server-side languages to choose from in the ever increasing and diversifying market of dynamic web site production. Fortunately, Dreamweaver MX 2004 can help you create your web pages in many of these languages, and because of its extensible architecture. You can add even more to the list, which already includes:

- ASP/VBScript

- ASP/JavaScript

- VB.NET

- C#.NET

- JSP

- PHP

- ColdFusion

Server-Side Technology in Dreamweaver MX

The creation of dynamic data-driven web sites relies on the ability to connect to a data source and to extract the required data. Dreamweaver MX 2004 makes it incredibly easy to do this. With the use of its server-side technologies you can

- Create connections to data sources, which are reusable throughout your site

- Build recordsets to hold the data you want to use on your web pages

- Create database interactions such as inserts, updates, and deletes

- Use basic server-side data objects such as data submitted from a form or session variables

Through the use of an intelligent interface that lets you build only the objects that are permitted for your chosen server-side language, you can quickly create dynamic web applications that utilize the strengths of your chosen development platform.

If you are developing in ColdFusion, you can

- Set up a ColdFusion site automatically

- Create, edit, inspect, and utilize ColdFusion components

- Use internal trace and debug utilities through the Live Server Debugging panel

- Browse database structures and transfer files to and from ColdFusion servers through RDS (Remote Development Services)

If you are developing in ASP.NET you can

- Create `DataSet`, `DataGrid`, and `DataList` objects to enable complex data display and manipulation

- Develop web form tags to allow advanced visualization and editing

- Import custom tags and view their structure attributes

For JSP developers, there is support for JavaBeans introspection, which enables you to integrate them with JSP applications.

In addition, there are commonly shared abilities for each of the server-side development languages, such as recordset creation and data manipulation.

Why You Need Dreamweaver MX 2004

Teamwork is key to the structure of Dreamweaver MX 2004. The check in/out features enable teams of developers to work more productively using visual clues to see who is working on what. The close ties with other applications in the Studio MX 2004 suite also enable team members to more easily contribute to the other areas of application development. Whether you approach web design from a visual design perspective, a coding perspective, or perhaps even a mix of both, Dreamweaver MX 2004 offers many advantages that will empower you to do more in a shorter period of time and more cost-efficiently than previously possible with a single tool.

With Dreamweaver MX 2004, the design elements are in place to enable the easy visual creation of web pages, and the code elements are in place to enable the coding teams to take a visual concept and make it a reality. It packs an impressive punch in terms of its capabilities. but perhaps most importantly, it is a single piece of software that every member of a web development team can use to build the application.

Designing

The integrated workspace is a familiar environment in which to work and is the same across all Macromedia MX products. This makes the transition between Flash MX 2004 and Fireworks MX 2004 to Dreamweaver MX 2004 much easier, which enhances productivity. The content and visuals you create in these Macromedia products are easily brought into the Dreamweaver environment through tight integration.

There are many elements that you can use to quickly visualize sites in Dreamweaver MX 2004, including the quick start elements that can help you lay out single pages or entire sites.

You can utilize the new template features to keep the visual style of a set of pages consistent. Templates are developed through the creation of sophisticated rules, enabling you to manage and update page content without losing control of the design.

An integrated file explorer gives you quick and easy access to any files on your desktop, file system, or network, meaning that no matter where the media you need to incorporate into your page is located, it can be utilized in your page as long as it is accessible on your network. Any media brought to the site from outside of your site structure will automatically be added to the default images location defined when you set up your site.

Coding

Dreamweaver MX 2004 affords you complete control over your code and offers greatly increased editing support through code hints and customizable syntax with coloring for tags, attributes, and more.

- You have an editable, customizable Tag library into which you can add custom tags.

- Tag editors enable you to edit the relevant attributes of specific tags in HTML, CFML, and ASP.NET.

- Code libraries are available to help you visually create your web sites using the leading server-side technologies, including ASP, PHP, ASP.NET, ColdFusion, and JSP.

- The Reference panel houses reference books for each of the server-side technologies, along with several other useful items, such as HTML, JavaScript, SQL, and CSS.

- The Database panel enables you to view the structure of your databases prior to building queries that will draw on their content.

- You have instant access to a large quantity of code snippets that come with the product and are as easy as point-and-click to use. You can also store your own code snippets for reuse. You can even assign keyboard shortcuts to your snippets.

- You can validate documents in many markup languages, including HTML, XHTML, XML, WML, SMIL, and CFML. Creating and editing documents utilizing these languages (and many more) is made easier by Dreamweaver's support for Flash ActionScript coding.

Homesite+ is included with Dreamweaver MX 2004.

Moving Around in Dreamweaver MX 2004

The engineers at Macromedia put a lot of work into the Dreamweaver MX 2004 workspace.

The MDI

The MDI, or **Multiple Document Interface**, as shown in Figure 1-2, brings everything together in a very intuitive way from a development standpoint, so no matter what you need; it is only a mouse-click away.

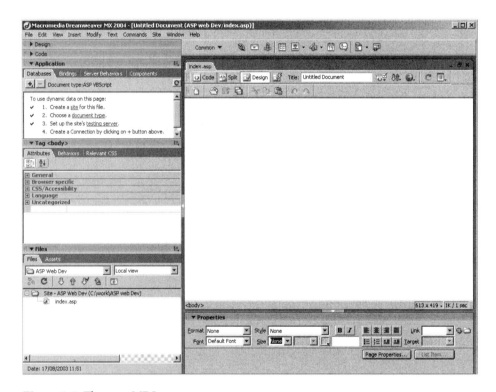

Figure 1-2. The new MDI

As was mentioned earlier, the floating panels layout that was available in previous versions of Dreamweaver has been retired in favor of the MDI interface. When you install and set up Dreamweaver MX 2004, you decide on which side of the main document window to put the panel groups. This can be changed at any time so don't worry about getting it wrong. You can have the panels grouped on the left of the main document window or on the right. This is defined in Dreamweaver MX 2004 as **Designer** (panels grouped on the right) or **Coder** (panels grouped on the left) as shown in Figure 1-3.

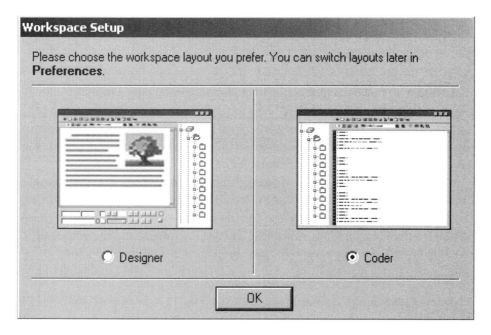

Figure 1-3. The workspace setup preference screen

Neither option will stop you from being able to drag panel groups to the left and right of your workspace to get exactly the working environment you want. The way you arrange your panel groups is entirely up to you.

The main difference between Designer and Coder layouts is what happens when you open a page. In Designer mode, you open a page in Design view by default. In Coder mode, you get the Code view by default.

If you are in the fortunate position of having a multiple monitor configuration, the ability to place panels on multiple screens can give you instant access to even more panels at the same time.

Each panel group has a gripper in its top left corner, which is used to drag panels into position in your environment. The gripper is shown in Figure 1-4.

Figure 1-4. The panel's gripper

When you open a document, the main document toolbars appear. In Dreamweaver MX, each document had a tab at the bottom of the page that had shortcuts to commonly used file options, such as Save, Save As, Close, and so on. In Dreamweaver MX 2004, these tabs are at the top of the document. They have a new look and also have added functionality.

The document that is active in the document window has a solid gray tab; all other open documents have text links. Clicking the text link focuses that document.

The extended functionality of the document tabs includes the ability to close all documents, close all but the currently focused document, and revert the current document's changes back to the last saved version as shown in Figure 1-5.

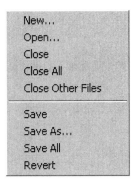

Figure 1-5. The context menu of the Document tab

The Panels

There are 18 panels that make up the Dreamweaver MX environment. Fortunately, you don't have to have them all open at once—that might take up a few monitors worth of space.

The MDI is a fantastic interface because you get to pick and choose which panels are important to your work flow and then group them together exactly how and where you want. You can even rename the panel groups! Let's look at the main panels.

The Tag Inspector Panel

The Tag Inspector panel group contains three panels that cannot be grouped outside that panel group. Nor can you group other panels with this panel group. This is because the Tag Inspector is contextual—the panel group offers relevant items for the currently selected tag in the current document as shown in Figure 1-6.

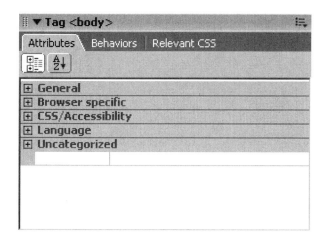

Figure 1-6. The Tag Inspector panel

The first of these three panels is the Attributes panel, the content of which you can display grouped by category or as a list of attributes. The second panel is the Behaviors panel, and the third panel is called Relevant CSS. These are fairly self-explanatory.

The Insert Panel

In Dreamweaver MX, the Insert panel became a tabbed panel that separated the insertable items into their own categories such as Common, Forms, Scripts, and so on.

The Insert panel, now the Insert bar in Dreamweaver MX 2004 doesn't have the tabbed interface by default, instead, it uses a menu similar to that found in the floating panel days of Dreamweaver 4 as shown in Figure 1-7.

Figure 1-7. The Insert panel

If you prefer the tabbed version from Dreamweaver MX, shown in Figure 1-8, click Show as tabs at the bottom of the menu.

Figure 1-8. The Insert panel shown as tabs

Redisplay the menu version by right-clicking in the blue area of the tabbed bar and selecting Show as menu from the options.

Some items on the Insert bar have been conveniently grouped to make them easier to find. For example, the Image button contains a menu of items, including items that used to be separate icons on the Insert bar. It also contains other relevant options, such as image map tools, as shown in Figure 1-9.

Once you have selected an option from the menu, it becomes the default option for that button. The button is split into two parts (shown in Figure 1-10)—the left portion will insert the selected item onto the page, whereas the right portion brings up the menu again so that you can select a different option, which then becomes the default action for that button.

Another great improvement is the Favorites option that has been added to the Insert bar. Here you get to build your own personal toolbar that contains your commonly used Insert bar items (shown in Figure 1-11).

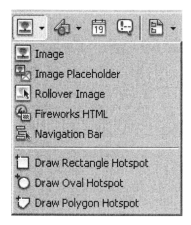

Figure 1-9. The Image button group

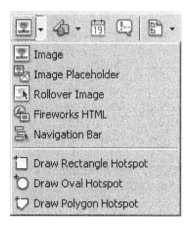

Figure 1-10. The Image button group after its first use

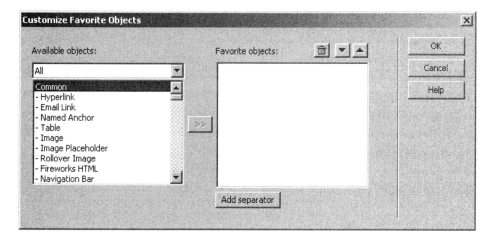

Figure 1-11. The Customize Favorite Objects dialog box

You can start building your favorites bar by right-clicking the gray part of the Insert bar and choosing Customize favorites. Certain Insert bar items are only available for certain server-side language types, and the Insert bar adapts accordingly. You will never see an icon on the Insert bar that cannot be used in your current application.

The Application Panel Group

For the development of dynamic web applications, the Application panel group (shown in Figure 1-12) is very important. It contains a panel that shows your data sources and their structure (databases), the bindings that each page has made to that data source (bindings), and the server-side logic you applied to each page (server behaviors).

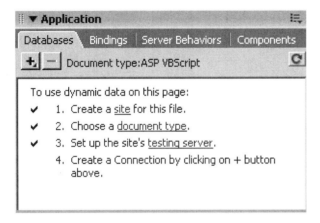

Figure 1-12. The Application panel group

You also have the Components panel grouped here, but if you code in a server-side language that doesn't use components such as ASP/VBScript, you can close it to make room for something else.

The Code Panel Group

The Code panel group contains two panels to help you with the coding side of your development. They are Snippets (shown in Figure 1-13), where you can store reusable lumps of code, and Reference, which is a veritable library!

The Snippets panel comes with many prebuilt code snippets for you to use in your projects.

The Reference panel includes 11 reference books that cover a wide array of topics that you may need. The titles include the following:

- *Macromedia CF Function Reference*

- *Macromedia CFML Reference*

- *O'Reilly ASP.NET Reference*

- *O'Reilly CSS Reference*

- *O'Reilly HTML Reference*

- *O'Reilly JavaScript Reference*

- *O'Reilly PHP Pocket Reference*

- *O'Reilly SQL Language Reference*

- *UsableNet Accessibility Reference*

- *Wrox ASP 3.0 Reference*

- *Wrox JSP Reference*

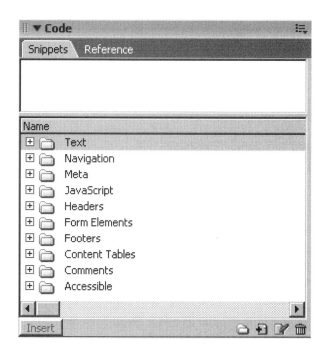

Figure 1-13. The Code panel group with the Snippets panel selected

The Files Panel Group

Your site can be viewed in the traditional full-screen mode or as a panel in your workspace environment (see Figure 1-14). This option gives you access to all your sites' documents and constituent elements as you work on the pages.

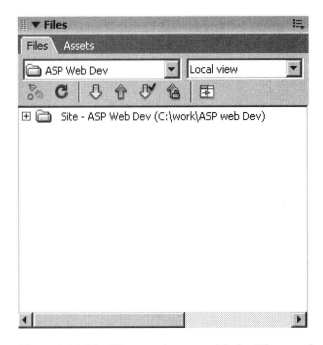

Figure 1-14. The Files panel group with the Files panel selected

The Files panel has all the functionality of the full-screen version with the added bonus of making the drag and drop features of Dreamweaver MX 2004 work even more to your advantage. You can browse your images folder, find an image, and then drag it onto the page, the Properties inspector, or Code view. It is a much more comfortable way of working when you have multiple files open at the same time.

The Files panel also has an integrated file browser that enables you to gather content from anywhere on your local computer or network. Dreamweaver MX 2004 is also smart enough to put any media you find outside of the defined site into your default images folder (which you specify when you define a site—more on that later), bringing that new content into an easily found place within your site. The link-tracking features help you keep your documents up-to-date if you decide to move any item to a new location.

You can use the Files panel for all the standard file maintenance operations, including

- Creating new documents

- Moving files or opening them in their native applications

- Creating, editing, and deleting items such as folders and files

- Transferring files between your local site, your remote site, and your testing server

The Tag Selector

The Tag Selector is located in the status bar at the bottom of the document window, as shown in Figure 1-15.

Figure 1-15. The Tag Selector bar

The Tag Selector displays a hierarchy of tags that starts from the opening <body> tag and ends with the current selection in Design view. In Figure 1-15, the cursor is in a cell of a table which, in turn, is in a form called form1.

Clicking any of the tags listed highlights the content of that tag, whereas right-clicking the tags will display a context menu that enables you to edit the contents of the selected tag, remove the selected tag (and its contents), or set the ID or class (CSS style) of the selected tag.

You can also display the Window Sizes menu from the status bar. You can use this to resize the current document window to any of the listed sizes. You can also add your own sizes to this list. This design tool is useful for visualizing your pages at different screen sizes but it does not affect your code in any way. The menu options are only selectable when your document window is not maximized.

To the right of that menu, on the status bar, there are two figures that represent the estimated document size and the estimated download time based on your preferences. You select a modem speed to use in this calculation by going to Edit ➤ Preferences ➤ Status Bar ➤ Connection Speed (a drop-down menu). The estimated document size is calculated by including all files that make up the document, including but not limited to images, JavaScript, and CSS. The download speeds are estimated on theoretical speeds rather than actual speeds, which can bias the result slightly. Bearing that in mind, it does give you a reasonable indication as to the time your page will take to load.

The Document Toolbar

The Document toolbar gives you instant access to many development tools quickly and easily, as shown in Figure 1-16.

Figure 1-16. The Document toolbar

The three buttons on the left of the toolbar allow you to switch between the three document views: Code, Split, and Design. Let's go through the remaining buttons in order, from left to right.

- The **Live Data View** button is a very powerful feature that allows you to view actual data from your database on the page you are creating, while you are creating it. You can make design changes (or code changes) to your page and see in real time what presentational effect the changes will have on the data being displayed.

- The **Browser Check** button enables you to check your document for compatibility with your target browsers. You can specify exactly which browsers you are targeting and the checker will keep you informed about errors it finds in your document. You can also set it to check your document when you open it. If any errors are found, the icon changes from a green checked check box to a yellow warning triangle. Selecting Show all errors from the menu opens the Results panel and displays the errors that were found. Double-clicking the error in the Results panel locates and highlights the problem in the code.

- The **File Management** button is used for quick access to file actions such as Get, Put, Check in, Check out, and Locate in the site.

- The **Preview/Debug in Browser** button allows you to launch one of the browsers listed for preview/debugging purposes. You can also edit the browser list from this menu.

- The **Refresh Design View** button is there for you to bring the Design view into line with any changes you may have made in Code view. Most of the changes you make will be reflected in Design view but for those times that they are not, this button does the trick.

- The **View Options** button lets you decide how you want certain visual elements to be displayed. You use this menu to specify which of the visual aids that Dreamweaver MX 2004 has to offer you want to use. If you work in Split view, you also have the option of setting Design view to be above or below the code window.

The Standard Toolbar

The Standard toolbar is another useful addition that includes often-used file, clipboard, and page-based commands, as shown in Figure 1-17.

Figure 1-17. The Standard toolbar

From left to right, the first four buttons are: New, Open, Save, and Save All. Next is the clipboard section, including the Cut, Copy, and Paste buttons. Finally, there are the page commands Undo and Redo. A few useful items that are missing from this toolbar includes a Save As button, a Close All button, and a Close Other Files button—these commands can only be accessed from the File menu or by right-clicking the document tab at the top of a maximized document and selecting that command from the menu.

The quickest way to activate the Standard toolbar is to right-click the Document toolbar. A pop-up menu will appear showing a check mark next to the name of each visible toolbar. Make sure the relevant selection is ticked by simply selecting it from that menu.

The Results Panel Group

When you run a validation check or a report on your documents or your entire site, the details are output to the relevant panel of the Results panel group (as shown in Figure 1-18). When results are displayed, you can double-click a line of the report to go directly to that part of the specified document. If that document isn't open yet, it will be opened for you, usually in Split view so you can see the exact part of the code referenced.

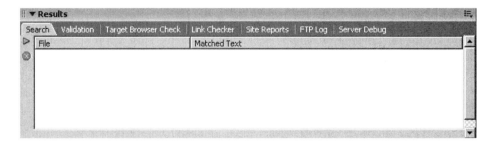

Figure 1-18. The Results panel group

As Figure 1-18 shows, there are seven panels in the panel group, which we'll discuss now.

Search Panel

The Search panel reports every match from Find and Replace actions. The green Play button just below the tab displays the Find and Replace dialog box only if you have a document open. You can also display that dialog box from the context menu (right-click the item) in Code view or the code portion of the Split view. Just below the green Play button is a Stop button that is active only when a Results panel task is running. These and other buttons are available on all except the FTP Log panel and the Server Debug panel. Other buttons you might see in this area are a More info button, which is a white speech bubble with an "i" in it, a Save report button that uses a disk icon, and a Browse report button, which uses a globe icon.

Validation Panel

The Validation panel gives you quick access to the validation options in Dreamweaver MX 2004. The green Play button on this panel has a small black down arrow signifying a submenu is available to you. Clicking the green Play button displays the submenu giving you the following four options:

- **Validate Current Document**: This validates the document that currently has the focus.

- **Validate Entire Site**: This validates the entire site.

- **Validate Selected Files in Site**: This validates all the currently selected files in the site window.

- **Settings**: This launches the Validator section of the preferences palette, allowing you to modify your validation settings .

Target Browser Check Panel

The Target Browser Check panel helps you to check for browser-specific issues with your pages. The default installation of Dreamweaver MX 2004 checks your documents against Internet Explorer 5.0 and Netscape 4.0. You can change these settings to whatever suits your needs, of course, by selecting the relevant options in the Target Browsers dialog box, as shown in Figure 1-19. When you run the browser check, any markup deemed invalid by Dreamweaver MX 2004 will be flagged by a red underline for your attention.

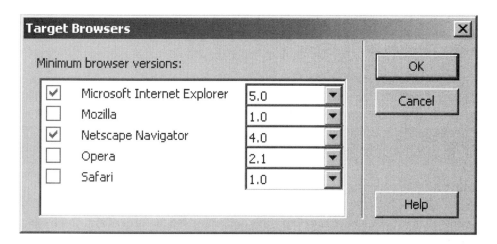

Figure 1-19. The Target Browsers dialog box

These browser profiles are stored in text files and are, of course, extensible, so as new browser versions are released, new profiles can be added to enable you to validate your documents against them.

Link Checker

The Link Checker gives you the option of checking links within the currently open document, within the entire site or within selected file/folders and will report any broken ones.

Site Reports Panel

The Site Reports panel enables you to run various reports on the current document, the entire site, selected files in the site, or a folder, and it can help you quickly identify common mistakes in your HTML files. Once the report is run, you can right-click a row in the Results panel and select More Info from the context menu. This might open up the Reference panel and display the relevant usability reference material that corresponds with your report selection, or it could just display a dialog box that contains information about the problem. Double-clicking a row will display the section of offending code.

FTP Log Panel

The FTP Log panel is a useful tool if you use Dreamweaver MX's FTP tools. Every FTP command issued through Dreamweaver MX is recorded in a log file and this panel can help you find the cause of any problems that occurred during FTP.

Server Debug Panel

The Server Debug panel is only for ColdFusion pages and helps you in your debugging efforts by presenting several pieces of useful information, such as a list of all the pages the server had to process in order to render the page, all the SQL queries that were executed, and all the server variables and their values.

Summary

In this chapter, you saw many of the new and improved features of and you have hopefully gained some insight into the various new technologies that are available to you with this new release.

The design and code features that enable you—as a lone developer or as part of a development team—to work faster and more efficiently have all received attention, along with the updated interface and many of the constituent panels.

The extensibility of Dreamweaver MX 2004 means that a growing number of developers will release extensions that increase its functionality. Some will be free and some will be commercial but they will all bring added value to Dreamweaver.

We will cover building a couple of useful, timesaving extensions in Chapter 9 of this book.

Standards compliance, accessibility, and page validation are strongly featured in Dreamweaver MX 2004 along with tools that enable you to produce pages of code that can be seen by anyone on the Internet.

Speaking of which, this leads us neatly into Chapter 2 where we'll cover web standards and the production of valid XHTML and CSS in Dreamweaver MX 2004.

CHAPTER 2

Web Standards in Dreamweaver

WITH THE LAUNCH OF Dreamweaver MX 2004, Macromedia moves further toward web standards support, incorporating more features that enable web designers to put best practices to work when developing web sites. Using clean, standard markup and separating content from presentation by way of Cascading Stylesheets (CSS) can make your job as an application developer far easier. For example, if you are creating an application that allows clients to update their own pages, CSS controls how that content is formatted so it is more likely to fit the look and feel of the whole site. In this chapter, we will focus on the use of XHTML and CSS when working in Dreamweaver. You will discover

- Why developing in XHTML instead of HTML is a good idea

- How to start working in valid XHTML Transitional

- How to use CSS within Dreamweaver

- How to create a tables-based layout in Dreamweaver using XHTML Transitional

- How to convert that layout to XHTML Strict, using CSS to replace elements that are not allowed in a document that uses a strict DOCTYPE

- How to create a site with a CSS layout in Dreamweaver

- How to handle older browsers when using advanced CSS

Authoring Valid XHTML

This chapter assumes that you are working in XHTML, however, most of the following is equally valid if you are working in HTML because Dreamweaver will add the correct markup depending on the type of DOCTYPE declaration you are using. The DOCTYPE specifies which version of (X)HTML you are using.

If you haven't made the change to XHTML yet, here are some reasons why you might want to make that move.

- **Cleaner markup**: HTML allows developers to write markup in a very flexible manner. Although web browsers are good at interpreting and displaying markup, it can be very difficult to manipulate the document in any other way because the flexibility that current desktop browsers allow can lead to untidy, sloppy markup. A valid XHTML document can easily be read by traditional browsers as well as other devices (such as PDAs and other mobile devices) that lack the processing power needed to interpret sloppy markup.

- **Greater platform independence**: XHTML's insistence on clean, structured markup makes it far easier to port documents to different environments. As mentioned earlier, not all devices have the power of a traditional web browser to interpret incorrect or convoluted markup and display it correctly. XHTML's strict nature means it is far more likely to be displayed correctly on all devices.

- **Accessibility**: XHTML documents must adhere to strict rules. This makes it easier for alternative devices such as Braille readers, screen readers, and other assistive technologies to interpret the content and present it to the user in a useful and navigable manner. A valid XHTML document leaves no room for non-standard markup, therefore eliminating the chance of anything in the document interfering with its accessibility. A side effect of making your document accessible for users of alternate devices is that it becomes more accessible to search engine spiders. Clean, correct markup is far easier for a robot to index, which gives it a better chance of finding the real content of your site.

- **Forward compatibility**: There will be no future version of HTML. Browser manufacturers are looking toward the future with new releases, and although it is unlikely that we will see support for HTML dropped any time soon, it is always a good idea to work to the newest standards. By doing so, your pages are far less likely to break when the next versions of the major browsers appear on the scene. As you will see later in this chapter, working with the Transitional DOCTYPE enables you to create XHTML documents that will be displayed properly in older browsers, while still creating a document that validates against an XHTML DOCTYPE.

- **Learning the rules of XML**: XML is here to stay. By writing XHTML documents, you are adhering to the strict rules of XML markup, which will stand you in good stead in the future. Getting into the habit of creating well-formed documents will make creating XML documents for different applications in the future second nature to you.

- **Integrating with other XML applications**: XHTML allows the incorporation of tags from other XML definitions, such as MathML (Mathematical Markup Language), SMIL (Synchronized Multimedia Integration Language), and SVG (Scalable Vector Graphics). This might not seem particularly useful to many designers and developers today, but it is likely to become more important as uptake and use of other XML applications grows. Learning XHTML at this relatively early stage will make your résumé and skills look very up to date.

- **Page load time**: Valid XHTML documents load faster because the browser does not need to reinterpret bad markup. HTML is lenient about unclosed tags and improperly nested markup, so it leaves more to the interpretation of the browser. Additionally, HTML's inherent flexibility encourages sloppy markup, which in turn can add load time onto the page through increased file size. As you move toward creating XHTML pages that follow the Strict Document Type Declaration (DTD), you need to move style and presentation aspects into CSS, thus trimming your pages down further. Despite the increasing numbers of people with broadband high-speed connections, page-load time is still an important issue. Although writing valid, well-structured HTML will also enable faster-loading pages, XHTML enforces that strictness and prevents sloppiness from creeping in. Dreamweaver MX 2004 makes it very easy to switch from working in HTML to working in XHTML, and there is no reason why the change should be problematic for you. Sites written in XHTML perform just as well in older browsers as HTML 4 sites, so there are no issues with backward compatibility. If you are about to start work on a new site with the help of this book, why not take the plunge and go XHTML!

The Rules of Writing XHTML

For anyone with a reasonable understanding of HTML, XHTML is not difficult to learn and, of course, Dreamweaver MX will help you all the way. All you need to do is follow a few simple rules that are common to all XML (and therefore XHTML) documents.

Document Type Declaration

An XHTML document must validate against one of the following three XHTML DTDs:

- XHTML Strict
  ```
  <!DOCTYPE html PUBLIC "-//W3C//DTD XHTML 1.0 Strict//EN"
  "http://www.w3.org/TR/xhtml1/DTD/xhtml1-strict.dtd">
  ```

- XHTML Transitional
  ```
  <!DOCTYPE html PUBLIC "-//W3C//DTD XHTML 1.0 Transitional//EN"
  "http://www.w3.org/TR/xhtml1/DTD/xhtml1-transitional.dtd">
  ```

- XHTML Frameset
  ```
  <!DOCTYPE html PUBLIC "-//W3C//DTD XHTML 1.0 Frameset//EN"
  "http://www.w3.org/TR/xhtml1/DTD/xhtml1-frameset.dtd">
  ```

As you will see later in this chapter, XHTML Strict doesn't allow any deprecated elements or framesets, XHTML Transitional supports deprecated elements (those elements that have been flagged for removal in future versions of (X)HTML) but not frames, and XHTML Frameset is the transitional version that supports deprecated elements and frames. There must be a DOCTYPE declaration in the document above the `<html>` tag, and it must reference one of the XHTML DTDs. Dreamweaver MX inserts the XHTML Transitional DTD as default when you create a document with the Make Document XHTML Compliant check box selected in the New Document dialog box, as shown in Figure 2-1. However, if you are creating a frameset, it will insert the Frameset DTD.

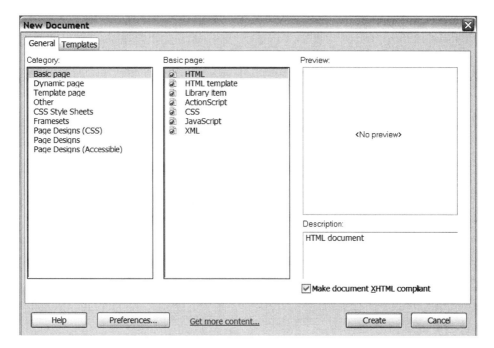

Figure 2-1. The New Document dialog box

Today's web contains a varied mix of web sites; some are written to the new standards of HTML 4.01 or XHTML, and others are a mixture of HTML versions utilizing browser-specific tags and quirks for specific effects. In order to cope with this, the latest browser releases use the DOCTYPE to decide whether the document's author expects a standards-compliant browser to render the page or whether the page was written for older, non standards compliant browsers and might rely on quirky, non-standard behavior. DOCTYPE "sniffing" as it has come to be described, relies on the fact that most of these quirky documents either have no DOCTYPE or use an old DOCTYPE.

Using any of the XHTML examples shown earlier will cause modern browsers to switch into standards-compliant mode and render your pages relatively close to the W3C specifications. Please note that using the XML declaration or prolog (<?xml version="1.0" encoding="UTF-8" ?>) at the top of your document will switch Internet Explorer 6 back into Quirks mode, causing IE6 to presume that you want to display your pages as they would appear in older versions of browsers, whereas Netscape 6+ and Mozilla will display your pages in a standards-compliant manner. This was added in the previous version of Dreamweaver, so if you want to work to standards-compliant mode, the best advice is to remove it. Your pages will still be valid XHTML documents without it.

If you are still working in HTML, you can also work in standards-compliant mode by using a complete HTML 4.01 DOCTYPE (that contains a URL).

```
<!DOCTYPE HTML PUBLIC "-//W3C//DTD HTML 4.01 ↵
Transitional//EN" "http://www.w3.org/TR/html4/loose.dtd">
```

If you use an incomplete DOCTYPE (like the one displayed as follows) or no DOCTYPE at all, IE 6, Mozilla and Netscape 6 will presume that you want your pages to look as they did in older versions of browsers and revert to their Quirks mode.

```
<!DOCTYPE HTML PUBLIC "-//W3C//DTD HTML 4.01 Transitional//EN">
```

Quotation Marks

All attribute values must be enclosed in quotation marks. In the following `<img>` tag, the height and width attributes are incorrectly defined:

```
<img height=100 width=300 alt="my logo" src="logo.gif" />
```

This is the correct way to do it:

```
<img height="100" width="300" alt="my logo" src="logo.gif" />
```

Although previous versions of Dreamweaver tended to quote attributes correctly, you may find that code snippets that you or other developers on your team use may not be as carefully written. Selecting Commands ➤ Clean Up XHTML will add quotation marks where they are needed in your document.

Case Sensitivity

Element and attribute names must be in lowercase. Both of these lines are incorrect.

```
<IMG HEIGHT="100" WIDTH="300" ALT="my logo" SRC="logo.gif" />
<img HEIGHT="100" WIDTH="300" ALT="my logo" SRC="logo.gif" />
```

Here is the correct XHTML.

```
<img height="100" width="300" alt="my logo" src="logo.gif" />
```

If you have always written your HTML tags in uppercase to easily differentiate between tags and content, you may find this change difficult at first. JavaScript event handlers such as `onclick` or `onmouseover` must also be written in lowercase.

The following JavaScript is incorrect:

```
onMouseOver="MM_swapImage('img1','','i/button01b.gif',1)
```

This is the correct way to do it:

```
onmouseover="MM_swapImage('img1','','i/button01b.gif',1)"
```

When working with an XHTML document, Dreamweaver MX will generate lowercase code, including JavaScript. If you are working in HTML, you can choose whether to use uppercase or lowercase for HTML tags in the Preferences dialog box. However, it is not a bad idea to begin to work in lowercase, even in HTML, because it will be necessary in the future.

Closing Tags for Non-Empty Elements

A non-empty element is a tag that contains something between the start tag and the end tag. Some HTML elements can be written without the closing tag, for example, the closing `</p>` tag of the paragraph element is optional and therefore omitted by many HTML authors. In XHTML however, all elements must be closed.

The following, although valid in HTML, is incorrect in XHTML:

```
<p>This is some text formatted in a paragraph.
<p> This is the second paragraph.
```

This is the XHTML way of marking up the same text:

```
<p>This is some text formatted in a paragraph.</p>
<p> This is the second paragraph.</p>
```

Dreamweaver MX closes all non-empty elements whether you are working in HTML or XHTML, and will add closing tags when you run the Clean Up HTML command.

Empty Elements

Empty elements are those HTML tags that stand alone and do not include any-thing between the beginning and end tag, such as `<br>` and `<hr>`. In XHTML these need to be closed—`<br>` and `<hr>` become `<br />` and `<hr />` in XHTML.

> **NOTE** *There is a space after the tag and before the forward slash. Although it is also correct to close your tags without this additional space, the space will allow those browsers that do not recognize XHTML to display your content correctly.*

Dreamweaver uses the correct syntax for empty tags such as `<br />` when gen-erating markup in an XHTML document and also when cleaning up XHTML.

Nesting

An XHTML document must be well formed. This means that all tags must nest correctly—the first tag you open should be the last tag you close. Incorrect nesting is illegal in SGML-based languages but was tolerated by browsers.

This is an example of badly formed markup.

```
<p><strong>This is bold text.</p></strong>
```

This is the proper way of nesting the tags.

```
<p><strong>This is bold text.</strong></p>
```

Dreamweaver nests elements correctly and will also correct nesting of ele-ments when cleaning up XHTML.

Attribute Minimization

Attribute minimization is the practice of writing only the attribute's name without specifying a value, which sets the attribute to its default value. Attributes in valid XHTML documents cannot be minimized. All attributes should be written as name/value pairs even where this means that the value is the same as the name.

This is incorrect in XHTML.

```
<input type="checkbox" name="checkbox" id="checkbox" value="True" checked />
```

This is the corrected version.

```
<input type="checkbox" name="checkbox" id="checkbox" value="True"
      checked="checked" />
```

Dreamweaver inserts this correct markup and also converts minimized attributes to name/value pairs if you convert an HTML document into XHTML.

Here is an example of an XHTML document that complies with the guidelines.

```
<?xml version="1.0" encoding="iso-8859-1"?>
<!DOCTYPE html PUBLIC "-//W3C//DTD XHTML 1.0 Transitional//EN" ⤷
"http://www.w3.org/TR/xhtml1/DTD/xhtml1-transitional.dtd">
<html xmlns="http://www.w3.org/1999/xhtml">
  <head>
    <title>My XHTML Document</title>
  </head>
  <body>
    <p><strong>Hello! World</strong></p>
  </body>
</html>
```

Best Practices for Markup

In the future, we will all need to think more about the various devices that are accessing our web sites: not just devices to enable people with disabilities to access the web, but also the PDAs, phones, and similar devices that are now being used. Using HTML tags inappropriately causes enough problems when the content is being accessed with traditional web browsers; the problems are even greater when the content is accessed by devices likely to have a more limited capacity.

Working in a visual development environment enables rapid development of documents and web sites. However, it can cause us to forget what is actually happening in the code as we move things around the document window, aiming for the right look and feel for our latest project. By structuring a document badly or using tags inappropriately, your document may validate, but it could still cause accessibility problems for those on alternative devices.

Deciding whether your document is structured logically isn't something that an automated validator can do easily, however, it is very easy to do yourself. Simply turn off CSS in your browser or remove your stylesheet link, and see whether the content in your document is still logically presented once it defaults to the browser's standard way of styling the elements.

In addition to checking that it looks sensible and well structured, you can also consider the following points.

Do Not Use Font Tags for Styling and Sizing Text

Today's widely used browsers can all use CSS for styling text. Although you may be reluctant to move to CSS for page layout, there is simply no reason to ignore the huge benefits of using CSS instead of `<font>` tags for text styling. The cleaner markup that results from the removal of font tags leads to faster downloads and easier maintenance and redesign of a site. All standard desktop browsers released in the last five years have CSS support for text styling so there is no point in using font tags.

Use Heading Tags for Structure

The heading levels (`<h1>` to `<h6>`) provided by (X)HTML are designed to give structure to the document; they are not supposed to be an easy way to have different sized titles. Although you may use CSS to alter the appearance of these tags, make sure that you are using them logically within the document so that any browser or device that does not recognize the CSS can still follow the structure of the document correctly. A related issue is the use of `<p>` tags with a larger font size used as a heading. If the text is a heading, use a heading tag for it.

Do Not Use Block Quotes for Indentation

For the same reasons that you should not use the heading tags simply for sizing, `<blockquote>` (and lists) should not be used to indent text. A nontraditional browser may well interpret `<blockquote>` as a quote; if you want to indent text for appearance only, use CSS to create a custom class for this purpose. For example in Dreamweaver, create a new CSS class named `.indent`. Give this class a padding of 40 pixels on the left. To indent any paragraph, simply apply this class.

```
<p class="indent">This is my paragraph that I would like to be indented.</p>
```

This gives you far more control over the indentation than simply using `<blockquote>`, and it ensures that your document remains understandable.

Mark Lists as Lists

In HTML 4.01 and XHTML there are three, non-deprecated list definitions to choose from: Ordered list, Unordered list, and Definition list. It is important to use the correct type of list when entering your information—do not simply choose one for visual effect. Once again, if you are going for a certain look, use CSS to achieve it.

Ordered Lists

Use Ordered lists for a list of items numbered in sequential order, for example, a list of step-by-step instructions or ranked items.

```
<ol>
        <li>list item one</li>
        <li>list item two</li>
</ol>
```

This is displayed in most browsers, as shown in Figure 2-2.

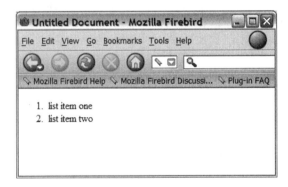

Figure 2-2. Ordered list in a browser

Unordered Lists

Use Unordered lists for a list of unordered items, for example, a list of attributes.

```
<ul>
        <li>list item one</li>
        <li>list item two</li>
</ul>
```

This is displayed in most browsers, as shown in Figure 2-3.

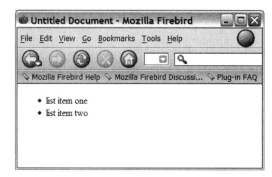

Figure 2-3. Unordered list in a browser

Definition Lists

Use a Definition list if you have a list of items and explanations. By using this type of list, you make it clear to someone using an assistive technology such as a screen reader (or other device that can only see the structure of the document) that the list contains items and their definitions.

If you create this kind of list just by altering the presentational aspects of the page, your intentions may not be clear to someone who cannot see that presentation. The definition list includes <dt> tags for terms and <dd> tags for definitions.

```
<dl>
        <dt>the term</dt>
        <dd>the definition</dd>
        <dt>another term</dt>
        <dd>another definition</dd>
</dl>
```

This markup is displayed in most browsers as shown in Figure 2-4.

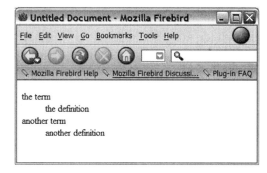

Figure 2-4. Definition list in a browser

Special Characters

When inserting special characters such as brackets (< >) or the ampersand (&),
you should always use the correct Unicode character entities. When you enter
common characters into Design view, Dreamweaver MX enters the correct character code for you, for example adding < in place of < and & in place of &. However, if you are working in Code view or need to insert a character that is not on
your keyboard, there are additional characters available from the Text tab of the
Insert toolbar that you can insert into the document. The Text tab is shown in
Figure 2-5.

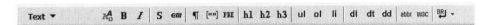

Figure 2-5. Character entities in Insert toolbar

The more unusual characters can be found by clicking the button on the right
of the Characters tab (or clicking the arrow on the far right and selecting Other
Characters), which opens a panel of characters for you to choose from and insert
into your document, as shown in Figure 2-6.

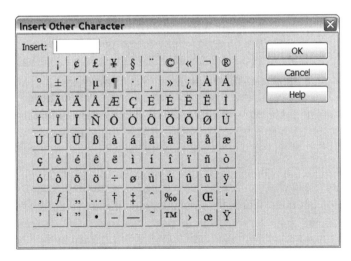

Figure 2-6. More character entities

XHTML in Dreamweaver MX 2004

Whether you are new to XHTML or an experienced developer looking for a quicker way of working, Dreamweaver MX can help you write valid XHTML quickly and accurately.

Setting Preferences

Setting your preferences will ensure that Dreamweaver MX is working with you to create valid XHTML or HTML documents right from the outset. To access the Preferences dialog box, select Edit ➤ Preferences.

The General Pane

In the General pane of the Preferences dialog box, make sure that the "Use <strong> and <em> instead of <b> and <i>" option is checked.

The<b> and <i> tags won't cause your page to be invalid, but from a best practices point of view, it is suggested that you use <strong> and <em> instead. Why? Because <b> for bold text and <i> for italic text are presentational tags designed to tell the browser how something should look. The <strong> and <em> tags are logical tags that tell the browser or device that the document author wants a word or statement to have particular emphasis. A screen reader, for example, may interpret these tags differently, with an inflection designed to give the person listening to the page the same understanding as someone seeing bold or italic text.

Your page should look exactly the same in a conventional browser whichever choice you make, so this is one place where making a small change can really lift the accessibility of your web site without you needing to do anything that might alter the look of the pages.

While in this pane, make sure that the Allow Multiple Consecutive Spaces check box is well and truly unchecked! If this is checked, pressing the spacebar will insert multiple   into your code, which is really annoying! From a best practices viewpoint, indentation of page elements should be created with CSS, and not by adding non-breaking spaces.

The Accessibility Pane

In the "Show Attributes when inserting" area of the Accessibility pane, ensure that the Images check box is checked. For your documents to validate against accessibility requirements they must have alt text. This dialog box will remind you to add that text each time you insert an image. If you are keen to create valid and accessible code, you may want to check the Form Objects, Frames, Media, and Tables check boxes too. These features will be discussed further in Chapter 4.

The New Document Pane

If you want to use XHTML for future work, you can set Dreamweaver MX to make new documents XHTML-compliant automatically. To do so, check the Make document XHTML compliant check box in this pane. Alternatively, you can choose to make documents XHTML-compliant each time you create a new document in Dreamweaver MX, although the original default will be HTML.

The Validator Pane

In this pane, you can set which DTD you want to validate against with the internal validator. Check the DTD that you will most often use—you can always go back and change it if you are working on a site with a different DTD.

Authoring Valid CSS

CSS allows the separation of content and structure from the presentation. HTML was originally designed as a language to allow creation of easy-to-read, structured documents. Formatting tags (such as <font>) were added by the browser companies (notably Netscape) to extend the capabilities of HTML, and many of these later became part of the official specifications. The CSS1 specification covers basic CSS mainly for text styling. This specification is widely implemented across all the main browsers. The CSS2 specification builds on CSS1 and adds support for positioning elements. Although much of this specification is implemented across browsers, you still need to test thoroughly when using it because it is newer and has been implemented slightly differently between browsers.

Why Use CSS?

If you are working to standards (and especially if you want to validate against a Strict DOCTYPE) you will need to replace presentational tags and attributes in your (X)HTML with CSS. This may sound like a lot of extra work, but it brings many benefits.

Separating Document Structure from Presentation

You will see this phrase a lot wherever stylesheets are discussed. In practice, it means that all information describing how the document *looks* is removed from the HTML and put into stylesheet rules. All information that defines the content and document structure remains in the HTML. Elements such as headings `<h1>` through to `<h6>`, paragraphs (`<p>`), tables for tabular data (`<table>`), and so on are used to describe the structure and content of the document. Other elements and attributes are typically used for presentational purposes, such as the `color` and `font` attributes for setting text colors and fonts, and `align`, `margin`, `border`, and `padding` attributes for positioning content.

By removing these presentational HTML elements and attributes and replacing them with stylesheets, your pages will become smaller and far easier to read and debug.

Accessibility

CSS allows precise control over layout, obviating tag misuse. Screen readers and other technologies interpret the markup by using the HTML tags that are present on the page. If inappropriate markup is used, a person who is blind will find your page confusing because the structure and meaning of your document is not clear.

Modern browsers allow users to override your styles with a user stylesheet. You might not think this is a good idea at first—why would you want users to replace your carefully crafted stylesheet with theirs? But users with low vision can apply a stylesheet that uses large fonts or high contrast, allowing them to interact with your site much more easily.

By using CSS, you can easily change the font size, colors, and even layout of your site simply by changing the stylesheet. Many sites now offer different themes, for example, providing a high-contrast color scheme or large text in order to assist those who would have difficulty reading your site otherwise. One example of this is `http://www.zeldman.com`. By displaying different stylesheets, designers aren't so restricted in their design choices when attempting to make their sites both visually appealing and accessible to people with disabilities or alternative devices. We will return to the issue of displaying different stylesheets later in this chapter.

More Flexibility in Design

Using HTML tags to lay out and style your pages gave you limited ways in which to resize and position page elements. Using `<font size="xx">` allows resizing, but CSS enables you to specify the spacing between words, letters, and lines of text, and add or reduce the amount of padding around `<h1>` or other structural tags. CSS2 goes even further, allowing positioning of page elements outside of the grid layout made necessary by using tables as a layout tool.

Smaller File Sizes

Moving to CSS allows you to control the visual appearance of all the elements across your entire site with one stylesheet. More advanced use of CSS can produce effects that previously would have required an image such as the layering of page elements.

Browser Support

CSS is very browser friendly. If a browser or device does not support CSS the browser just ignores the stylesheet and renders the content with its default settings. Apart from certain bugs in traditional web browsers (which we will discuss later), the use of CSS will not render your pages inaccessible to someone who is using an older browser or device that does not support CSS.

Shortening Development Time

Once you have set up a stylesheet for the common elements across your site, adding new pages that are consistent with the rest of the site is simple because any page that has the stylesheet linked will adopt the same styles for headings, paragraphs, borders, and other elements. Should you want to change the font or the color scheme used throughout the site, only one stylesheet needs to be altered for the changes to be reflected across the entire site consistently.

The Basics of CSS

Before you dive into working with CSS within Dreamweaver MX, you should understand some of the basic concepts of CSS design. If you used CSS in the past, this section will serve as a refresher.

Ways to Implement CSS

There are three ways in which to implement CSS in your web site or document: inline, embedded, or externally.

Inline Stylesheets

An inline style definition is a one-time style definition placed in your code to style only the element to which it is attached. By using this method you will lose many of the benefits of CSS because you will need to style each element individually, which is the same way that you use font tags or other presentational HTML.

```
<h1 style=" font-family: Verdana, Arial, Helvetica, sans-serif; color: #663366;">
```

This markup only affects that particular `<h1>` tag on that page. If this were the only time that you ever used this style in your site, you might consider using an inline style. If it is going to be used more than once, however, it would be better to make this into a class and apply it to the `<h1>` tag because you could reuse the class for other instances of this style. Using an inline style will override anything you have defined for this tag in your stylesheet for this instance of the tag, so it can be useful if you want just one `<h1>` tag to look different to the others. See the "Cascading Stylesheets" section for more information.

Embedded Stylesheets

An embedded stylesheet controls only the elements on that page, and the CSS code is placed in the head of the document. In the following code example, any `<h1>` tags in the document will be colored purple. However, this CSS will not be applied to any other pages on the site.

```
<head>
<title>CSS Example</title>
<style type="text/css">
<!--
h1 {
```

```
    font-family: Verdana, Arial, Helvetica, sans-serif;
    color: #663366;
}
-->
</style>
</head>
```

If you want to use this style on every page of your site and were using the embedded method, you would need to add this code to every page, meaning that changing the ‹h1› from purple to orange would involve changing it on every page of the site.

External Stylesheets

An external stylesheet is the most useful and flexible way to use CSS. By linking to a single external stylesheet from all pages of your web site, each page uses the definitions from that stylesheet. Changing the purple ‹h1› tags to orange throughout the site involves one simple change to the external stylesheet. A simple link to an external stylesheet looks like this.

```
<link href="global.css" rel="stylesheet" type="text/css" />
```

We will discuss the design and implementation of external CSS further later in this chapter.

Cascading Stylesheets

The "cascading" in CSS refers to the fact that styles defined closer to the element will overwrite any other rules set. For example, consider the following:

```
h1 {
    font-family: Verdana, Arial, Helvetica, sans-serif;
    color: #663366;
}
```

If you set this in an external stylesheet, but decide that on one particular page you want all ‹h1› tags to be a different color, you could add a style rule in an embedded stylesheet in the head of that document that would override the external stylesheet rule. If you then decide you wanted a single specific ‹h1› tag on this particular page to be yet another color, you could use an inline style on that specific tag and it would take precedence over styles set in the embedded and external stylesheets.

Redefining How HTML Tags Look in the Browser

You have already seen how redefining HTML tags with CSS rules can change the way these structural tags are rendered and preserve the structure of your markup. This method provides a simple way of creating and maintaining a consistent look and feel for your site without bloating the HTML with presentational markup. If you are working with several authors who each add content to the site, redefining tags means that their content will fit with the rest of the site because the content will use the formatting defined in your stylesheet.

Creating CSS Classes

CSS classes allow you to create rules for page elements that have classes applied to them. For instance, if in the stylesheet you have the following:

```
.myborder {
  border-width: 1px;
  border-color: #000000;
  border-style: solid;
}
```

Then any element, such as the following `<img>`, with a class of border applied will have a one-pixel wide black border around it.

```
<img alt="me" height="80" width="40" src="me.jpg" class="myborder" />
```

> **TIP** *Netscape 4 renders this border in a strange way and will cause the image to become non-clickable if it is a link. This is just one of the problems that you may encounter while using CSS with Netscape 4. Later in this chapter we will discuss ways to cope with old browsers.*

CSS Tools in Dreamweaver MX 2004

Dreamweaver has a variety of tools that make working with CSS easier.

Setting Preferences

The following preferences will enable you to become comfortable working within the Dreamweaver environment with CSS.

CSS Styles

Open the Preferences dialog box (shown in Figure 2-7) by selecting Edit ➤ Preferences then selecting the CSS Styles category.

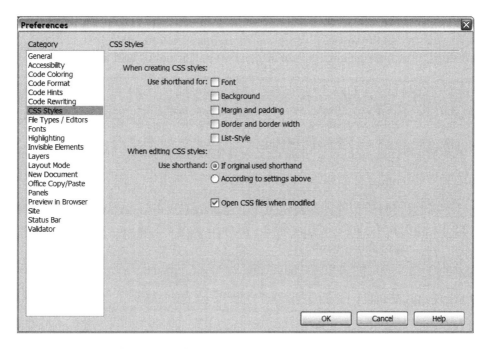

Figure 2-7. The Preferences dialog box

CSS allows shorthand and longhand syntaxes for either brevity or clarity. A snippet of CSS code in longhand syntax looks like this.

```
.longhand {
font-family: Arial, Helvetica, sans-serif;
  font-size: small;
  color: #660066;
  text-decoration: underline;
}
```

In this dialog box, checking the Use Shorthand For boxes forces Dreamweaver to use the shorthand syntax.

```
.shorthand {
  font: small Arial, Helvetica, sans-serif;
  color: #660066;
  text-decoration: underline;
}
```

These rules are displayed in exactly the same way in any browser.

More important are the radio buttons at the bottom. If you are creating a stylesheet in another editor such as TopStyle but then make edits in Dreamweaver, you should make sure that any rules Dreamweaver adds are consistent with the style you used in the rest of your stylesheet. In this situation, select the "When editing CSS style: Use Shorthand: if original used shorthand" option.

> **TIP** *You may find that certain rules work when declared in shorthand and not in longhand in certain browsers, particularly in older browsers such as Netscape 4. If you are using the shorthand syntax to handle these problems, it is important to make sure Dreamweaver is set up to assist you with this.*

If you check the final check box on this dialog box, Dreamweaver will open the CSS file when it is modified. This means you can keep a close eye on what the software is adding to your stylesheet.

File Types/Editors

To specify another editor as your default CSS editor, go to Preferences ➤ File Types/Editors, as shown in Figure 2-8.

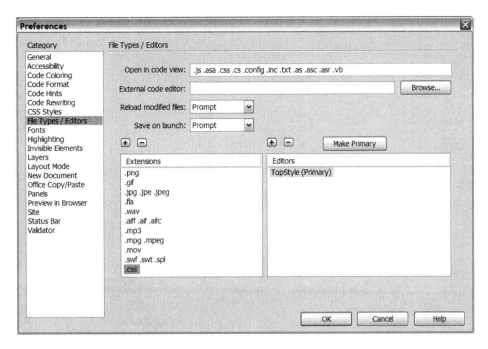

Figure 2-8. File Types/Editors

We will discuss integrating an external editor later in this chapter.

The CSS Panel

The CSS panel enables you to attach stylesheets to your page, create new styles (either in a new stylesheet, an existing stylesheet, or embedded in your document), and edit styles already created.

Creating a Simple Stylesheet in Dreamweaver

To create a new stylesheet click the New CSS Style button, which is the second button from the left on the CSS panel, as shown in Figure 2-9.

Figure 2-9. The CSS panel with New CSS Style button highlighted

This displays a New CSS Style dialog box, as shown in Figure 2-10.

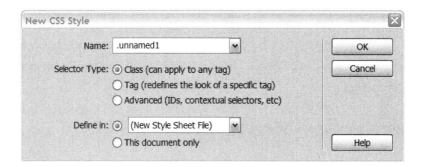

Figure 2-10. The New CSS Style dialog box

You will need to create a style definition in order to create a new stylesheet, so a good place to start is with the basic font styles for the body text of the page. Select the Tag (redefines the look of a specific tag) radio button. Next, in the drop-down menu at the top of the page, select Body. Then select the radio button to "Define in New Style Sheet File" and click OK.

Because this is a new stylesheet, a Save As dialog box will appear so that you can save your stylesheet. Make sure that you add the `.css` extension on the end of your stylesheet name (in other words, save as `global.css` and not just `global`). Once you have saved it, the dialog box shown in Figure 2-11 appears.

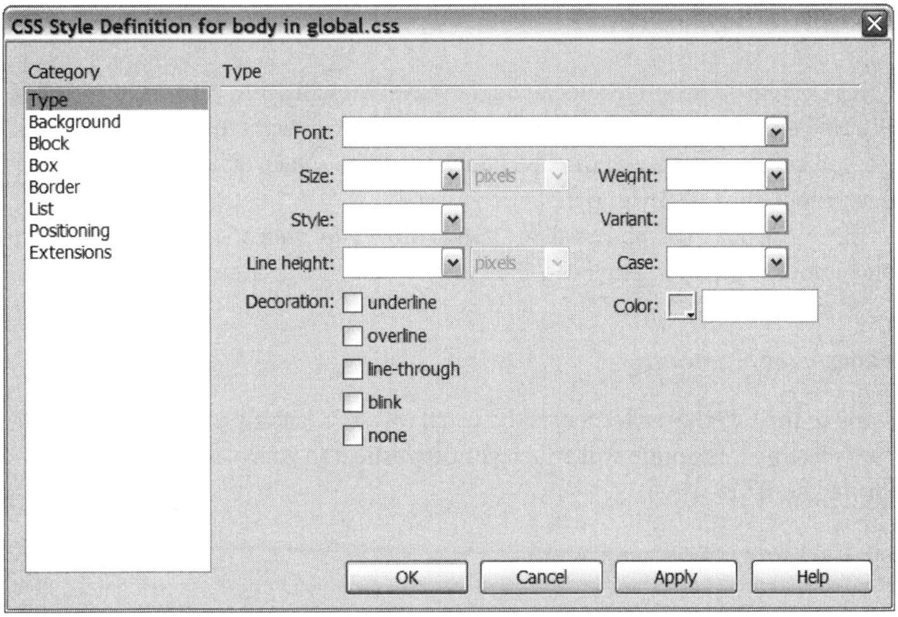

Figure 2-11. The CSS Style Definition dialog box

In this CSS Style Definition dialog box, you can set the rules for the tag or class that you are working with. For the body text, select Type in the left list and then choose a font face, size, and color, and then click OK. You can redefine the look of any HTML tags that you want by following these steps.

To edit a CSS style, select it in the CSS panel and then click the Edit button (second from the right at the bottom of the panel) to open the CSS Style Definition dialog box. Double-clicking the style in the tree view in the CSS panel opens the stylesheet in Dreamweaver so that you can make changes to the stylesheet itself.

Creating Classes

Creating classes in Dreamweaver is as simple as redefining an HTML tag. Open the New CSS Style dialog box once again, and select the Class (can apply to any tag) radio button. Next, in the textbox at the top of the dialog box, enter a name for your class. This needs to begin with a period.

Click OK and the familiar dialog box will open, allowing you to set the properties for this class. Set some properties and click OK. Your new class will appear in the CSS Styles panel.

Attaching a Stylesheet

When you create a new stylesheet, Dreamweaver attaches it to your page automatically. However, if you already have a stylesheet that you want to attach to the page, you can attach it using the CSS panel. Click the Attach Style Sheet button on the bottom of the CSS Styles panel.

The dialog box that appears allows you to browse for your stylesheet. Use the two radio buttons to select whether you want the stylesheet to be linked or imported.

Linking to the Stylesheet

Linking to the external stylesheet is the usual way of attaching a stylesheet to your page. Selecting this option will attach your stylesheet to your page by way of the following markup:

```
<link href="global.css" rel="stylesheet" type="text/css" />
```

This way of attaching a stylesheet is supported by all CSS-enabled browsers, and is what you should do if you need to support browsers such as Netscape 4 with your web page.

Importing the Stylesheet

If you choose import, the stylesheet will be attached using the following markup:

```
<style type="text/css">
  <!--
    @import url("global.css");
  -->
</style>
```

This way of attaching a stylesheet is not recognized by the older version 4, browsers, but you can use this to your advantage when you have to deal with buggy CSS support in these older browsers. We will return to this subject later.

The Property Inspector

In Dreamweaver MX 2004 the old-style Property inspector that allowed you to add font tags to your documents is gone. In its place is a far more useful Properties inspector, shown in Figure 2-12, that allows you to add classes to page elements far more quickly than before.

Figure 2-12. Properties inspector

The Format drop-down menu lets you add the structural (X)HTML markup to elements. If you select an element in Design view and then choose Heading 1 from this list, the element will become a level 1 heading (`<h1>`). Other structural markup that can be added using the Properties inspector is as follows:

- Click B to wrap an element in `<strong></strong>` tags, making it appear bold in a browser.

- Click I to wrap an element in `<em></em>` tags, making it appear italicized in the browser.

- Click the unordered list icon to turn an element into an unordered list.

- Click the ordered list icon to create an ordered list.

The Text Indent and Text Outdent buttons add and remove `<blockquote>` elements. This should not be used to indent text but rather to markup a quote. To indent text, you should use a left padding setting in a CSS class.

The font, size, and color drop-down menus should be used with caution. As already mentioned, the use of font tags has been removed from the Properties inspector so if you change the font of an element using this menu, Dreamweaver creates a class in the head of your document and then applies it to the element. You would be better advised to create your own classes for text that needs to be specially formatted, or create a special element using these menus, copy the resulting CSS out of the head of your document and into your external stylesheet, where it will be available to any pages that have this stylesheet attached.

The Style drop-down menu picks up any classes that you have created and gives you an easy way to apply them to page elements. Select an element in Design view, select a class from this drop-down menu, and it will be applied to the element.

The Page Properties Dialog Box

The Page Properties dialog box can be launched from the Properties inspector as well as by selecting Modify ➤ Page Properties. This dialog box gives you a quick way to set CSS properties for your document. Once again, these will appear in the head of your document, and because you are usually aiming for a unified look and feel throughout your site, you should copy them across to your external stylesheet.

Design Files: Pre-Made CSS Stylesheets

Dreamweaver MX ships with a set of ready-made design files. These include pre-made stylesheets. If CSS seems like a rather abstract concept at this point, or if you just want a way to quickly get started, these files are really useful.

To use a ready-made stylesheet, select File ➤ New, and then select CSS Style Sheets from the New Document dialog box. A list of pre-made stylesheets is displayed in the center selector box, as shown in Figure 2-13.

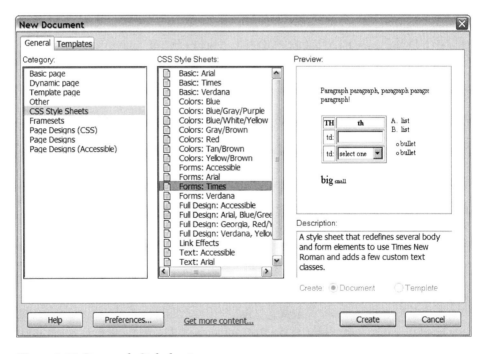

Figure 2-13. Pre-made Stylesheets

Clicking any of the stylesheet names will display some of its elements in the Preview panel. After choosing one that you want to work with, click Create, and the stylesheet is created as a new document in Dreamweaver. You will need to save this stylesheet within your site.

To get started using your stylesheet, attach it to your page. Any redefined tags will adopt the rules set in the stylesheet, and any custom classes defined will be available for your use.

Design Files: Page Designs (CSS)

Dreamweaver also ships with full CSS pages designs ready for you to use. These are an excellent way to start using CSS layouts because they give you a starting point from which you can experiment. To use one of these layouts select File ➤ New ➤ Page Designs (CSS) and pick one of the designs. You can see a preview of the layout in the Preview panel, as shown in Figure 2-14. Click Create, save the HTML document, and copy the CSS file into your site.

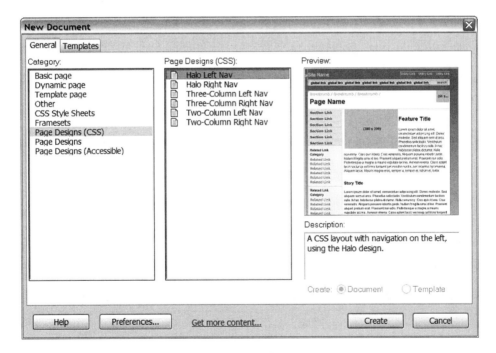

Figure 2-14. Page designs in the Preview panel

The layout will appear in Design view and you can edit the HTML and CSS to your own requirements. Changes made to the CSS file now will not affect the master CSS file that is used to create the layout in the first place so feel free to experiment as much as you like.

Design-Time Stylesheets

Design-time stylesheets allow you to apply a stylesheet that will not be visible when the site goes live. They are useful when working on a site that has multiple stylesheets attached, such as sites that use different stylesheets for different browsers or sites that allow a user to select one of several stylesheets. If you are writing the link to the stylesheet dynamically with ASP (or PHP, or JavaScript, etc.), Dreamweaver will not be able to render that stylesheet during the design process, so using a design-time stylesheet allows you to work visually in the Dreamweaver environment.

Working with a Design-Time Stylesheet

You can open the Design Time Style Sheets dialog box by either right-clicking (CMD-clicking on a Mac) the CSS Styles panel and selecting Design Time in the context menu, or choosing Text ➤ CSS Styles ➤ Design Time Style Sheets. The dialog box shown in Figure 2-15 appears.

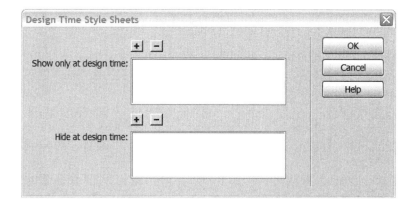

Figure 2-15. The Design Time Style Sheets dialog box

As shown in Figure 2-15, you can select stylesheets saved within your site to be shown or hidden at design time. To display a CSS stylesheet at design time, click the (+) plus button above Show Only at Design Time, to open a dialog box that will allow you to browse for and select this stylesheet. To hide a CSS stylesheet, click the plus sign (+) button above Hide at Design Time, and browse for the stylesheet.

You can remove the stylesheet simply by selecting the stylesheet and clicking the minus sign (–) button.

The CSS Styles panel is updated with the selected stylesheet's name, along with an indicator (hidden or design) to reflect the stylesheet's status. This only affects the view of the document within Dreamweaver; no changes are made to your code.

Integration with TopStyle CSS Editor

Although you can select any editor to be your external editor for CSS, Dreamweaver MX has a close integration with the popular TopStyle CSS editor. A trial version of TopStyle is included on the CD with Dreamweaver MX, and it can be downloaded from http://www.bradsoft.com/. It is a very useful application for anyone working extensively with CSS.

Unfortunately, TopStyle is currently a Windows-only product. There are Mac alternatives (including Style Master, available at http://www.westciv.com/style_master/index.html), but it doesn't currently offer the tight integration of TopStyle with Dreamweaver MX.

If you are working with TopStyle, you will find that changes made to your stylesheet in TopStyle will automatically be updated in Dreamweaver's Design view, and new classes that you add will be available for use immediately.

Creating Valid Markup

In this section, we will look at the tools available for laying out web pages. You will create a document using XHTML 1.0 Transitional, tables for layout, basic CSS for text styling, and rollover graphics for navigation.

You will then see how to move this document to XHTML Strict—removing any presentational attributes from your pages. Removing presentational attributes and markup from your pages means that you need to replace them with something, so we will explore replacing them with CSS.

Finally, we will look at more advanced CSS and re-create our layout using CSS positioning, also replacing the images rollovers with CSS.

A New XHTML Document

To create a new XHTML document select File ➤ New from within Dreamweaver MX to open the New Document dialog box. Select the first two options—Basic Page in the first category list and HTML in the second list. Check Make Document XHTML Compliant at the bottom of the New Document dialog box, as shown in Figure 2-16.

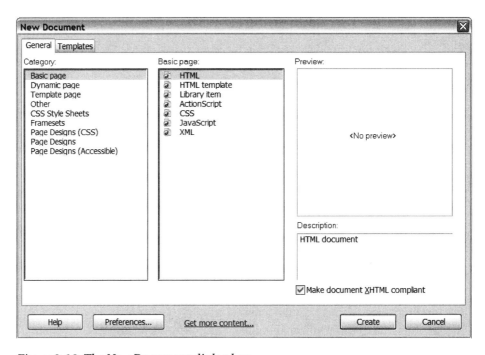

Figure 2-16. The New Document dialog box

Laying Out a Page

To insert a table (in this instance for layout) into your page, switch the Insert toolbar to the Layout panel, as shown in Figure 2-17.

Figure 2-17. Insert toolbar's Layout panel

There are three options for creating tables based layouts—Standard, Expanded, and Layout. Layout mode might look like a good idea because you can drag table cells. However, it tends to create very messy mark-up—something you want to avoid! Therefore, start in Standard mode. Click the Table icon on the Insert toolbar to open Table dialog box, as shown in Figure 2-18.

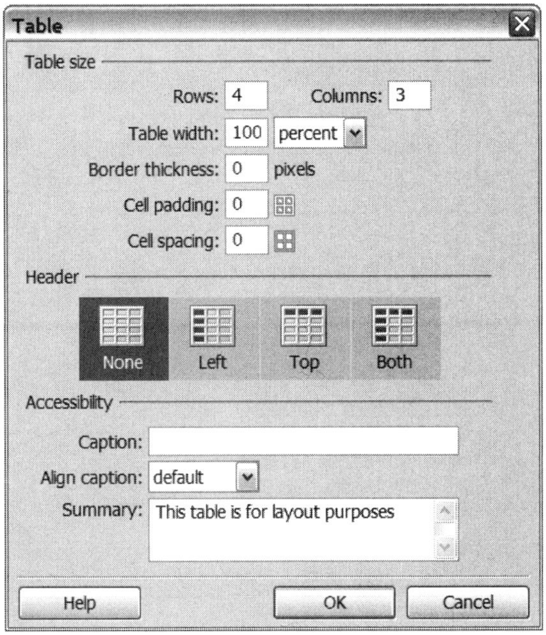

Figure 2-18. The Table dialog box

In the Table dialog box, enter the properties of your table as follows:

- **Rows**: 4

- **Columns**: 3

- **Table width**: 100 percent

- **Border thickness**: 0 pixels

- **Cell padding**: 0

- **Cell spacing**: 0

- **Header**: None

In the Summary text box, type **This table is used for layout purposes only**.
Click OK and your table will appear in Design view, as shown in Figure 2-19.

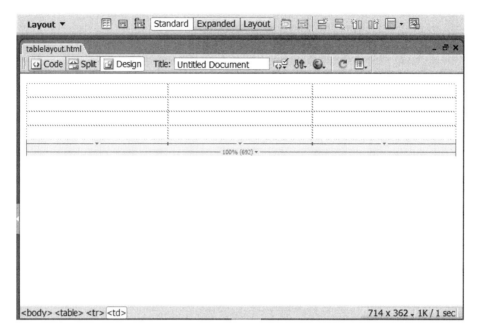

Figure 2-19. Design view after inserting the table

Setting Page Properties

Before continuing, let's set some basic page properties. These include removing
the margin that you can see between the table and the edge of the browser window. To open the Page Properties dialog box (shown in Figure 2-20), either click
the Page Properties button in the Properties inspector or select Modify ➤ Page
Properties.

Enter the properties of your page as follows:

• **Page font**: Verdana, Arial, Helvetica, sans serif

• **Size**: .9 ems

• **Text color**: #333333

• **Background color**: #ffffff

- **Left margin**: 0

- **Right margin**: 0

- **Top margin**: 0

- **Bottom margin**: 0

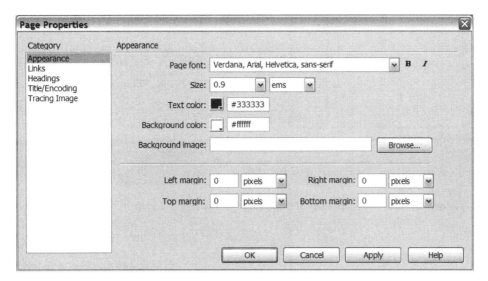

Figure 2-20. The Page Properties dialog box

Click OK to see the changes in Design view. If you switch into Code view you will see that these properties have been added with CSS and are in a stylesheet within the head of the document. Because you are likely to want to apply the same properties to multiple pages, it is wise to place these properties into an external stylesheet. To do so, select File ➤ New ➤ Basic Page, and select CSS to open the New Document dialog box, as shown in Figure 2-21.

Click Create to open an empty stylesheet in Dreamweaver. Copy the styles from the head of the document (do not copy the comment or <style> tags that enclose them) and paste them into your new stylesheet. Save the stylesheet as global.css. Return to your document and delete the <style></style> tags and everything inside them. Return to Design view.

Now attach your new stylesheet to the page by selecting Attach Style Sheet from the CSS panel and browsing to and selecting the global.css document that you created.

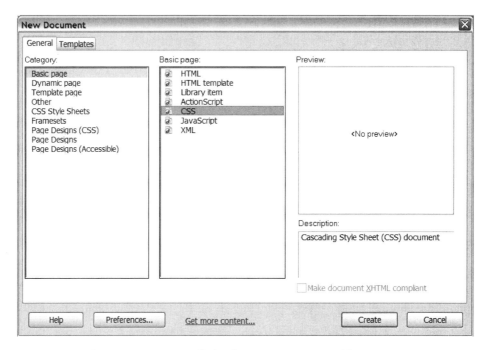

Figure 2-21. The New Document dialog box, creating a CSS file

The Layout

You are going to create a layout with a banner at the top of the page and a navigation menu on the left side. To create the banner, select the top row of table cells and click Merge Cells in the Properties inspector.

> **NOTE** *The bottom half of the Properties inspector changes to reflect the current selection in Design view.*

Repeat this process for the next two rows so your table ends up with three rows containing one cell each, and a fourth row containing three cells, as shown in Figure 2-22.

Figure 2-22. The table

Click the left cell of the bottom row. This will be the menu. In the Properties inspector, set this cell's width to 200 pixels, as shown in Figure 2-23.

Figure 2-23. Setting table properties in the Properties inspector

Click the bottom right cell. Set this cell to 40 pixels wide. The middle cell is where your page content will go.

Click the very top cell and set it to 20 pixels in height. Do the same to the third cell down. Finally, set the middle cell to 80 pixels in height.

The Banner

This middle cell will be the banner across the top of the page. You could simply set a background color for the table cell, however, it is a better idea to do this using CSS instead—if you create additional pages from this template page, you can change the color of the banner on every page with one change in the stylesheet.

To set the background color using CSS you need to create a class. Create a new class and name it .banner. In the Background category of the CSS Style Definition dialog box, select a color for the banner; then go to the Border category and give the banner a top and bottom border, as shown in Figure 2-24.

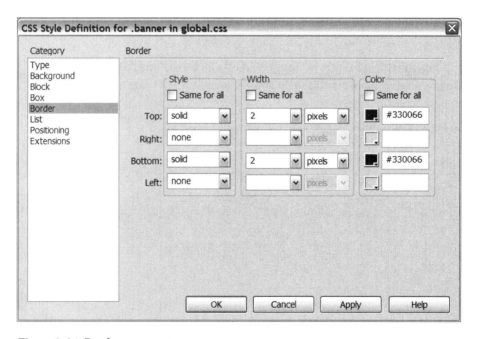

Figure 2-24. Border category

Click OK. Next, using the Properties inspector's Style drop-down menu, apply the .banner class to the banner table cell.

Adding Page Content

In order to see how your content will look, add some dummy content, including a level 1 and level 2 heading to the main content area of the page (the middle cell of the bottom row).

When you paste in your content it will take on the font of the style that you set for page's preferences. You can now set styles for your level 1 and level 2 headings by going to the New CSS Style dialog box, choosing Tag, and then choosing the h1 or h2 tag, as shown in Figure 2-25.

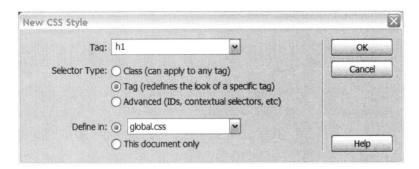

Figure 2-25. The New CSS Style dialog box

The Navigation

Click the cell on the bottom left. In the Properties inspector, select center from the Horz (align) drop-down menu, and top from the Vert (valign) drop-down menu.

Insert another table into this cell, containing four rows and one column, and a summary: "This table contains the navigation." In Design view, the table looks as shown in Figure 2-26.

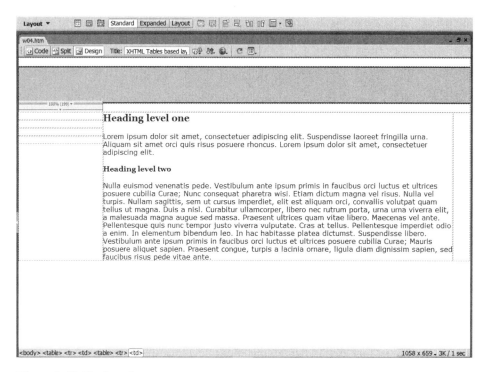

Figure 2-26. Design view

Adding Rollover Images

To make the navigation more interesting, let's add some rollover buttons. Dreamweaver makes it simple to add such effects. First, insert the navigation images into the cells. Name them in the Properties inspector as you insert them.

To add the rollover effect, expand the list of behaviors in the Behaviors panel by clicking the plus sign (+) icon, and choose Swap Image. Next, browse to the image you want to appear when the mouse rolls over the button and click OK, making sure that Preload Image (which will load your images as the page loads so there is no delay when the mouse pointer rolls over it) and Restore Images onMouseOut (which will roll the image back to its previous state when the mouse pointer is no longer rolling over the button) are both checked, as shown in Figure 2-27.

> **TIP** *When adding images to your page, be sure to add alt text to the image. If you have set your preferences to prompt you for Accessibility attributes when you insert an image, you will get a dialog box requesting the alt text—otherwise you can add it in the Properties inspector.*

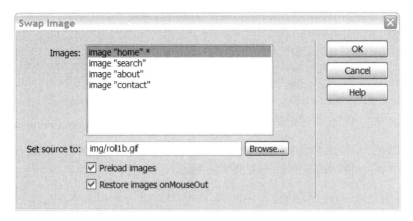

Figure 2-27. The Swap Image dialog box

After adding the images, this simple layout is complete, as shown in Figure 2-28.

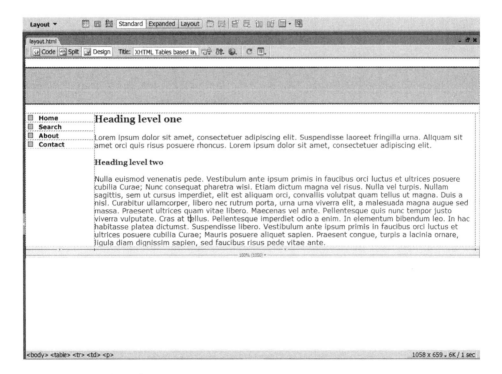

Figure 2-28. Design view

The XHTML markup behind this document looks like this.

```
<!DOCTYPE html PUBLIC "-//W3C//DTD XHTML 1.0 Transitional//EN" ⏎
"http://www.w3.org/TR/xhtml1/DTD/xhtml1-transitional.dtd">
<html xmlns="http://www.w3.org/1999/xhtml">
<head>
<title>XHTML Tables based layout</title>
<meta http-equiv="Content-Type" content="text/html; charset=iso-8859-1" />
<link href="global.css" rel="stylesheet" type="text/css" />
<script language="JavaScript" type="text/JavaScript">
<!--
function MM_preloadImages() { //v3.0
  var d=document; if(d.images){ if(!d.MM_p) d.MM_p=new Array();
    var i,j=d.MM_p.length,a=MM_preloadImages.arguments; for(i=0; i<a.length; i++)
    if (a[i].indexOf("#")!=0){ d.MM_p[j]=new Image; d.MM_p[j++].src=a[i];}}
}

function MM_swapImgRestore() { //v3.0
  var i,x,a=document.MM_sr; for(i=0;a&&i<a.length&&(x=a[i])&&x.oSrc;i++) ⏎
x.src=x.oSrc;
}

function MM_findObj(n, d) { //v4.01
  var p,i,x;  if(!d) d=document; if((p=n.indexOf("?"))>0&&parent.frames.length) {
    d=parent.frames[n.substring(p+1)].document; n=n.substring(0,p);}
  if(!(x=d[n])&&d.all) x=d.all[n]; for (i=0;!x&&i<d.forms.length;i++) ⏎
x=d.forms[i][n];
  for(i=0;!x&&d.layers&&i<d.layers.length;i++) x=MM_findObj(n,d.layers[i].⏎
document);
  if(!x && d.getElementById) x=d.getElementById(n); return x;
}

function MM_swapImage() { //v3.0
  var i,j=0,x,a=MM_swapImage.arguments; document.MM_sr=new Array; ⏎
for(i=0;i<(a.length-2);i+=3)
   if ((x=MM_findObj(a[i]))!=null){document.MM_sr[j++]=x; if(!x.oSrc) ⏎
x.oSrc=x.src; x.src=a[i+2];}
}
//-->
</script>
</head>

<body onload="MM_preloadImages('img/roll1b.gif', 'img/roll2b.gif',⏎
'img/roll3b.gif', 'img/roll4b.gif')">
<table width="100%"  border="0" cellspacing="0" cellpadding="0" ⏎
summary="This table is used for layout purposes only">
```

```
    <tr>
      <td height="20" colspan="3"> </td>
    </tr>
    <tr>
      <td height="80" colspan="3" class="banner"> </td>
    </tr>
    <tr>
      <td height="20" colspan="3"> </td>
    </tr>
    <tr>
      <td width="200" align="center" valign="top"><table width="100%"  border="0" ↵
cellspacing="0" cellpadding="0" summary="this table contains the navigation">
        <tr>
          <td><a href="javascript:;" onmouseover="MM_swapImage↵
('home', '', 'img/roll1b.gif',1)" onmouseout="MM_swapImgRestore()"><img ↵
src="img/roll1a.gif" alt="Home" name="home" width="160" height="20" border="0" ↵
id="home" /></a></td>
        </tr>
        <tr>
          <td><a href="javascript:;" onmouseover="MM_swapImage↵
('search', '', 'img/roll2b.gif',1)" onmouseout="MM_swapImgRestore()"><img src=↵
"img/roll2a.gif" alt="Search" name="search" width="160" height="20" border=↵
"0" id="search" /></a></td>
        </tr>
        <tr>
          <td><a href="javascript:;" onmouseover="MM_swapImage↵
('about', '', 'img/roll3b.gif',1)" onmouseout="MM_swapImgRestore()"><img ↵
src="img/roll3a.gif" alt="About" name="about" width="160" height="20" border="0" ↵
id="about" /></a></td>
        </tr>
        <tr>
          <td><a href="javascript:;" ↵
onmouseover="MM_swapImage('contact', '', 'img/roll4b.gif',1)" ↵
 onmouseout="MM_swapImgRestore()"><img src="img/roll4a.gif" alt="content" ↵
 name="contact" width="160" height="20" border="0" id="contact" /></a></td>↵
        </tr>
      </table></td>
      <td> <h1>Heading level one </h1>
        <p>Content here</p></td>
      <td width="40"> </td>
    </tr>
</table>
</body>
</html>
```

Validating the Document

After creating any layout, particularly if you are going to create multiple pages based on the same layout, it is a good idea to validate it before continuing. Dreamweaver has its own validator to make this easy. Before using the validator, make sure that you have checked XHTML 1.0 Transitional to validate against in Edit ➤ Preferences ➤ Validator. To run the validator, open the Results panel and click the small, green arrow, shown in Figure 2-29.

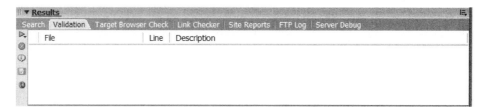

Figure 2-29. Dreamweaver's validator

You can also validate your document by selecting File ➤ Check Page ➤ Validate Markup (for HTML) or File ➤ Check Page ➤ Validate as XML (for XHTML).

You can choose to validate the current document, the entire site, or just selected files in the site. The validator preferences can also be set here. The document should validate as XHTML 1.0 Transitional without needing to be edited by hand.

Using the W3C Validator

Although the internal validator is a useful tool when working on your documents within Dreamweaver, validating at the W3C makes a good final check. The URL for the W3C HTML Validator is `http://validator.w3.org`.

The W3C tool allows you to validate by entering the URL of the page that requires validation or by uploading the document. The easiest way to validate your pages is to FTP them to your web site and then enter the URL into the appropriate box at the validator. If you are using the Dreamweaver validator as you work on your site, you will probably only need to check with the W3C validator as part of your final testing to ensure that all documents, including those that contain dynamic data, are valid.

Moving to XHTML Strict

The XHTML Transitional DTD allows the use of deprecated attributes that will be removed from future versions. The Strict DTD does not allow the use of these deprecated attributes.

To convert your document from the Transitional DTD to the Strict DTD, you must work in Code view. Dreamweaver MX creates XHTML Transitional markup in recognition of the fact that most developers still need to create pages that are backward compatible with older (pre–version 5) browsers. However, the changes that you will need to make are relatively simple.

Change the Document Type Declaration

In Code view, change the `DOCTYPE` at the top of the page to

```
<!DOCTYPE html PUBLIC "-//W3C//DTD XHTML 1.0 Strict//EN"
 "http://www.w3.org/TR/xhtml1/DTD/xhtml1-strict.dtd">
```

Revalidate Your Page in Dreamweaver

In Edit ➤ Preferences ➤ Validator, select the check box to validate against XHTML Strict. Run Validate as XML again. This time you will get a list of errors shown with a red exclamation mark, as seen in Figure 2-30.

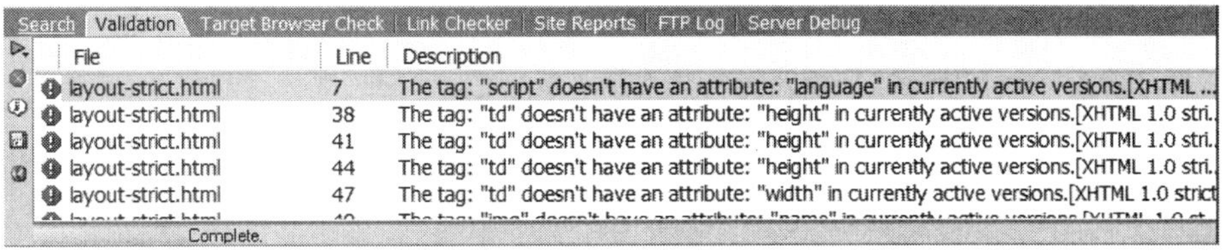
Search
Validation
Target Browser Check
Link Checker
Site Reports
FTP Log
Server Debug
File
Line
Description
layout-strict.html
7
The tag: "script" doesn't have an attribute: "language" in currently active versions.[XHTML ...
layout-strict.html
38
The tag: "td" doesn't have an attribute: "height" in currently active versions.[XHTML 1.0 stri...
layout-strict.html
41
The tag: "td" doesn't have an attribute: "height" in currently active versions.[XHTML 1.0 stri...
layout-strict.html
44
The tag: "td" doesn't have an attribute: "height" in currently active versions.[XHTML 1.0 stri...
layout-strict.html
47
The tag: "td" doesn't have an attribute: "width" in currently active versions.[XHTML 1.0 strict
Complete.

Figure 2-30. Validator showing the errors

> **TIP** *You can also save this list (right-click (on PC) and Command-click (on Mac), and select Save Results) or open the list in a browser (select Open Results in Browser), which is useful if you are validating a large document or entire site because you can use the list as a check list to ensure that you have caught all instances of invalid code.*

The validator at the W3C site gives a similar list of errors, as shown in Figure 2-31.

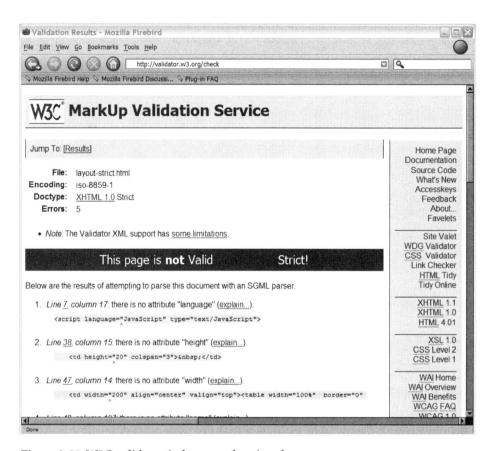

Figure 2-31. W3C validator in browser showing the errors

These "errors" are simply the tags and attributes that have been removed from the Strict DTD. They are mainly elements that have to do with how the document looks and therefore should be replaced with CSS. This list is very helpful in making your page validate against the XHTML Strict DTD because it gives you a quick way to see the deprecated elements. (The document validates as XHTML Transitional, so it conforms to the rules of being well formed.)

Table 2-1 shows the errors that the validator flagged, and how these are solved.

Table 2-1. Validator Errors and Solutions

Error	Solution
Attribute {}language is not declared for element script	This refers to `<script language="JavaScript" type="text/JavaScript">`; the language attribute is deprecated and should be removed.
Attribute {}width is not declared for element td	This refers to `<td width="80">`: the width attribute of the `<td>` tag has been deprecated because it can be replaced by CSS. All width attributes of table cells should be removed.
Attribute {}border is not declared for element img	Refers to `<img border="0" [. . .] >`. We have become used to using border="0" on images that are also links to remove the unsightly border around the image. It is possible to use CSS to do this and so border must be removed from all images.
Attribute {}name is not declared for element img	Dreamweaver MX inserts both a name attribute and an id attribute when you name an image. The name attribute is still used by older browsers and ensures backward compatibility, whereas the id attribute is the attribute in the specification. To use both is valid in XHTML Transitional, but in Strict the deprecated name attribute has to go.

After removing these deprecated attributes you should find that your page validates as XHTML 1.0 Strict, but it looks a bit funny—the banner isn't as tall and there are big blue borders around the images. You can fix this by replacing the deprecated attributes with CSS.

Remove Borders Around Images

In the days of HTML, you would use border="0" to remove borders on images with links; now you can create the same effect with CSS. Open the New Style dialog box and select Tag and img, as shown in Figure 2-32.

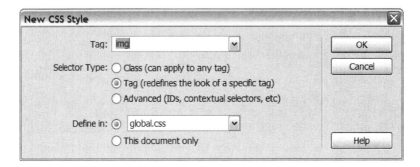

Figure 2-32. The New CSS Style dialog box

After clicking OK, select the Border category in the CSS Style Definitions dialog box. In the Style list, select the value none in the top drop-down menu and make sure that Same for All is checked, as shown in Figure 2-33.

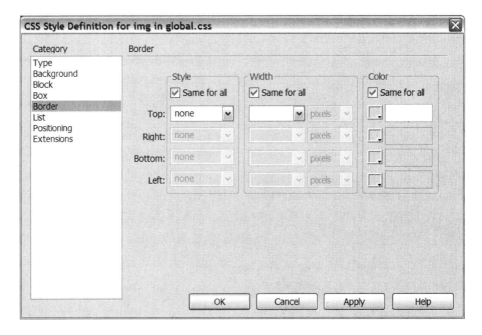

Figure 2-33. CSS Definitions for Border

Click OK and your image borders disappear in the Dreamweaver Design view.

> **TIP** *Dreamweaver adds a* `border="0"` *attribute to any image that is a link. If you need to validate to XHTML Strict or simply do not want this attribute there, you will need to remove it when it appears.*

Setting Properties of Table Cells

You can use CSS to replace the `width` and `height` attributes of table cells. You already have a class for your banner, so you can simply add the height that we want it to be to that class. Select the `.banner` class in the CSS Styles panel and click the Edit Style icon.

The dialog box that opens will contain the rules that you already set for this class. Go to the Box category and in the height box, type **80 pixels**, then click OK. You can create classes for any table cells that you want to change.

Move JavaScript to an External File

Dreamweaver inserts all JavaScript required by its behaviors into the head of your document. This is not ideal. For instance, the JavaScript in the document you created in this chapter that enables the rollover effect is 23 lines long. That same block of script will need to be inserted into every page of the web site and loaded each time.

Removing this JavaScript to a central file that is linked to all pages will trim down the load times of your pages. It also means that search engine spiders do not have to crawl through lines and lines of script to find your content, and pages are easier to maintain and keep consistent.

To move the JavaScript to a central file, simply copy the JavaScript onto the clipboard and open a JavaScript document in Dreamweaver by clicking File ➤ New, selecting Other, and selecting JavaScript. Once you have a JavaScript document, save it, for example, as `functions.js`, and paste the contents of the clipboard into it. You can now return to the original XHTML document and delete everything between the `<script>` tags. If you are working in HTML or XHTML Transitional, You should just be left with the following:

```
<script language="JavaScript" type="text/javascript"></script>
```

If you are working in XHTML Strict, you should just be left with

```
<script type="text/javascript"></script>
```

Now all you need to do is add a link within the `<script>` tags to the source of the JavaScript.

```
<script language="JavaScript" type="text/javascript" src="functions.js"></script>
```

If you are using XHTML Strict, that will need to be

```
<script type="text/javascript" src="functions.js"></script>
```

If you add any other behaviors to other page elements, Dreamweaver will continue to add them to your document. However, you can add as many different functions to your external JavaScript file as you like. Just copy and paste them to your file and remember to delete any additional `<script>` tags that Dreamweaver inserts.

Now when you want to create a new page that utilizes any or all of the functions in your `functions.js` file, all you need do is paste the link to the functions file into the head of your document and the functions will be available to that page. This is an excellent way to work with templates because you can create your template file with all the JavaScript in the head of your document, move the JavaScript to a functions file, and just have the link to that file in the head of the template document. When you create new pages from your template, they will automatically contain all the necessary JavaScript.

CSS for Layout

One of the reasons for building and validating an XHTML Transitional and Strict document is to show that you can still work to standards even if you are not ready to go with CSS for layout yet. However, CSS for layout is the way of the future and learning to use CSS in this way is going to be important for the future career of anyone working in this industry. Dreamweaver MX 2004 supports CSS for layout in a far more advanced way than previous versions, making it far easier to get started.

> **TIP** *You may also hear people talking about layers in Dreamweaver. Layers are simply content structured using inline CSS positioning. They are less useful than positioning your page elements in an external stylesheet, for reasons discussed earlier (for example, reduced code portability and added document size).*

To get started building a layout using CSS, create a new XHTML document in Dreamweaver and attach to it the stylesheet that you created for our tables-based layout.

Creating the Banner

You can use the styles you created for your banner table cell. First open your stylesheet in Dreamweaver and change `.banner` to `#banner`.

To create the banner, add a `<div>`—a `<div>` simply marks an area of the document, which you can then style. To insert a `<div>` for the banner, select the Layout pane of the Insert toolbar and click the Insert Div Tag icon, as shown in Figure 2-34.

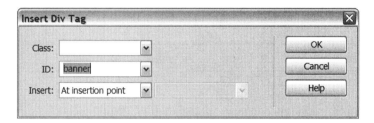

Figure 2-34. The Insert Div Tag dialog box

You will see that the banner shows up as an `id`—this is because a pound sign (#) denotes an `id` in the stylesheet, whereas a period (.) denotes a class. Select the `id` banner and click OK.

> **TIP** *An* id *needs to be unique in your document, so it is perfect to use for an area of the page that will only occur once in each document, such as a banner or navigation block. A class can be present multiple times in one document so you use a class for elements that may appear more than once, such as styles for links, a box-out style to highlight terms, and so on.*

You should see the familiar banner appear in Design view. It contains the text Content for `id` "banner" Goes Here, as shown in Figure 2-35.

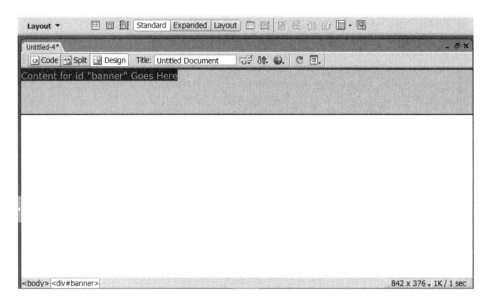

Figure 2-35. Design view

If you switch into Code view you can see the markup that Dreamweaver added.

```
<div id ="banner">Content for id "banner" Goes here</div>
```

Delete the placeholder text. In the tables-based layout, there was some white space above the banner. You can reproduce this with CSS by adding a margin to the top of the banner. Edit the #banner id again and select the Box category. Uncheck the Same for All check box in the Margin section and then set the following properties, as shown in Figure 2-36.

- **Top**: 20 pixels

- **Right**: 0 pixels

- **Bottom**: 20 pixels

- **Left**: 0 pixels

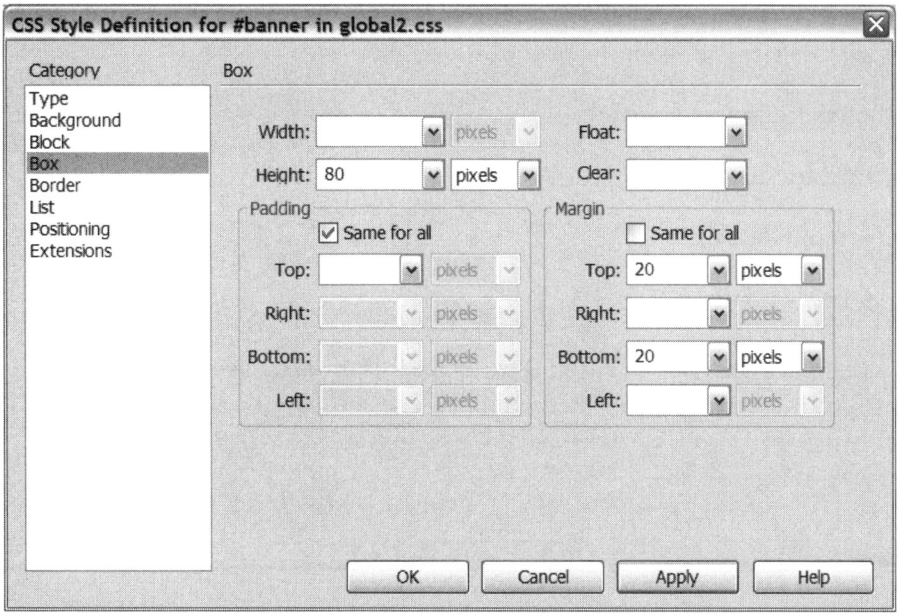

Figure 2-36. The Box category

Click OK to see the change in Design view.

Create the Navigation

Create a new CSS class; this time select Advanced under Selector type and under Selector type **#nav**, as shown in Figure 2-37.

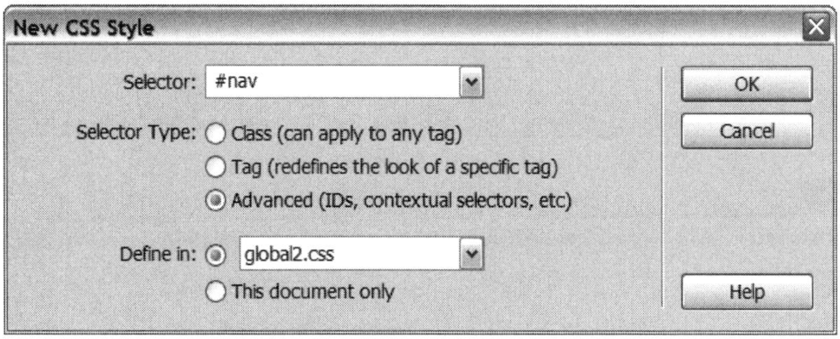

Figure 2-37. The New CSS Style dialog box

Click OK—this set of rules is for your navigation block. Now select the Positioning category and set the following properties:

- **Type**: absolute

- **Width**: 200 pixels

- **Top**: 140 pixels

- **Left**: 4 pixels

Then click OK. Click the Insert Div icon once again, and this time in the id fields, click nav. Under Insert, select After start of tag and choose <div id="banner"> to ensure that this <div> is created outside the banner and doesn't get nested inside it, as shown in Figure 2-38.

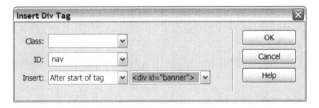

Figure 2-38. The Insert Div Tag dialog box

Click OK and you should see the <div> appear underneath the banner on the left, as shown in Figure 2-39.

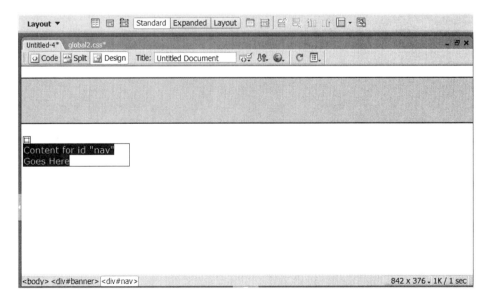

Figure 2-39. Design view

CSS Navigation Buttons

One way to trim down file sizes and improve the accessibility of your document is to use CSS for navigation that would have previously required images. You will use CSS in this way to create your navigation. Your navigation is simply a list of places where the user can go, and as such, using a list to markup the content is a good choice. So, in the #nav <div> create a list, and make each item a link, as shown in Figure 2-40.

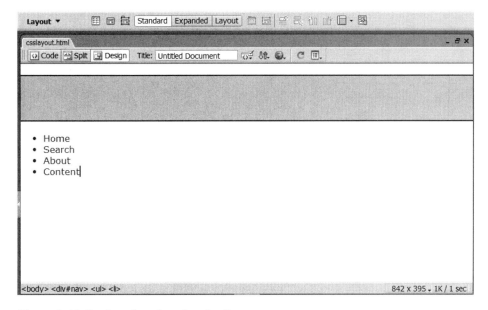

Figure 2-40. Design view showing the list

First you will style the list itself. Create a new CSS style, choose Advanced, and in the Selector box, type **#nav ul**, as shown in Figure 2-41.

Figure 2-41. The New CSS Style dialog box

Using the selector #nav ul means that you are creating styles for all <ul> tags within the div #nav. Any <ul> within that division will be styled in this way, but those not inside this area of the page will retain their default formatting.

Go to the Box category of the CSS Styles Definition dialog box and set Margin Left to 0 pixels and Padding Left to 0 pixels. Click OK and then create a new CSS Style, this time for #nav li, which styles any list item that is inside the id #nav.

Go to the List category of the CSS Style Definition dialog box and under Type select none to remove the bullet from the start of each list item. Next, in the Box category, set Padding to Same for All 3 pixels and Margin, uncheck Same for All, and set Bottom to 4. To add a border to each item, use the Border category, as shown in Figure 2-42.

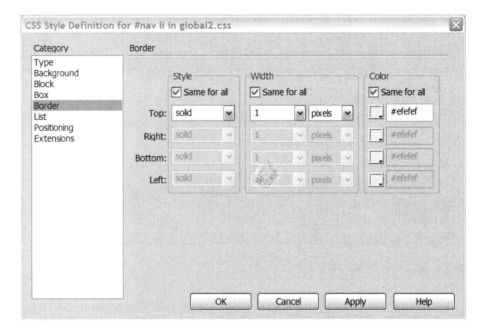

Figure 2-42. Setting properties

You now need to style the anchor tag—the actual navigation link itself. Create a new CSS class, select the Advanced radio button, and type **#nav a:link**. You can now style this menu in any way you choose. Using the Type category, style the text of the link and set the color. You can also set the navigation link to have no underline by choosing none under Decoration, as shown in Figure 2-43.

After setting up #nav a:link you should repeat this process for #nav a:visited, #nav a:hover, and #nav a:active. If you want your navigation to be highlighted when the user holds their mouse pointer over the link, duplicating the look of the rollover buttons, set a different color for the #nav a:hover state.

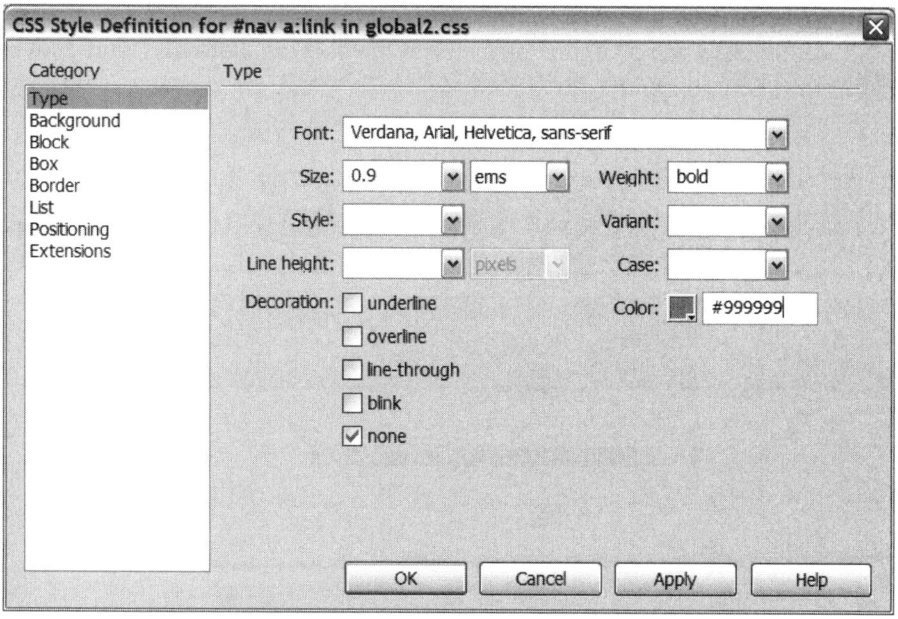

Figure 2-43. Setting text properties

> **TIP** *When setting different properties for the hover state take care not to change the size of the text. If you do, you will end up with a jiggling effect as the page elements are shifted around by the change in size of the link.*

The Content Area

Finally, for this simple layout, you need to place the content on the page. Create a new CSS style, select the Advanced radio button, and type **#content** into the Selector box. You want your content to be liquid and stretch to fill the users screen width, so in the Box category, uncheck Margin Same for All and set the following properties:

- **Top**: 50 pixels

- **Left**: 260 pixels

- **Right**: 40 pixels

Now click OK, and insert the `<div>` content after the tag `<div id="nav">`. You should see the `<div>` appear in the main area of the page, as shown in Figure 2-44. Add some dummy content.

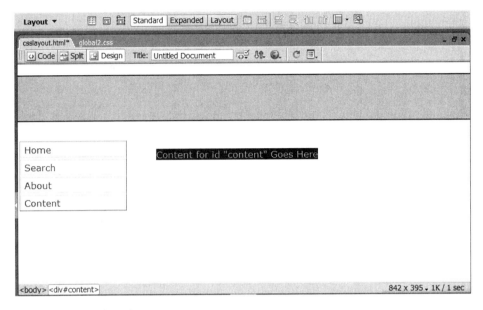

Figure 2-44. Design view

As you may have realized, you didn't use absolute positioning or anything else to position this content. You simply used a margin to clear it from the navigation, which is absolutely positioned. This works because absolute positioning takes an element out of the flow of the document. The content without any margins applied to it would have simply laid over the top of the navigation as if the navigation wasn't there.

All you needed to do to get this to be displayed nicely and as a liquid layout that resizes with the users screen size was to make sure that the content left space for the absolutely positioned navigation.

This is a very simple layout, but hopefully it has given you an idea of the tools that are available in Dreamweaver to work with CSS layouts. If this is your first experience of working with CSS, you may find the concepts a little tricky, but the best way to become accustomed to any new way of working is simply by experimenting and trying things out. In the "Resources" section at the end of this chapter there are several sites listed that provide CSS layouts that you can experiment with. There are also the CSS page designs within Dreamweaver that you can take as starting points for your own experiments.

Browser and Device Issues

Browser issues are cited as the main reason that people do not implement CSS on their web sites, however, this excuse is fast becoming outdated. Even so, we will look at how to address these issues in this section.

Although browsers with no support for CSS should render your content in a readable fashion, there are problems with browsers that have partial or buggy support for CSS, and it is these browsers, particularly Netscape 4, that you need to consider.

Versions of Netscape 4 may crash when encountering certain valid CSS declarations, or they may render your page so that it is unusable or just plain ugly! Thankfully there are ways around this problem.

Netscape 4

Earlier, we looked at two ways of attaching a stylesheet to a page: linking it and importing it. Netscape 4 does not recognize @import, and you can use this fact to your advantage by attaching two stylesheets to the page: one basic, Netscape 4 friendly stylesheet that you link to your page, and another, more advanced stylesheet that you attach using @import, which is invisible to Netscape 4.

To attach two stylesheets to your page in this way using Dreamweaver, you need to attach the basic Netscape 4-friendly stylesheet first, using the link method, as shown in Figure 2-45.

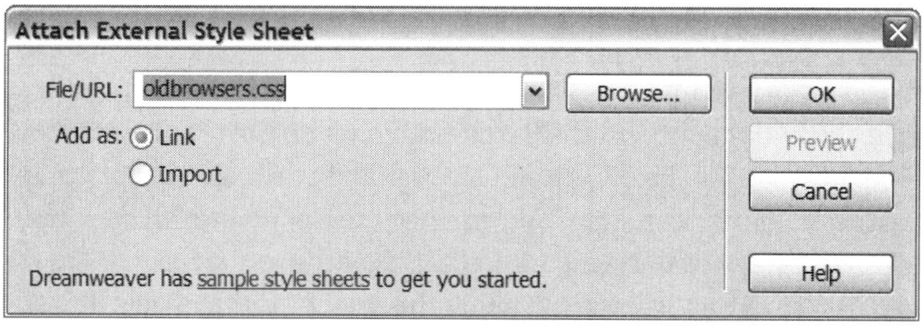

Figure 2-45. The link method

Then attach the second stylesheet with the declarations for newer browsers using @import, as shown in Figure 2-46.

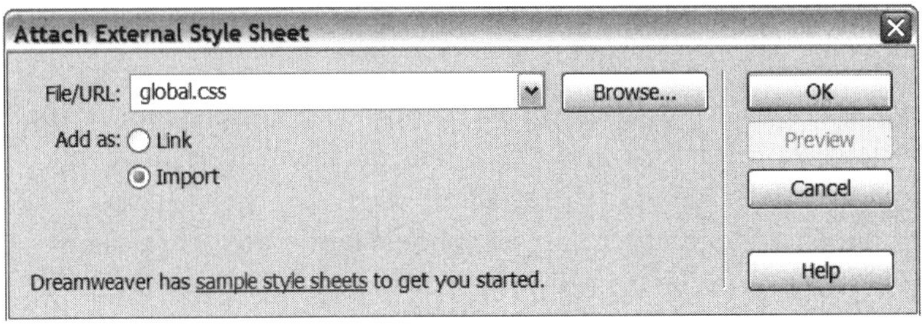

Figure 2-46. The import method

You have to specify the imported stylesheet after the linked stylesheet, so that the basic Netscape 4 friendly CSS is overridden by the second stylesheet. In Code view the generated code looks like this

```
<link href="oldbrowsers.css" rel="stylesheet" type="text/css" />
<style type="text/css">
<!--
@import url("newbrowsers.css");
-->
</style>
```

Any CSS that you want to be different for newer browsers must be included in the imported stylesheet. The browser will use the values in the linked stylesheet if no values are found in the imported one for that element.

JavaScript Techniques

It is possible to use JavaScript to detect what browser is being used and write an appropriate stylesheet for that browser. This method relies on the user having JavaScript turned on, but it can be very useful if you find that a bug in a particular browser causes a crash or other problem and you need to isolate that browser by attaching a stylesheet designed to be friendly to it.

You can also use JavaScript to detect whether the user is visiting with a newer, more standards-compliant browser or a pre–version 5 browser, and display stylesheets accordingly. This method checks to see whether the browser supports the W3C DOM, which newer browsers do, and then writes the appropriate stylesheet into the page.

```
<script language="javascript" type="text/javascript">
if (!document.getElementById) {
document.write('<link rel="stylesheet" href="oldbrowsers.css" type="text/css" />');
```

```
}
else
{
document.write('<link rel="stylesheet" href="newbrowsers.css" type="text/css" />');
}
</script>
```

The first stylesheet in the code just shown should be the stylesheet for those older browsers that do not support the W3C DOM; the second stylesheet is for all newer browsers.

Media Descriptors

Media descriptors allow you to specify how a document is presented on different media: monitor screens, paper, screen readers, Braille readers, or other devices. For example, you can specify that one stylesheet is used if a page is being printed and another is used when it's displayed in the browser window. A media descriptor allows a stylesheet designed with speech synthesis rules to be served to screen readers, and stylesheets designed with Web TV or PDAs in mind to be served appropriately.

Whether a browser or device understands the media descriptor varies between devices at present, but there is good support for print (the media descriptor you will currently find most useful) and learning to use this method of serving appropriate presentational rules should become more useful in the future as device support grows.

The media descriptors as listed in the CSS2 specification are shown in Table 2-2.

Table 2-2. CSS2 Media Descriptors

Descriptor	Media
all	All devices
aural	Speech synthesizers (screen readers)
braille	Braille tactile feedback devices
embossed	Paged Braille printers
handheld	Handheld devices (small screen, monochrome, limited bandwidth)
print	Documents to be printed
projection	Projection devices
screen	Color computer screens—standard web browsers
tty	Media using a fixed-pitch character grid or portable devices with limited display capabilities. These are typically older mobile devices; most current devices would fall into the handheld category
tv	Television

You can use media descriptors either by specifying a separate stylesheet for each type that you want to use or by using @import.

Specifying a Separate Stylesheet for Each Media Descriptor

If you already have a stylesheet linked to your page for presenting your document in a browser and you want to add a stylesheet that will only come into play when the document is printed, you can add a second linked stylesheet for print. You will also need to add the media descriptor screen to your existing stylesheet so that the browser knows that the screen stylesheet is to be used in the browser, but the print stylesheet should be used when the page is printed.

```
<link rel="stylesheet" type="text/css" media="screen" href="screen.css" />
<link rel="stylesheet" type="text/css" media="print" href="print.css" />
```

Using a print stylesheet allows you, for instance, to hide navigation when a document is printed, change the font from a sans-serif typeface (which is more readable on screen) to serif typeface (which is more readable in print), and remove a background color or images that would cause the printing to take longer.

Media Descriptors with Imported Stylesheets

The method just outlined means that you need to create a separate stylesheet for each browser. However, by using @import instead, you can specify certain elements within one stylesheet to apply to different types of media. To use the @import method, attach your stylesheet to the page.

```
<style type="text/css" media="all">@import "all.css";</style>
```

Within the all.css stylesheet you add attributes for each media descriptor, by using @media as shown here.

```
@media print {
  body { font-size: 10pt; }
}

@media screen {
  body { font-size: 12px; }
}

@media screen, print {
  body { color: #000000; }
}
```

The declarations just shown give a font size of 10 points when the page is printed and 12 pixels when the page is viewed in a regular browser. Both screen and print will use #000000 (black) as the color of the body text.

Working with Dynamic Data

Later on in this book, you will immerse yourself in developing dynamic sites in Dreamweaver MX 2004. Developing with valid XHTML or HTML should make your life easier when incorporating dynamic data into your page. When data is being pulled from a database, small errors such as unclosed tags and badly nested elements can wreak havoc across your site and become difficult to debug, so starting out with a solid framework as you design your layout should save you time later on in the development process.

A combination of valid (X)HTML and CSS is ideal for a dynamic site, especially those sites that allow users to add information (such as content management systems or client-updateable news pages) because your stylesheets ensure that consistency is maintained across your site.

What to Watch Out For

There are some issues to watch out for when working with dynamic pages.

- When selecting an area to create a repeat region (a dynamic, repeating block of code pulled from a database), ensure that you selected the entire block of code that you want to be repeated, and that the tags are still properly closed and nested when the page is viewed in a web browser.

- When creating areas of your page that will be displayed conditionally, ensure that all tags are closed correctly when the page is loaded under each possible condition.

- If you are creating pages to which users or content authors will add content via an administration section, take extra care in the design of the application so that the authors do not add anything invalid, or add HTML markup where you are working in XHTML. If you are using ASP, careful use of the Replace function can allow you to replace offending items (such as special characters, or if you are allowing people to enter HTML tags, non-valid tags or attributes) with their valid versions.

Validating Dynamic Pages

Dynamic pages should be validated with the online validator at the W3C. If the pages include conditional regions, validate each possible way that the page can be displayed if at all possible. Your server-side code will not cause you any validation problems with the validator because by the time it has been parsed by the server, the validator sees only is the (X)HTML generated from the server-side code.

If you are maintaining a dynamic site, pages that are frequently modified, either by users or content authors, should be validated occasionally in order to check that you're effectively counteracting invalid items inserted by content authors.

Summary

With Macromedia Dreamweaver MX 2004, creating valid and accessible web sites with HTML and XHTML is within the reach of every designer and developer's abilities. In this chapter, we discussed

- How to write valid XHTML in the Dreamweaver environment

- How to create standards-compliant, table-based layouts in Dreamweaver

- How to use CSS to replace elements that are deprecated in the transitional DOCTYPE and not allowed if you validate to Strict

- How to use CSS for layout

This chapter provided some essential building blocks for good practices in web development, which will assist you as you move onward to styling your pages with CSS and adding dynamic data to your web sites. By following best practice, not only will your web sites be more accessible to all web users, but you will also find your working and debugging methods are streamlined and simplified.

Resources

There are many resources available online for those who want to further explore the subjects discussed in this chapter.

- **The Web Standards Project**: `http://www.webstandards.org`. The WaSP web site provides news and information about web standards and many helpful resources to help you to work with standards in your own projects.

- **NYPL Style Guide**: `http://www.nypl.org/styleguide/`. This style guide, created for the New York Public Library, is an easy-to-understand explanation of how to use web standards.

- **Macromedia Devnet**: `http://www.macromedia.com/devnet/`. Keep an eye on this site for tutorials, specifically about using XHTML and CSS with Dreamweaver. There are whole sections devoted to CSS and accessibility.

- **W3Schools**: `http://www.w3schools.com`. Check out the CSS and XHTML tutorials here. This site has lots of information on many web technologies, presented in a clear and easy-to-understand manner.

- **CSS-Discuss**: `http://www.css-discuss.org/`. A mailing list for CSS discussion. Try searching the archives here if you are having a problem with CSS. If you don't find an answer, posting to the list will get some of the best CSS brains in the world looking over your problem for you. To get useful help on this mailing list and others like it, it is a good idea to ensure that you have validated your document and CSS file before posting because it makes it easier for people to see whether your problem is an error on your part or perhaps a browser bug for which there is a workaround.

- **CSS Zen Garden**: `http://www.csszengarden.com`. Inspiration for CSS layouts.

- **Real World Style**: `http://realworldstyle.com/`. CSS layouts, tips, and techniques, many of which work in Netscape 4.

- **CSS Panic Guide**: `http://www.thenoodleincident.com/tutorials/css/`. A good place to go when it all seems to be going wrong, or when you want to find more resources on CSS.

CHAPTER 3

Accessibility and
Dreamweaver MX 2004

CREATING ACCESSIBLE WEB PAGES has never been more important than it is today. With the recent adoption of accessibility standards in the United States, Canada, the European Union, Australia, Japan, and Brazil, designers and developers face mandates to ensure that people with disabilities can access the contents of web sites and web applications.

In addition, ensuring that web sites are accessible to people with disabilities is simply the right thing to do. For people with disabilities, the Internet can be a tremendously valuable tool. It can provide access to the world around us, as well as a level of independence not previously possible.

Consider the task of reading a newspaper. Prior to the Internet, a blind person who wanted to read the paper had two choices. He could get a Braille version of the paper—often expensive and hard to find—or he could ask someone to read the paper to him. Today, a blind person is able to use screen reader software to read the news to him from a web site each day. Dependence on others is eliminated.

From a commercial perspective, creating accessible sites is valuable in two respects. First, an accessible site offers an edge over competitors who might not have an accessible site. Providing access to users with disabilities broadens existing markets and potentially opens new ones. Second, an accessible site ensures all visitors have access. For many people with disabilities, accessibility is not about convenience. It is about access to employment, education, and the community.

Dreamweaver MX 2004 provides the most complete set of tools available for building, editing, and maintaining accessible web sites and web applications. Dreamweaver MX 2004 includes tools that prompt designers to provide important accessibility information when inserting images, forms, media, tables, and frames.

Dreamweaver MX 2004 helps designers understand and comply with accessibility standards by including features that provide a reference guide, templates, code snippets, and a built-in accessibility validation tool.

Dreamweaver MX 2004 also introduces a new way of coding Cascading Stylesheets (CSS) and provides improved integration with Macromedia Contribute. CSS provides designers with a comprehensive set of tools for formatting and laying out pages while allowing end users control over the page. This has tremendous benefits for users with disabilities. Pages coded using CSS allow users to modify specific aspects of the page, such as text size and color, or replace the formatting altogether to best meet their individual needs.

Finally, Dreamweaver MX 2004 makes it easier than ever for people with disabilities to create web sites and web applications. With improvements to the authoring environment, Dreamweaver MX 2004 now works with assistive technologies, such as the Window-Eyes™ screen reader from GW Micro (http://www.gwmicro.com/) and the JAWS screen reader from Freedom Scientific (http://www.freedomscientific.com/).

This chapter will introduce the topic of accessibility and review the accessibility features of Macromedia Dreamweaver MX 2004. Topics include

- Defining disabilities

- Accessibility preferences options

- Accessibility validation

- Accessibility reference

- Cascading Stylesheets

- Accessible templates

- Accessible authoring environment

Accessibility Overview

In general terms, accessibility describes how well web sites work for people with disabilities. An accessible site is one in which design elements such as color, font size, or layout do not obscure the site's content. An accessible web site is also compatible with the assistive technologies used by people with disabilities.

More specifically, policies such as Section 508 of the U.S. Rehabilitation Act (http://www.section508.gov/) and guidelines such as the Web Accessibility Initiative, or WAI (http://www.w3.org/TR/WCAG10/) specify what constitutes an accessible site with a series of checkpoints. Each checkpoint addresses issues for specific disabilities and technologies.

This section reviews some of the reasons for incorporating accessibility into web site design, provides a more complete definition of accessibility in terms of the range of disabilities commonly found among web users, introduces some of the assistive technologies used by persons with disabilities, and presents the policies governing web accessibility.

Why Is Accessibility Important?

For most people, the reasons for creating an accessible web site are simple: it is the right thing to do and it is the law. It is often helpful, however, to point out the additional benefits of creating an accessible web site. The following is a list of reasons many find compelling:

- Accessibility offers benefits for *all* users, not just those with disabilities

- Accessibility uses innovative technology

- Accessibility creates market opportunity

Accessibility Is the Right Thing to Do

Accessibility represents an important step toward independence for individuals with disabilities. Accessible web pages provide access to fundamental government services and information such as tax forms, social programs, and legislative representatives. Accessible web pages also make possible a broader range of employment and educational opportunities by enabling persons with disabilities to use the Internet as a means of communication. In addition, accessibility allows users with disabilities to participate in day-to-day activities many people take for granted, such as reading a newspaper or buying a gift for a loved one.

Accessibility Is the Law for Many Institutions

With new national requirements in the United States, Canada, and the European Union, and more to come in the near future, there are numerous legal mandates for accessibility. These policies will likely expand in scope. In the U.S., for instance, Section 508 sets standards for web pages designed or maintained by federal agencies. State and local governments as well as educational and non-profit institutions around the U.S. are considering their own accessibility policies. For example, in 2001, the University of Wisconsin at Madison adopted an accessibility policy requiring all pages published or hosted by the university to conform to all Section 508 guidelines.

Accessibility Offers Benefits for All Users

As with many improvements intended for individuals with disabilities, the enhancements of accessible design offer benefits for all users of the web. Anyone who has pushed a shopping cart out of a grocery store can attest to the value of automatic doors and ramps cut into curbs. Similarly, accessible web pages are often easier to read, easier to navigate, and faster to download because they are optimized for ease of use. They also tend to contain fewer of the page elements that make sites large and slow to load, such as Flash movies and large images.

Accessibility Uses Innovative Technology

Accessible design is based on the premise that web pages must work with a range of browsers that includes more than just Netscape and Internet Explorer. A page must also be accessible when it is viewed through a screen reader, a refreshable Braille display, or a head pointer. Making pages work with non-standard browsers often makes them available to other consumer Internet devices, such as wireless application protocol (WAP)-enabled phones or handheld personal digital assistants (PDAs).

The techniques of accessibility are based on recent technologies and design strategies. Older, static HTML designs often intermix content with formatting on web pages. Accessibility guidelines encourage the separation of formatting from content through the use of CSS, which allows more flexible use of content and easier implementation of more powerful dynamic models. For more on the use of CSS for accessibility, refer back to Chapter 2 of this book.

Accessibility Creates Market Opportunity

Accessibility offers potential for organizations to reach new customers and new markets. As additional accessibility policies are adopted, governmental and educational institutions will continue to need goods and services that help them comply with the new laws. In the U.S., businesses providing goods and services to the government via the web or other information technology should understand Section 508. Businesses that understand accessibility issues and comply with Section 508 have a strong market advantage. This advantage is multiplied as local governments implement new policies.

Defining Disabilities

A 1997 report by the U.S. Census Bureau categorizes 19.6 percent of the United States population as having some sort of disability. This percentage is generally considered to be consistent with worldwide statistics. Within the broader category of disability are the following subcategories:

- Visual impairments

- Hearing impairments

- Motor impairments

- Cognitive impairments

Each of these subcategories includes a range of ability. For example, visual impairments include low vision, colorblindness, and blindness. The tools and techniques addressing issues for people who are blind are very different from those that address issues for people who are colorblind.

Perhaps the most diverse category is that of cognitive impairments. This group includes people with seizure disorders as well as people with learning or developmental disabilities. Building sites that are accessible to people with cognitive disabilities can be a complex task because the obstacles to comprehension often lie in the content as well as in the page design.

Disability categories can overlap and might also include temporary disabilities. For example, someone with a broken wrist may have difficulty using a mouse but still needs access to the web to meet day-to-day job requirements.

It is also important to keep in mind that as people get older, almost everyone will face a disability of some kind. Although nearly 20 percent of the total U.S. population has a disability, as the population ages, the proportion of people with disabilities grows higher (see Table 3-1). In fact, almost 75 percent of the population over the age of 80 has a disability. Thus, accessibility is not just about opening doors; it is about keeping them open. Accessibility allows people to maintain a level of independence that age might otherwise make difficult.

Table 3-1. Disability Statistics in an Aging Population[1]

	Total Number	With Disability	Percent with Disability
All Ages	267,665,000	52,596,000	19.7%
Under 15 years	59,606,000	4,661,000	7.8%
15 to 24 years	36,897,000	3,961,000	10.7%
25 to 44 years	83,887,000	11,200,000	13.4%
45 to 54 years	33,620,000	7,585,000	22.6%
55 to 64 years	21,591,000	7,708,000	35.7%
65 years and over	32,064,000	17,480,000	54.5%

Assistive Technologies

Users with disabilities frequently rely on specialized hardware and software tools to access web content. These tools, known as assistive technologies, range from screen readers to touch screens and head pointers.

Blind users frequently use software called a screen reader that reads the contents of a web page out loud. Two common (and previously mentioned) screen readers are JAWS, from Freedom Scientific, and Window-Eyes, from GW Micro. Screen readers enable users to hear, rather than view, the contents of a web page; however, a screen reader can read only text, not images or animations. It is essential, therefore, that images and animations be assigned text descriptions that screen readers can read. These text descriptions are called **alternative text**, or alt text.

Users with impaired mobility may rely on the keyboard instead of the mouse to navigate web pages. In Internet Explorer, pressing Tab moves the focus of the browser among all available links on a page. The border around links in IE lets the user know where the current focus of the browser is positioned. Pressing Enter activates links, giving the same effect as clicking a mouse button. In Figure 3-1, notice the border around the link for the Apress TechZone logo.

Assistive devices include a touch screen, which allows an individual to navigate the page using her or his hands without requiring the fine-motor control needed to use the mouse, and a head pointer, which is simply a stick placed in a person's mouth or mounted on a head strap that the person uses to interact with a keyboard or a touch screen.

---

1. Source: http://www.census.gov/hhes/www/disable/sipp/disab97/ds97t1.html

Figure 3-1. Note the border indicating the current focus.

In these cases, it is very important that essential components of the page work without a mouse. Rollovers, drop-down menus, and interactive simulations are all examples of elements that typically depend on the mouse for user interaction. The designer or developer of these elements must ensure that keyboard-defined events are included with mouse-defined events. A quick test using the keystrokes available in IE can provide a valuable glimpse of the difficulties a web page may present for users with disabilities who cannot use a mouse. For example, a user can move to any focusable object, including links, form controls, and embedded objects, by pressing the Tab key; pressing the Enter key will activate selected links. Pressing Ctrl+Tab moves between frames. This replicates some of the ways users who cannot use a mouse must interact with a web page.

Accessibility Standards

Accessibility policies vary from country to country, but many countries, including the United States, Australia, Canada, the European Union, and Japan have adopted policies based on standards developed by the **World Wide Web Consortium (W3C)**. In 1994, the W3C began investigating accessibility issues that might be encountered by people with disabilities on the emerging world wide web. This group led to the formation of the **Web Accessibility Initiative (WAI)**. The WAI consists of several efforts to improve the accessibility of the web. Perhaps the most widely used document is the **Web Content Accessibility Guidelines (WCAG)**. WCAG is comprised of 14 accessibility guidelines that are further broken down into prioritized checkpoints.

- Priority 1 checkpoints are the actions designers *must* take to make a site accessible.

- Priority 2 checkpoints are the actions designers *should* take to make a site accessible.

- Priority 3 checkpoints are the actions a designer *might* take to improve the accessibility of a site.

The priority 1 checkpoints of the WCAG serve as the basis of accessibility standards in almost every country where a formal policy has been adopted. The exceptions are Canada and the United Kingdom, where web designers for the national governments are required to follow both the priority 1 and priority 2 checkpoints of the WCAG.

In the United States, the law governing web accessibility is commonly referred to as Section 508. Section 508 of the U.S. Rehabilitation Act prohibits federal agencies from buying, developing, maintaining, or using electronic and information technology that is inaccessible to people with disabilities. Originally enacted in 1988, Section 508 made little progress until Congress passed the Workforce Investment Act ten years later. This amendment to Section 508 mandated standards for accessibility. It also gave members of the public and government employees with disabilities the right to sue agencies in federal court and file administrative complaints for noncompliance.

As of June 21 2002, all federal web sites were expected to comply with the standards mandated under Section 508. These standards are based on the priority 1 checkpoints of the WCAG, with one priority 3 checkpoint thrown in for good measure. Section 508 does not make any provision for priority 2 checkpoints of the WCAG.

The difference between Section 508 and the WCAG is subtle but important. Section 508 was intended to define when a problem was severe enough to serve as the basis of a lawsuit. The WCAG defines a set of goals for accessible design. As a result, the Section 508 standards are designed to be evaluated more easily. This has made the Section 508 standards a popular basis for accessibility policies at the state, local, and institutional level. Designers in these settings are often under no federal mandate to follow the Section 508 standards. Instead, their local accessibility policy may require use of these standards. This distinction can be confusing but it is important. The consequences for noncompliance may vary significantly from place to place.

The Section 508 standards consist of six parts. Each part addresses a different type of technology. The full set of standards for each section may be found at the following URLs:

- **1194.21 Software applications and operating systems**:
  `http://www.section508.gov/index.cfm?FuseAction=Content&ID=12#Software`

- **1194.22 Web-based intranet and internet information and applications**:
  `http://www.section508.gov/index.cfm?FuseAction=Content&ID=12#Web`

- **1194.23 Telecommunications products**: `http://www.section508.gov/`
  `index.cfm?FuseAction=Content&ID=12#Telecommunications`

- **1194.24 Video and multimedia products**: `http://www.section508.gov/`
  `index.cfm?FuseAction=Content&ID=12#Video`

- **1194.25 Self contained, closed products**: `http://www.section508.gov/`
  `index.cfm?FuseAction=Content&ID=12#Self`

- **1194.26 Desktop and portable computers**: `http://www.section508.gov/`
  `index.cfm?FuseAction=Content&ID=12#Desktop`

Most relevant to this discussion are the standards for web content outlined in section 1194.22. These standards are listed as follows. It is important to note that in cases where plug-ins such as Macromedia Flash content are used, the Software and Operating System standards outlined in section 1194.21 apply. To learn more about the Section 508 standards, visit `http://www.section508.gov` or `http://www.macromedia.com/macromedia/accessibility/`.

§ 1194.22

The section 508 standards for web-based intranet and Internet information and applications are as follows:

- A text equivalent for every nontext element shall be provided (e.g. via "alt," "longdesc," or in element content).

- Equivalent alternatives for any multimedia presentation shall be synchronized with the presentation.

- Web pages shall be designed so that all information conveyed with color is also available without color, for example, from context or markup.

- Documents shall be organized so they are readable without requiring an associated stylesheet.

- Redundant text links shall be provided for each active region of a server-side image map.

- Client-side image maps shall be provided instead of server-side image maps, except where the regions cannot be defined with an available geometric shape.

- Row and column headers shall be identified for data tables.

- Markup shall be used to associate data cells and header cells for data tables that have two or more logical levels of row or column headers.

- Frames shall be titled with text that facilitates frame identification and navigation.

- Pages shall be designed to avoid causing the screen to flicker with a frequency greater than 2Hz and lower than 55Hz.

- A text-only page with equivalent information or functionality shall be provided to make a website comply with the provisions of this part, when compliance cannot be accomplished in any other way. The content of the text-only page shall be updated whenever the primary page changes.

- When pages utilize scripting languages to display content or to create interface elements, the information provided by the script shall be identified with functional text that can be read by assistive technology.

- When a web page requires that an applet, plug-in, or other application be present on the client system to interpret page content, the page must provide a link to a plug-in or applet that complies with §1194.21(a) through (l).

- When electronic forms are designed to be completed online, the form shall allow people using assistive technology to access the information, field elements, and functionality required for completion and submission of the form, including all directions and cues.

- A method shall be provided that permits users to skip repetitive navigation links.

- When a timed response is required, the user shall be alerted and given sufficient time to indicate more time is required.

Skip navigation mechanism enables people using screen readers to avoid listening to every link in the navigation bar on each page. Typically, designers create skip navigation by linking a small transparent image at the top of a page to an anchor just before the main content. The Alt text description for this image would read, "skips to content" or "skip navigation."

Accessibility in Dreamweaver MX 2004

For designers trying to build accessible web sites, Dreamweaver MX 2004 is an ideal tool. Dreamweaver MX 2004 automates many elements of creating accessible sites and prompts designers to provide information when necessary. Dreamweaver MX 2004 also includes a powerful validation and reference tools to help designers ensure that their sites are designed properly for accessibility. Another advantage of Dreamweaver MX 2004 is that it has been modified to provide better keyboard access and to work with screen readers. Dreamweaver is the first professional design tool to be accessible to individuals with disabilities.

This section outlines the accessibility features implemented in Dreamweaver MX 2004. Each of the features will be explained and described in terms of the benefits for people with disabilities and for the designers themselves.

Accessibility Preferences Options

Accessibility features such as alt text are often overlooked when creating web sites. Dreamweaver MX 2004 allows designers to set preferences that remind them to provide accessibility information as they are building the page. By activating the Accessibility options in the Preferences dialog box (on the Edit menu), designers and developers will be prompted to provide accessibility-related information for form objects, frames, media, images, and tables as they insert each of these elements (see Figure 3-2).

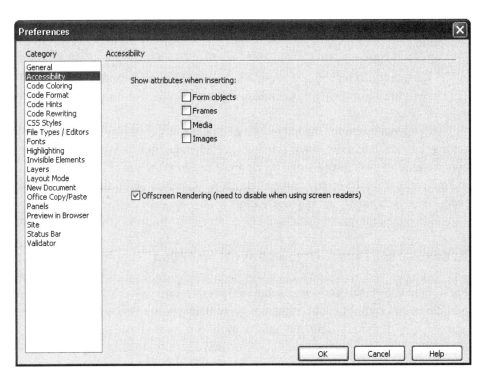

Figure 3-2. Accessibility options in Dreamweaver MX 2004

Adding Images

When the Images option is selected, users are asked to provide a text equivalent and a description for each image in the dialog box shown in Figure 3-3.

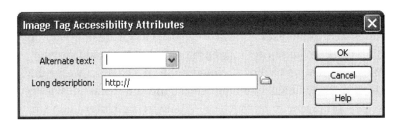

Figure 3-3. Adding image descriptions in Dreamweaver MX 2004

A screen reader reads the contents of the `alt` attribute in place of the image. In general, it is desirable to describe the image in terms of its function rather than its appearance. This helps the content flow better as it is read to the user. It also spares the user from long descriptions that are not relevant to the content.

In general, alt text (contained in the `alt` attribute of an element) should be limited to about 50 characters. If further details are required to convey the content of the image, the designer should consider using a long description. The `longdesc` attribute is a link to a longer description stored on a separate page. Although the long description is not visible to sighted users, screen reader users are notified of the existence of the link. In Figure 3-4, the source code listed shows an image with both an `alt` attribute and a `longdesc` attribute. The image shows a diver near a coral reef with alt text that reads, "Safe diving near a coral reef." There is also a link to a long description file, `scuba.htm`, that includes a more detailed discussion of the techniques demonstrated in the photo.

```
Label: <img src="/images/scuba.gif alt="Photo: Safe diving near a coral reef"
longdesc="scuba.htm">
```

Figure 3-4. Photo and alt text

For images that convey no content, such as spacer images, the appropriate `alt` attribute is `alt=""`. To set an empty `alt` attribute, Dreamweaver MX 2004 has a new drop-down menu on the Image Tag Accessibility Attributes dialog box and the Properties inspector. From this drop-down menu, the designer or developer can select `<empty>` as the value for the `alt` attribute, as shown in Figure 3-5.

Image Tag Accessibility Attributes ☒

Alternate text: | ▾

Long description: <empty> ☐

OK

Cancel

Help

Figure 3-5. Selecting an empty `alt` *attribute*

Adding Media

Under Section 508 standards, any content that is delivered using a plug-in is considered a piece of software. Therefore, media elements such Flash or Shockwave files must be evaluated using the software standards. For more information on the software standards, visit `http://www.section508.gov`.

In addition, designers might want to provide more information about the media element. As with images, when a media element is inserted, a dialog box appears to collect accessibility-related information (shown in Figure 3-6).

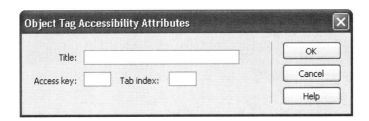

Object Tag Accessibility Attributes ☒

Title:

Access key: ⬚ Tab index: ⬚

OK

Cancel

Help

Figure 3-6. Providing accessibility information on media objects.

The `title` attribute is similar to the `alt` attribute for images, and it is useful in the design of forms when objects such as radio buttons and form fields need description.

Access key (the `accesskey` attribute) provides keyboard users with a quick means of moving directly to the element on the page. For example, if the access key for a Flash movie is set to P, users who rely on the keyboard rather than the mouse could press Alt+P to go directly to the Flash movie. It is necessary, however, for the designer to notify the user of the existence of the access key. In a form, underlining a letter in the label generally identifies the access key; however, media elements do not usually have labels associated with them. Consequently, the designer will have to provide this information on the page itself or on a separate page that provides directions for users with disabilities.

Tab index (the `tabindex` attribute) is a very helpful when working with Flash content. The tab index allows the designer to specify the order in which a user encounters the contents of a page when using Tab to navigate. With Flash content, a problem may arise if the ActiveX architecture traps the cursor inside the Flash movie. If a user presses Tab to enter a Flash navigation bar at the top of a page, it is likely that the user will be unable to access the links on the page. A common way around this problem is to set the Flash element to appear at the end of the tab order. It is important to remember, however, that a tab order must be set for all links, input elements, and objects in this instance.

Adding Frames

There was a time when frames posed a serious challenge to screen readers; however, most screen readers today can handle frames perfectly well. Most of the challenges that people with disabilities encounter with frames are the same as those for people without disabilities. It is difficult to link to individual pages, and the use of the Back button may be problematic.

Ironically, frames can provide a real benefit for accessibility. Most designers use them to segment the page by content. Often the banner appears in one frame, navigation in another, and the content in a third. A screen reader user can easily move from one frame to another, skipping over titles and links to get to the information the user wants.

However, frames are only helpful if titled properly. In Dreamweaver MX 2004, as a designer inserts a frameset, he or she is prompted to provide a title for each frame (see Figure 3-7). The drop-down menu at the top of the dialog box contains a list of all the frames in the frameset. For each of these frames, the designer will need to specify a different name. The names do not have to be long or detailed, but they should be meaningful. Names as simple as *banner*, *nav*, and *content* will suffice.

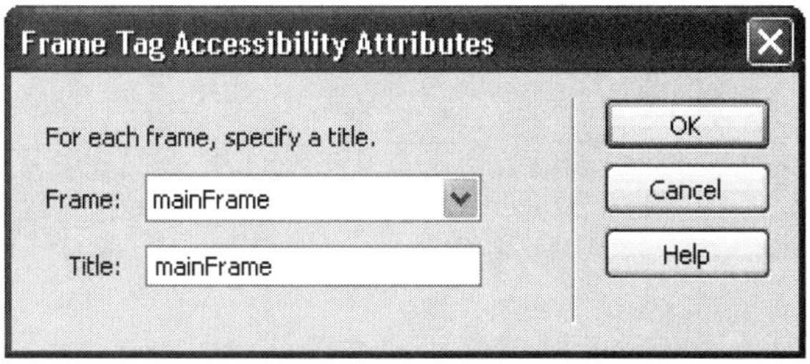

Figure 3-7. Specifying titles for each frame in a frameset

Adding Forms

Creating accessible forms is easy with Dreamweaver MX 2004. With the Forms option selected in the Preferences dialog box, designers are prompted to provide a label for each form element along with an access key and the position in the tab order.

Traditionally, labels for form elements are simply placed to the left of the element itself. If the layout is more complex, however, and labels are placed away from the corresponding elements, people using a screen reader can have a very difficult time determining the purpose of each element. When the designer uses the dialog box shown in Figure 3-8 to add the label for an element, Dreamweaver MX 2004 also adds HTML markup that formally associates the text label with the element.

There are two styles available for this label-element association. The first option, Wrap with label tag, is used when the text label is immediately next to the form object. The second, Attach label tag using 'for' attribute, is used when the layout is more complex.

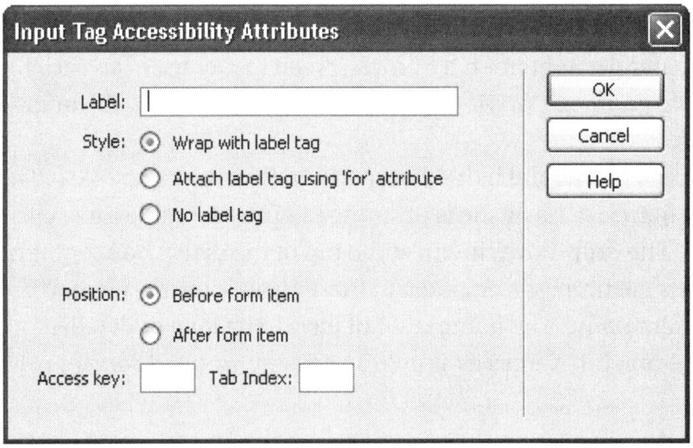

Figure 3-8. Adding accessible form labels

Let's take a simple example. We'll create a form with a single form field for an email address and a Submit button. In this example, the text label is immediately to the left of the form field so the designer would use to first option, Wrap with label tag, to create the form, shown in Figure 3-9.

Figure 3-9. A simple form example

The code to generate this form is shown as follows. Notice that the `<label>` element contains both the text label *Email* and the `<input>` element itself. Also, notice that the Submit button has no label. This is because screen readers will read the contents of the `name` attribute as the label for the Submit button.

```
<form name="form1" method="post" action="">
  <p>
    <label>Email
    <input type="text" name="textfield">
    </label>
  </p>
  <p>
    <input type="submit" name="Submit" value="Submit">
  </p>
</form>
```

In the next example, the layout is slightly more complex. The text label is placed above the form element using a table, as shown in Figure 3-10. In this case, the method just described won't work. Instead, the designer should use the `for` and `id` attributes to associate the text label with the form field. This is most easily accomplished by choosing the second option, Attach label tag using 'for' attribute in the Input Tag Accessibility Attributes dialog box.

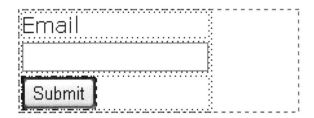

Figure 3-10. A slightly more complex form example

The code used to generate this example is shown as follows. Notice that the `<label>` element contains only the text label, *Email*. The `for` attribute within the `<label>` element has the same value as the `id` attribute in the `<input>` element, `textfield`. This is how the screen readers will know which label should go with which form field in complex layouts such as this one.

```
<form name="form1" method="post" action="">
  <table width="10" border="0">
    <tr>
      <td><label for="textfield">Email</label></td>
    </tr>
    <tr>
      <td> <input type="text" name="textfield" id="textfield"></td>
    </tr>
    <tr>
      <td><input type="submit" name="Submit" value="Submit"></td>
    </tr>
  </table>
</form>
```

Adding Tables

Creating accessible tables for presenting data is perhaps the most complex issue for designers. Dreamweaver MX 2004 has greatly simplified this process by providing fields for adding all the necessary markup for simple tables with one or two sets of headers.

When inserting a data table within Dreamweaver MX 2004, designers are immediately asked to provide a caption, summary information, and the position of headers in the table. A table caption is used to provide a title for the table. These captions are visible and placed at the top of the table. Summaries should be used to provide a general description of the data in the table. This information is not visible but is easily accessible to screen reader users.

Identifying headers makes it significantly easier for screen readers to navigate tables. This step is tremendously important but often overlooked by designers. When the designer specifies a header using the Table in the figure dialog box (shown in Figure 3-11), Dreamweaver MX 2004 identifies the row or column of headers and adds the `scope` attribute for that header. The `scope` attribute associates data in the data cells with the corresponding headers so that a screen reader will read the headers along with the data.

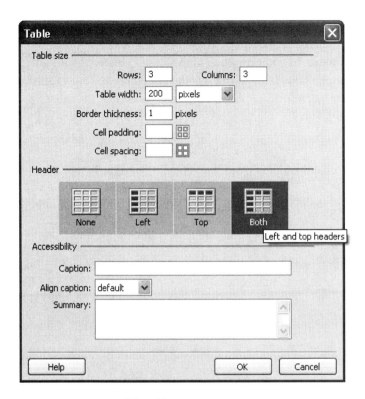

Figure 3-11. Accessible tables in Dreamweaver MX 2004

Figure 3-12 is a relatively simple table with a single row of headers. Under these headers, there is a brief list of individuals.

Participants 2003

Last Name	City	State
Flynn	Raleigh	NC
Marsh	Madison	WI
Gandin	Madison	WI
Rick	Columbus	OH

Figure 3-12. A simple table

In the code used to generate this table, all the cells in the first row use the `<th>` element. This lets the screen reader know that these cells are headers for the information displayed below them. In addition, each of these `<th>` elements contains the scope attribute with the value set to col. This lets the screen reader know that the header organizes a column of information, as opposed to a row and that all of the cells below use this header.

```
<table width="150" border="1" summary="This table shows three
 columns of data displaying last name, city and state.">
  <caption>Participants 2003</caption>
  <tr>
    <th scope="col">Last Name</th>
    <th scope="col">City</th>
    <th scope="col">State</th>
  </tr>
  <tr>
    <td>Flynn</td>
    <td>Raleigh</td>
    <td>NC</td>
  </tr>
  <tr>
    <td>Marsh</td>
    <td>Madison</td>
    <td>WI</td>
  </tr>
  <tr>
    <td>Gandin</td>
    <td>Madison</td>
    <td>WI</td>
  </tr>
  <tr>
    <td>Rick</td>
    <td>Columbus</td>
    <td>OH</td>
  </tr>
</table>
```

Accessibility Validation

Dreamweaver MX 2004 includes a comprehensive set of tools that can validate the accessibility of a single page, a group of pages, or even an entire site. The new Accessibility Reports tool (shown in Figure 3-13) validates web pages for compliance with Section 508 standards and the WCAG Priority 1 checkpoints.

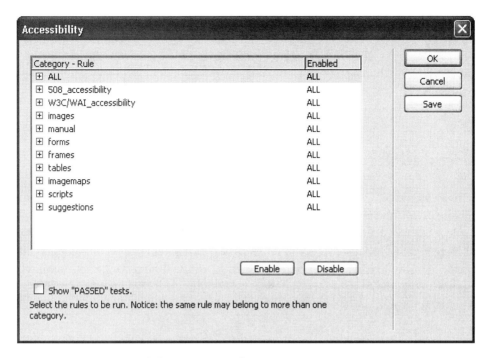

Figure 3-13. The Accessibility Reports tool

The accessibility report (shown in Figure 3-14) identifies all areas with obvious errors, such as missing alt text, as well as areas that require a manual evaluation, such as color combinations. In addition, when a designer or developer selects an individual item from the report, the corresponding part of the page is highlighted to point the designer directly to the area in need of attention.

Figure 3-14. An accessibility report

Beyond the validation tools built into Dreamweaver MX 2004, there are a variety of third-party products available that perform more sophisticated types of validation functions and help automate the repair of sites. One such product is LIFT for Dreamweaver from UsableNet (http://www.usablenet.com/). LIFT allows designers to validate a page as it is being constructed, pointing out problems as they appear on the page. LIFT also helps designers automate the repair of some of the most complex accessibility issues. For example, LIFT offers designers the ability to quickly repair complex tables using the headers and id attributes quickly, with a graphical interface. For designers who regularly work with these types of complex problems, LIFT can be a very valuable tool.

Accessibility Reference

Dreamweaver MX 2004 includes a built-in accessibility reference, as seen in Figure 3-15. This reference explains each of the rules used to check pages for accessibility and includes links to more detailed information about each issue. This reference tool makes it easier for designers to master the specific accessibility issues relevant to their sites. The reference tool can be used with the accessibility report so that the designer can request more information about a rule listed in the report, and view the response in the accessibility reference panel.

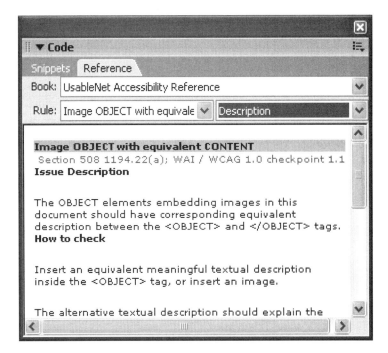

Figure 3-15. The Dreamweaver accessibility reference

Cascading Stylesheets

In Macromedia Dreamweaver MX 2004, Cascading Stylesheets are the default method for formatting text. This has significant implications for accessibility. Although use of CSS is not required under Section 508, it is required under policies in the UK, Canada, Germany, and several U.S. states. This section reviews some of the key benefits as well as the new features introduced in this latest release.

One of the central tenets of accessibility is the separation of presentation from structure. In very simple terms, this can mean using HTML to control the hierarchical organization of a document and CSS to control the formatting. As you saw in Chapter 2, CSS is a tremendously powerful technology because it allows the end user the capability to easily render the text in the manner that best meets his or her needs.

User-defined stylesheets are attached to a page by the user via the browser. They allow users to format text. Users with limited vision can change the text size and users who are colorblind can change the text and background colors.

The last stop in the cascade is HTML. This is important to note because HTML overrides all CSS styles, including user-defined styles. Using the `<font>` element to mark up text removes the user's control over the formatting of text. Mixing HTML presentation together with CSS limits the user's ability to control the formatting on the page. Even in a simple example such as the use of background images can serve as a tremendous obstacle. For colorblind users, black text on a white background can be significantly easier to read. However, if the background image is coded using HTML as opposed to CSS, they will not be able to use user-defined stylesheets to replace the background image, even if the text is formatted using CSS. The HTML will always override the CSS and thus the background image can not easily be removed by the user.

Dreamweaver MX 2004 uses CSS to format text by default. When choosing a font from the Properties inspector, an internal style is automatically created and added to the page. The size menu has also changed in this release. Designers can now specify sizes using a variety of units available via CSS. Finally, custom styles, also called **class selectors**, can be applied directly from the Style menu on the Properties inspector, as shown in Figure 3-16. This menu provides designers with a preview of each style to help facilitate consistent use of each style.

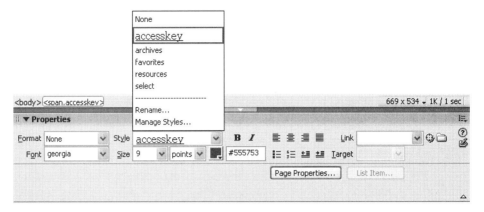

Figure 3-16. Previewing styles on the Style menu

There is one significant concern worth noting when it comes to the use of CSS—fixed units such as points and millimeters prevent the user from changing the text size on the screen. Although designers often want to exert precise control over text for layout and design reasons, it is important to remember that many users use the text size control in their browser to make small text easy to read. Using relative units such as ems and percentage provides users with a level of control over the text size.

Accessible Authoring Environment

A significant improvement to Dreamweaver MX 2004 over its predecessors is its cooperation with assistive technologies. With improved labeling and sequencing of buttons, Dreamweaver MX 2004 is now the most powerful web development environment for users of assistive technologies, such as the Window-Eyes and JAWS screen readers.

Several features have been added to Dreamweaver MX 2004 to make it easier for persons with disabilities to create web pages. Among these features are two new shortcut keys that allow users to access Dreamweaver MX 2004 panels using the keyboard. The first of these shortcuts, Ctrl+Alt+Tab, allows the user to access the panel groups in Dreamweaver MX 2004. For example, pressing Ctrl+Alt+Tab once displays the Design panel group. From there, pressing Tab moves the user among the buttons of the open panel. Pressing Ctrl+Tab displays the different panels in the group.

The second shortcut allows the user to redisplay the page window by pressing Ctrl+Alt+Home. Users will need this keystroke after moving among individual panels and panel groups.

Two other useful new features of Dreamweaver MX 2004 specifically support users with impaired vision, and who use a screen reader. Both of these options are available in Edit ➤ Preferences under the accessibility category. The first, Make Dreamweaver Use Large Fonts, increases the default font size within the Dreamweaver application. The menu options and panels are then easier to read for those with low vision.

The second, Offscreen rendering (Disable when using Screen Readers), offers improved performance for screen reader users in Dreamweaver MX 2004. To prevent flickering, Dreamweaver uses double buffering, which draws the screen in memory before displaying it to the user. Screen readers work best with this option disabled because they only read the foreground screen, not the screen generated in the background.

Summary

This chapter outlined the accessibility features in Macromedia Dreamweaver MX 2004. Dreamweaver MX 2004 is a powerful tool for people with disabilities who are creating web sites and for the development of accessible web sites and web applications. Dreamweaver MX 2004 automates many elements of creating accessible sites and prompts designers to provide information when necessary. Dreamweaver MX 2004 also includes powerful validation and reference tools to help designers ensure that their sites are designed properly.

The development of accessible web sites ensures that the site's content is not obscured by design elements; furthermore, an accessible web site is compatible with the assistive technologies used by people with disabilities, such as screen readers, touch screens, or head pointers. Dreamweaver MX 2004 was developed to provide better keyboard access and to work with screen readers, and it is the first professional design tool to be accessible to individuals with disabilities.

CHAPTER 4

Introducing ASP

THIS CHAPTER PROVIDES a swift introduction to the basics of coding dynamic web applications (using ASP/VBScript as the language of choice). This is essential to your Dreamweaver MX learning experience—before using the pre-built Dreamweaver MX server behaviors, it is important to have a firm understanding of how dynamic web pages work. This will enable you to use Dreamweaver MX to its fullest capacity and will also save you time! This book focuses on the classic ASP server behaviors and functionality of Dreamweaver MX—not the ASP.NET functionality, which is a different server model.

In this chapter, we will look at:

- Static versus dynamic web pages

- Variables

- Commenting code

- String, integer, and Boolean data types

- Built-in functions and typecasting

- Operators

- Conditional logic

- Looping logic

- HTML forms

- URL parameters

- Cookies

- Sessions

- Environment variables

No More Static

At this point in the book, you are ready to shed your old ways for the new. Have you ever wondered how to implement all those cool dynamic features you see on so many web sites these days, such as logins, registrations, personal folders, greeting cards, e-mail, and so on? By the end of this chapter, you will have working knowledge of how many of these cool features are done.

What's Wrong with HTML?

HTML is awesome! HTML is and will probably always be the main language of the Web. The question is not "What's wrong with HTML?" but rather "What can't HTML do?" The answer is: *a lot*, especially if you expect to offer user-interactive applications and/or data that will be constantly changing. Remember that HTML is not a programming language—it is a simple markup language, and its main job is to format text. How can we expect it to send an automatic e-mail when a user clicks the feedback button?

The only way we can expect something to happen automatically based on user interaction is by a program or **web application** that is built specifically for the task at hand. Web applications are built using one of the many web-scripting languages available. Dreamweaver MX supports five of the most popular—ASP, ASP.NET, JSP, ColdFusion, and PHP. In this chapter, we will be concentrating on the ASP server model.

Static vs. Dynamic

In simple terms, static means "fixed" or "stationary," whereas dynamic means "changing." Anything that only executes on the client browser is considered static, for example, the text contained in HTML cannot be manipulated unless the site's author goes into the source code and manually changes it. That's pretty darn "stationary." Although client-side JavaScript is much more sophisticated than HTML (it is an actual scripting language), it is also "stationary" because it only executes on the client browser. Even JavaScript programs are considered client-side unless they are used with Microsoft's Active Server Pages (ASP), which we will discuss later in this chapter (ASP is executed server-side). Client-side JavaScript programs execute wholly within the browser and can be viewed in the source code. This is why web developers usually refer to web development that utilizes these types of technologies as "client-side development."

On the other hand, "server-side" refers to web development that utilizes technologies that execute not within a client browser but on an actual live server. Server-side technology is considered dynamic because its execution can change depending on what it receives from the client. One of the most important aspects of server-side technology is that it allows you to connect to databases and view and update the data, all from the client browser.

The web scripting language is embedded within the source code with the HTML. It executes on the server once the page is accessed by a browser. The dynamic output and the generic HTML is then sent back to the clients. Here is an example in ASP.

```
<!-- sayHello.asp -->
<html>
  <body>
    <%
      Dim sayHello
      sayHello = "Hello friends!"
      response.write sayHello
    %>
  </body>
</html>
```

You could have simply written "Hello friends!" in the body, but instead, you stuffed the text into an ASP variable and then printed that variable. When a client accesses the page, the ASP engine reads the following ASP code:

```
    <%
      Dim sayHello
      sayHello = "Hello friends!"
      response.write sayHello
    %>
```

It then sends the text to the client browser as HTML. If you create this page and then execute it on a live server, you will not see any ASP in the source code; rather you will only see the following HTML:

```
<html>
  <body>
    Hello friends!
  </body>
</html>
```

This why they are called server-side languages: the server parses the embedded server-side script and sends the result as HTML to the client browser.

Now let's explore the workings of dynamic web pages in much more detail, looking at ASP in particular.

Exit Free CGI Hunting, Enter ASP

You will not have to learn all five web-scripting languages Dreamweaver MX supports to work through this book. Instead, we will show you how to construct dynamic pages in Dreamweaver MX using ASP.

As we said, ASP is one of Microsoft's server-side technologies. ASP files end with a .asp extension and are effectively HTML pages, but they have script contained within special delimiters (more on these later). ASP pages can be coded with any scripting language that has support for the ActiveX Scripting Engine—VBScript, JavaScript, JScript (Microsoft's version of JavaScript), Perl, Rexx, and Python. The two predominant choices are VBScript and JavaScript—both are supported natively by ASP.

VBScript seems to be the preferred one, and it is the one we will use throughout this book. It has gotten to the point where nearly all ASP resources use VBScript, so using VBScript makes it easier to find help when it's needed, especially for beginners. It is the default language for ASP.

Because Dreamweaver MX generates ASP code for you, you may wonder why you need to know anything about ASP at all. It's logical that you need a basic understanding of code and design before using a program that generates code and design for you. Dreamweaver MX speeds up your application building time if you know when and how to use it, but if you don't know what a recordset is, how can you know when and how to use the Dreamweaver MX Recordset Server Behavior? Take the time to learn a bit about web programming with ASP. Don't worry—you will soon see how to tell it to do all the "dummy" work for you.

Getting Started

Let's go straight to dynamic web programming with ASP/VBScript, Dreamweaver MX style.

What You Need To Get Started

To begin coding in VBScript all you need is any text editor (even Notepad will do). Because web-scripting languages execute on a live server, you need a web server to execute ASP.

- If you use Windows 95/98, there is a free mini-server called Personal Web Server (PWS). You can download it here: `http://www.microsoft.com/ msdownload/ntoptionpack/askwiz.asp`. You can choose the Windows 95 option for both 95 and 98.

- If you use Windows ME, Microsoft does not distribute PWS or support its use with this operating system. Please see this tech note: `http://support.microsoft.com/support/kb/articles/Q266/4/56.asp`. Although Microsoft does not recommend installing PWS on a Windows ME system, there are third-party tutorials on how to do so. Use these tutorials at your own risk. You can find one at `http://billsway.com/notes_public/PWS_WinMe.txt`.

- If you use Windows 2000, you are in luck. Although PWS will work fine for Windows 95/98 users, Windows 2000 comes with a full-blown web server called Internet Information Services (IIS). IIS is not installed by default on Windows 2000, but you can install it by completing the following steps:

  1. Click the Start button.

  2. Click Control Panel.

  3. Click Add/Remove Programs.

  4. Click Add/Remove Windows Components.

  5. Select the Internet Information Services check box.

  6. Click Next.

- If you use Windows XP Professional, you can install IIS by inserting the Windows XP Professional CD-ROM into your CD-ROM drive and following the same steps as for Windows 2000.

CAUTION *Please note that you cannot run ASP on Windows XP Home Edition.*

Unix does not support ASP out of the box, but there is software available that will enable the deployment of Active Server Pages on a Unix server. If you have to use a Unix server for ASP, you may find that your hosting company has the Sun ONE Active Server Pages installed (which used to be known as Chili!ASP)—found at `http://developers.sun.com/prodtech/asp/`.

Once you have completed your installations, make sure the server works by simply pointing your preferred web browser to http://localhost. If the installation was successful, you will see the default web server page.

Now let's try running an ASP through your web server. Create the following file and save it as `Myasppage.asp`:

```
<html>
  <head>
    <title>My ASP Page</title>
  </head>
  <body>
    Can you see me? I'm the first ASP page to be executed on this server!
  </body>
</html>
```

Place this file in the home directory of your web server. This is usually C:\inetpub\wwwroot—the folder wwwroot is the root of your virtual web site. Whenever your domain is accessed online, the server begins serving pages here. By default, the server will execute pages with the names default or index.

Point your browser to `http://localhost/Myasppage.asp`, and you should see a page similar to the one shown in Figure 4-1.

As long as the page loads and you see the text within the body, you're OK. If this is not your result, double check that you installed the web server properly. Make sure your web server is running by going to Control Panel ➤ Administrative Tools ➤ Internet Services Manager (or Personal Web Manager). You can start or shut down the web server by finding the default web site in the tree and using the Start and Stop buttons in the display. Once you have a web server running on your machine, take extra care to ensure that your computer is kept up to date with all service patches because any virus or exploit scanning for open, unpatched servers will find you just as it will find the web servers of a hosting company. Better still, install firewall software, or if you are using a DSL type of connection, connecting via a hardware router/firewall can give you additional peace of mind because they will hide your web server from the wider world.

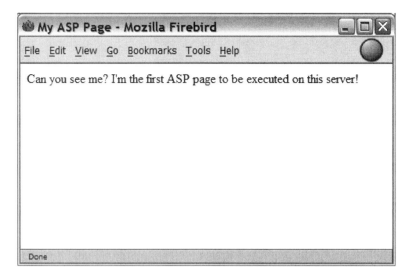

Figure 4-1. Page in browser

You should also make sure that the home directory has read access and can execute scripts. Right-click your default web site, select the Properties option, and click the Home Directory tab. Make sure the Read option is checked, and also make sure that Scripts only is selected from the Execute Permissions menu under Application Settings (Scripts and Executables will also work, but allowing others to execute programs on your web server can be a major security risk).

Creating a Virtual Directory

When you are working in ASP you need to think of each web site as an application. That application may be a collection of pages that are mainly static HTML that use a small amount of ASP for user identification, but they are still related. If you were to store all your ASP pages within the wwwroot directory, it would soon become very confusing. Therefore, you should start by creating a virtual directory whenever you begin a new application/site. The virtual directory allows you to execute ASP pages. You cannot simply store your files in any location on your computer and expect them to be parsed by the server; they have to go in locations that are set up as sites.

Create a regular directory on your computer where you will store the files you are working with throughout this virtual directory. Name this directory **webprodmx_files**. To set up a virtual directory:

1. Go to Start ➤ Settings ➤ Control Panel ➤ Administrative Tools ➤ Internet Information Services.

2. Expand the Web Sites folder , right-click the Default Web Site icon, and then select New ➤ Virtual Directory, as shown in Figure 4-2.

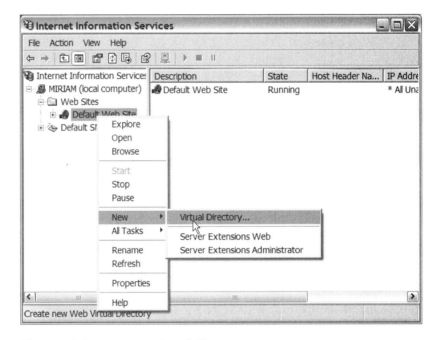

Figure 4-2. Create a new virtual directory

3. In the Virtual Directory Creation Wizard, type **webprodmx** as the alias.

4. Click Browse and select the directory named webprodmx_files.

5. Check Read and Scripts under Application permissions. Then click Finish.

You can now check that this virtual directory is working by pointing your web browser to `http://localhost/webprodmx`. When accessed through the browser, this directory will point to the physical folder webprodmx_files, so any ASP page you store within the webprodmx_files folder will be accessible via the URL `http://localhost/webprodmx/yourpage.asp`.

Setting Up Dreamweaver for ASP Development

Once your server is up and running, you then set up a site in Dreamweaver that uses ASP. This means that Dreamweaver will let you preview your dynamic pages from within Dreamweaver using live data.

Defining Your Site

1. With your web server running, open Dreamweaver and select Site ➤ Manage Sites. In the Manage Sites dialog box, click New Site, and then select Site to begin defining your new site. The first screen will ask you to name your site. Name it **webprodmx**.

2. In the next screen, select "Yes, I want to use a server technology" and select ASP/VBScript from the drop-down menu.

3. In the next screen, select the first radio button "Edit and test locally" and browse for the folder webprodmx_files.

4. In the next screen, enter the URL of the site locally—this is http://localhost/webprodmx—the virtual directory that you created.

5. Select No in the next screen.

6. Click Done to create your site.

If you copy the file you created earlier (Myasppage.asp) to test your server installation into your webprodmx_files directory, you should be able to view it by typing **http://localhost/webprodmx/Myasppage.asp**.

Open that page in Design view and click the Live Data button (which will appear beside the Design View button at the top of the document window). This view (shown in Figure 4-3) passes the page through the server and parses the ASP before displaying it so you do not have to keep previewing the page in the browser.

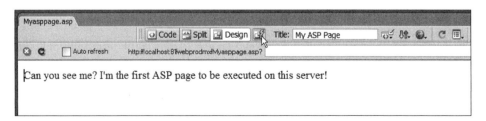

Figure 4-3. Live Data view displaying an ASP page

ASP/VBScript Basics

In this section, you will start to explore ASP and the scripting language VBScript, which is the language used throughout this book for ASP. Working through this section will give you a good overview of ASP and VBScript, and if you haven't used a scripting language before, you will develop an understanding of the various terms used to describe the parts of such a language. This will help you follow the rest of this book and get help when you need it.

Specifying Your Scripting Language

Because ASP web pages can be scripted using various languages, it is necessary to inform each page which language will be used. Because VBScript is the default language for ASP, it is not necessary to specify that you will be using VBScript, but it is good practice to specify it anyway. You specify a language besides VBScript by adding in a line of code at the top of your page with the following syntax: `<% @ Language = "language_name" %>`. For example, if you use VBScript, you would type

```
<% @ Language = "VBScript" %>
```

For JavaScript, you would type

```
<% @ Language = "JavaScript" %>
```

Keep in mind that this line must be the first line in your source code. If you do not specify your language at the top of each page, your page will throw an error when executed if it is coded in a language other than VBScript. Of course, it will also throw an error if you code with a language other than the one specified in this page directive.

Dreamweaver MX will automatically insert this line for you every time you create a new dynamic ASP web page using either VBScript or JavaScript.

The Delimiters

All ASP script code must appear between delimiters. Once the server sees the first opening delimiter, `<%`, the ASP script engine begins its work and continues until it reaches the closing delimiter, `%>`. Nothing but ASP scripting can go in between the delimiters. Here is an example:

```
<%
  Dim MyVariable
%>
```

You use the `Dim` statement to declare a variable—we'll explain more about variables later in this book. `Dim MyVariable` is one line. The following is equivalent to the previous example:

```
<% Dim MyVariable %>
```

You can also break up multiple lines with their own delimiter blocks.

```
<% Dim MyVariable %>
<% MyVariable = "Hello" %>
```

This is equivalent to

```
<%
  Dim MyVariable
  MyVariable = "Hello"
%>
```

You get the idea. It's up to you how you want to format your code—just remember to be consistent throughout your application and format your code in a manner that makes it easy for you and others to read. Try to keep as much ASP code as possible in one block when embedding ASP code within HTML; however, multiple blocks are sometimes necessary.

Keep in mind that one ASP line cannot be broken up into separate delimiter blocks. `<% Dim %> <% MyVariable %>` will throw an error because a variable must come after the `Dim` statement.

You can of course simply type code into the Code view. Throughout this chapter you will be working in Code view instead of Design view where Dreamweaver's built-in behaviors are available. If you want to cut down on typing, there are some code shortcuts on the ASP tab of the Insert toolbar, shown in Figure 4-4.

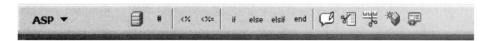

Figure 4-4. ASP pane of the Insert toolbar

To insert the `<% %>` delimiters, click the Code Block button.

Variables

Variables are among the most important concepts in any scripting language. A variable simply stores information that you can use later. In addition, the information in the variable may change during the course of the script.

For example, if you were writing a dynamic web application that deals with cars, for example, a database application that collects and stores details of people's cars, you would not know what kind of car will be introduced by the client/user. To account for all the different kinds of cars, you would use a placeholder that contains a value that could represent any kind of car.

Declaring Variables

It's time to declare your first variable in VBScript. Create a new dynamic page in Dreamweaver MX, and select ASP/VBScript. Select File ➤ New, and choose the options shown in Figure 4-5.

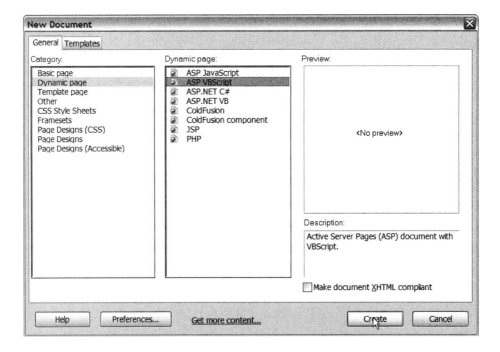

Figure 4-5.Create a new dynamic page

Keep the code and design panes in view. You will code your VBScript directly into the code pane. ASP code can go anywhere on your page, but for the examples in this chapter, all ASP code should be typed within the `<body>` tags of the document.

In VBScript, you declare a variable by using the `Dim` statement, as you saw earlier. Create a new ASP/VBScript page and save it as `my_variable.asp`. Type the following within the `<body></body>` tags:

```
<%
  Dim MyVariable
  MyVariable = "I am the value of an ASP variable"
%>
```

View the page live on your server. Press F12 to load the page in a browser window.

What did you see? If you said "nothing"…great! You shouldn't have seen anything but a blank screen because all you did was declare a variable called `MyVariable`, with a value of "I am the value of an ASP variable."

Now let's print out the value of the variable. Modify your code like this:

```
<%
  Dim MyVariable
  MyVariable = "I am the value of an ASP variable"
  Response.Write MyVariable
%>
```

The `Response.Write` statement simply an instruction to write the content of `MyVariable` on the page. View your page now. You should see the following displayed in your browser:

```
I am the value of an ASP variable
```

You can also include HTML within the value of a variable.

```
<%
  Dim MyVariable
  MyVariable = "I am the value of an <strong>ASP</strong> variable"
  Response.Write MyVariable
%>
```

Variables can be assigned values if they haven't been declared in a `Dim` statement, however, best practice suggests that by routinely "dimming" variables explicitly, it becomes easier to debug a page long after it has been written and published because the code is more readable and better organized.

The following example will work fine.

```
<%
  MyVariable = "I am the value of an ASP variable"
  Response.Write MyVariable
%>
```

Unfortunately, Dreamweaver MX does not stick to this convention. It often generates ASP code without declaring its variables.

Syntax Rules for Variables

There are some rules regarding the syntax of variables.

- Do not use spaces, periods, or dashes anywhere in the variable. `My variable` is unacceptable.

- Variables must begin with a letter. `2myvariable` is unacceptable.

- Reserved words cannot be used as variable names. For example "Dim" is unacceptable because it is reserved in VBScript. For a list of VBScript reserved words, see the following page: `http://support.microsoft.com/default.aspx?scid=kb;EN-US;q216528`.

Variable Naming Conventions

Some naming conventions that have become popular include naming variables according to their data types. You will learn more about data types later in this chapter.

If the variable is a string, adding `str` to the beginning of the variable name is not uncommon—for example, `strMyVariable` or `str_my_variable`. The same would go for an integer variable—`intMyVariable` or `int_myvariable`.

Some variables are named after the author. If your initials are RA, you might name your variable `RA_MyVariable` or `ra_my_variable`. You might also name it according to the application you are working on.

Macromedia adds `MM` to most of its variables so you will often find variables such as `MM_RedirectPage`, `MM_ConnectionString`, and so on.

Avoid naming your variables with initials only, such as `RP`, `ag1`, `str_cdp`, and the like. Make sure that what the variable represents is obvious just from glancing at it, such as `RedirectPage`, `ArabicGreeting`, and so on. Then you may feel free to add your own prefixes, however you want, for example `str_RedirectPage`, `OE_ArabicGreeting`, and so on. This makes your code far more readable, and you will not need to add so many comments to help others who read your code at a later date.

You'll get used to seeing this when sifting through the source code. It doesn't really matter how you name your variable. The best advice when naming your variables is to keep it simple, appropriate, and obvious—whether you add prefix letters to your variables is up to you. You can see an interesting article about naming conventions at `http://msdn.microsoft.com/library/default.asp?url=/library/en-us/script56/html/vbscodingconventions.asp`.

VBScript Is Case-Insensitive

Unlike JScript, VBScript is case-insensitive. This means that it doesn't matter whether you use lowercase or uppercase characters. `Dim Myvariable` is the same as `DIM mYvariaBle`. This makes things easier for the web developer, especially because it gives you one less thing to worry about when it comes to debugging time!

However, even though VBScript is case-insensitive you should maintain some sort of consistency within your code. Code becomes confusing to the eye when you have a variable written as `myvariable` in one place and then the same variable written `MYVariable` in another. Choose one style and stick with it.

Writing Data to the Page

You can use `<%=` in place of `Response.Write` as long as writing out this statement is the only action you want to perform inside a new block of code. For example, to print the date and time using the `Now()` VBScript function, this

```
<% Response.Write Now() %>
```

is equivalent to this

```
<%= Now() %>
```

You can also rewrite your variable declaration example to the following, utilizing the shortcut to output the variable:

```
<%
  MyVariable = "I am the value of an ASP variable"
%>


<%= MyVariable %>
```

This shortcut often comes in handy, as you shall see throughout the course of this chapter.

> **TIP** *You can insert the <%= %> code block from the ASP tab of the Insert toolbar by clicking the Output button, which has the <%= symbols on it.*

Commenting Code

Commenting code is a manner of including information about your code. Every programming/markup language offers the ability to comment code, even HTML. The following is an HTML comment:

```
<!-- This division is to hold the main navigation of the page -->
< div> home / about / contact </div>
```

Everything within the <!-- --> delimiters will not be parsed as HTML code. Of course, these HTML comments are viewable in the source code—as you can see, comments inform anyone viewing the code of the purpose of the different code sections.

ASP/VBScript comments are done by putting a single quotation mark in front of a line. This causes the entire line to be completely ignored by the web server. For example, let's add a comment to the my_variable.asp page, and comment the Response.Write line:

```
<%
  MyVariable = "I am the value of an ASP variable"

  'Response.Write MyVariable
  ' Here is a comment
%>
```

Dreamweaver MX should turn commented lines gray in Code view.

When you view this page in the browser now, the variable will not be outputted—only the first line will execute. Note that ASP comments are not viewable in the client browser at all because the server has already parsed the code.

Commenting code is very important, especially when it comes to debugging. It allows you to block out code quickly in case you want to test isolated code sections. It also gives you the opportunity to document your code. This is helpful when the time comes for you (or someone else) to look back through the code and update it.

> **NOTE** *Dreamweaver MX often comments code generated by its server behaviors.*

Concatenation Using the Ampersand (&)

You can also concatenate variables—concatenation simply means putting things together.

> **TIP** *Concatenation does not add things mathematically. It only puts them together, side by side.*

For example, let's try concatenating two strings into one variable. Create the following file and save it as `my_greeting.asp`:

```
<%
  Dim Mygreeting
  Mygreeting = "Hello" & " World"
  ' We need to leave a space before the W in World.

  Response.Write Mygreeting
%>
```

View the page in your browser and you should see the following appear:

```
Hello World
```

You concatenated two values into one for the `Mygreeting` variable. You can also concatenate two variables into the value of a third variable. Create the following file and save it as `my_second_greeting.asp`:

```
<%
  Dim MyHello, MyWorld, Mygreeting
  MyHello = "Hello"
  MyWorld = "World"
  Mygreeting = MyHello & " " & MyWorld

  Response.Write Mygreeting
%>
```

View the page in your browser and you should again see

```
Hello World
```

You can also concatenate variables with values during output. For example:

```
<%
  Dim MyHello
  MyHello = "Hello"

  Response.Write MyHello & " World"
%>
```

Every single part in concatenation must be separated by an ampersand (&). The following is incorrect and will throw an error:

```
<%
  Dim MyHello, MyWorld, Mygreeting
  MyHello = "Hello"
  MyWorld = "World"
  Mygreeting = MyHello & " " MyWorld
  ' there is a missing ampersand between the quotes and the MyWorld variable

  Response.Write Mygreeting
%>
```

Note that it is allowable to concatenate strings using the plus sign (+), but it is not preferred over the ampersand (&). Because the plus sign is also used to mathematically add integers, using the plus sign to concatenate integers can cause erroneous results.

Data Types: String, Integer, and Boolean

Every variable has a data type. It is important to know the difference between strings, integers, and Booleans. There certainly are more data types than these three but these are the ones you will usually be working with. Some other data types (that we will not be dealing with here) are: currency, date, object, decimal, byte, array, empty, null, long, single, and double.

Data type is also referred to as variable type. Variables act according to their types—you may try to do something with a string that will not give you the results you intended due to the data type.

Strings contain alphanumeric characters (strings must be surrounded by double quotation marks), integers contain whole numbers (integers are not surrounded by quotation marks), and Booleans hold values that are either true or false. Let's look at an example of each. Create the following page and save it as asp_datatypes.asp:

```
<%
  MyString = "Hi my name is Rachel!"
  MyInteger = 34
  MyBoolean = False
  ' notice how only strings are surrounded by quotes.

  Response.Write MyString & " I am not " & MyInteger & " That is " & MyBoolean
%>
```

You should see the following on your screen:

```
Hi my name is Rachel! I am not 34 That is False
```

Be aware that although strings can contain numbers, you can't perform any direct mathematical computations on them. Numbers with a string data type are not treated as integers; rather, they take on alphanumeric values. Let's take a look at an example—create the following file and save it as string_numbers.asp:

```
<%
  MyString1 = "20"
  MyString2 = "20"
  Response.Write MyString1 + MyString2
%>
```

You will see the following:

```
2020
```

The plus sign (+) will simply force a concatenation of the two strings. You didn't want 2020—you wanted 40! You can only receive this kind of response by giving the 20s integer data types. For example:

```
<%
  MyNumber1 = 20
  MyNumber2 = 20
  ' we must not add double quotes

  Response.Write MyNumber1 + MyNumber2
%>
```

This page should give you the following in your browser:

```
40
```

You might be asking "What if I wanted to add a quotation mark within the value of a string?" Of course you can do that, but you must escape it because once the ASP script engine hits the second double quote, it will think it is the end of the value and produce undesirable results. You can escape quotes within string values by adding another double quote in front of it. For example:

```
<%
  MyString1 = "Jennifer said, ""ASP is cool!"""
  ' double quotes have additional double quotes in front of them

  Response.Write MyString1
%>
```

VBScript's House of Built-In Functions

VBScript has a number of built-in functions that perform common tasks for you when called. They simplify things for you tremendously and give you the ability to manipulate your variables as required. These built-in functions include Date/Time functions, Conversion functions, Format functions, Math functions, Array functions, and String functions. For a complete list of the built-in functions VBScript has to offer, go to http://msdn.microsoft.com/library/default.asp?url=/library/en-us/dnexpvb/html/usingvbscriptfunctions.asp.

You don't need to remember all these functions—even experienced ASP developers use a reference! Once you understand how to use a few built-in functions, it should be obvious how to use others. Let's look at some examples.

Conversion Functions

This type of function converts one data type to another. For example, if you want to convert a string to an integer, you would use the CInt() function. Create the following file and save it as convert_to_int.asp:

```
<%
  MyString = "23"
  MyNewInt = CInt(MyString)
  'convert to integer data type, declare new variable

  Response.Write MyNewInt
%>
```

You should see the following in your browser:

```
23
```

The variable MyNewInt is now an integer. You took the number that had a string data type, converted it to an integer data type, and created a new variable out of it. This might be hard to believe unless you see it with your own eyes, so let's use the TypeName() function to display the data type of the variable.

Let's print out the data type of the variables before and after the conversion—add the following code to the last example:

```
<%
  MyString = "23"
  Response.Write TypeName(MyString)
  'print out variable data type

  MyNewInt = CInt(MyString)
  'convert to integer data type, declare new variable

  Response.Write MyNewInt
  Response.Write TypeName(MyNewInt)
  'print out variable and its data type
%>
```

You should see the following in your browser:

```
String23Integer
```

String Functions

String functions allow you to do some cool things with strings. Let's take a quick look at the following string functions: Len(), Trim(), and Left(). The Len() function returns the number of characters of a string. Create the following file and save it as len.asp:

```
<%
  MyString = "I am cool"

  Response.Write MyString
  Response.Write "<br>There are <strong>" & Len(MyString) & "</strong> ⏎
characters in the above statement."
%>
```

You should see the following results:

```
I am cool
There are 9 characters in the above statement.
```

Keep in mind that even empty spaces count as characters. The Trim() function removes spaces that may appear on both the left and the right side of a string. Create the following file and save it as trim.asp:

```
<%
  MyString = "  I am cool  "

  Response.Write "." & MyString & "."
  Response.Write "<br>." & Trim(MyString) & "."
%>
```

You should see the following results:

```
.  I am cool  .
.I am cool.
```

While printing the variables, we added a period before and after the string value so the empty spaces are more obvious. As you can see, the first printout still contains the empty spaces to the right and left, but the second printout does not because of the `Trim()` function. On this note, there are also `RTrim()` and `LTrim()` functions that can trim a specific side only.

The `Left()` function allows you to return a specified number of characters from the left. It accepts the number as an attribute after the string, For example, `Left(string, 5)`. Create the following file and save it as `left.asp`:

```
<%
  MyString = "I am cool. Didn't you know that I was valedictorian of my⤶
 High School class.."

  Response.Write Left(MyString, 10)
%>
```

You should only see the following results when printing the variable:

```
I am cool.
```

We cut the rest of the sentence. This comes in handy when you want to display only a certain amount of text, especially when text comes from a database field. (You will learn more about how to connect your pages to a database in Chapter 6.) Feel free to explore the many VBScript functions. They have a lot to offer.

Operators

Operators allow you to manipulate data within your code. Operators have three main classes: logical, comparison, and mathematical. The following sections discuss the most common operators. If you need to view the results of the examples live, type the code and save it in an ASP file.

Assignment

The equal sign (=) is the only assignment operator. It simply stores whatever is to the right of the operator inside the variable to the left. You have been doing this throughout the examples in this chapter, so you should be familiar with it by now. For example:

```
<%
  Dim myGreeting
  myGreeting = "Hello"
%>
```

The assignment operator just shown simply stores the string Hello inside the variable called myGreeting. Here is another example:

```
<%
  Dim myNumber
  myNumber = 23
%>
```

The assignment operator just shown simply stores the number 23 inside the variable called myNumber.

The equal sign can also be a mathematical operator that stands for equality when used in conditional logic, which we will cover later.

Logical

The logical operators are AND, NOT, and OR. Let's have a look at these in order.

AND

Logical operators join what is on the left to what is on the right. The following example checks to see whether the variables number1 and number2 equal 3. Because they don't both equal 3, false is returned.

```
<%
  number1 = 4-1
  number2 = 6-2
  If number1 AND number2 = 3 Then
    Response.Write "correct"
  Else
    Response.Write "false"
  End If
%>
```

OR

You can change the example by using OR (OR.asp).

```
<%
  number1 = 4-1
  number2 = 6-2
  If number1 OR number2 = 3 Then
```

```
  Response.Write "correct"
Else
  Response.Write "false"
End If
%>
```

This code checks to see whether 4–1 or 6–2 equals 3. Because at least one of them does, it prints out correct.

NOT

The NOT operator simply says the opposite of the statement to the right of it. For example (NOT_1.asp):

```
<%
  number1 = 4-1
  If number1 = 3 Then
    Response.Write "correct"
  Else
    Response.Write "false"
  End If
%>
```

Certainly, 4–1 equals 3 so correct will print out. Now let's add NOT to the code:

```
<%
number1 = 4-1
If NOT(number1 = 3) Then
Response.Write "correct"
Else
Response.Write "false"
End If
%>
```

Now false is returned—number1 still equals 3, but the NOT operator causes the code to return the opposite of what would otherwise be expected.

You will learn more about If. . .Then statements later in this chapter. Table 4-1 shows comparison operators.

Table 4-1. Comparison Operators

Comparison Operator	Meaning
=	Equal to
<	Less than
>	Greater than
<=	Less than or equal to
>=	Greater than or equal to
<>	Not equal to

For example:

```
<%
X = 1
Y = 3
If x < y Then
  [' Execute this code ]
End If
%>
```

Comparison operators compare two arguments and see if a specified condition is met. Table 4-2 lists mathematical operators.

Table 4-2. Mathematical Operators

Mathematical Operator	Meaning
^	Exponentiate
*	Multiply
/	Divide
\	Integer Divide
MOD	Modulus
+	Plus
−	Minus
&	Concatenate

For example:

```
x = 54
y = 67
z = x + y
Response.Write z
```

Mathematical operators perform a mathematical operation between what is on the left and right side of operators such as the plus sign (+).

The Divide (/) operator divides one number by another and returns the result, the Integer Divide (\) operator returns only the quotient and the Modulus (MOD) operator returns only the remainder.

For example, 5 divided by 3 is 1 with a remainder of 2. Integer Divide will return 1, and Modulus will return 2.

Let's use the following code to see this for ourselves (`divide.asp`):

```
<%
  number1 = 5/3 ' Divide
  number2 = 5\3 ' Integer Divide
  number3 = 5 MOD 3 ' Modulus

  Response.Write number1 & "<br>" & number2 & "<br>" & number3
%>
```

This gives us the following readout:

```
1.66666666666667
1
2
```

For further reading on VBScript operators, go to: `http://msdn.microsoft.com/library/default.asp?url=/library/en-us/script56/html/vbsoperators.asp`.

Operator Precedence

Operators execute according to their own order. This order is called **operator precedence**. Although comparison operators all have equal precedence (they execute in left-to-right order), mathematical and logical operators execute in order of precedence, regardless of a left-to-right order, as shown in Table 4-3.

Table 4-3. Operator Precedence

Precedence Order	Operation
Mathematical	
1	Exponentiation (^)
2	Multiplication (*), Division (/), Integer Divide (\)
3	Modulus (Mod)
4	Addition (+), Subtraction (-)
Logical	
1	Not
2	And
3	Or

For example (`operator_precedence1.asp`):

```
<%
  intOrderTest = 3 + 2 * 4
  Response.Write intOrderTest
%>
```

In left-to-right order the answer is 20, but because multiplication has a higher precedence than addition, the answer is 11. Using parentheses to group expressions allows you to force operators to execute before others that may be higher in precedence. For example, to force addition before multiplication, you could change the example to this (`operator_precedence2.asp`):

```
<%
  intOrderTest = (3 + 2) * 4
  Response.Write intOrderTest
%>
```

Expressions in parentheses are always evaluated before expressions that are not in parentheses. It is important to note that operator precedence is maintained between multiple expressions that are all in parentheses. You should always group expressions with parentheses instead of relying on the natural precedence to make your code more readable.

> **NOTE** *Multiplication, division, and integer divide will execute in left-to-right order when they occur together in the same expression.*

Conditional Logic

Conditional logic lets the coder control the flow of his or her program depending on certain criteria or conditions. This is particularly pertinent when working with dynamic web sites in which you have no idea how users will interact with your web applications. Let's take a look how you can control your output.

If. . .Then Statement

This is the mother of all control! It says "If this is true, do this." Create the following file and save it as if_then.asp:

```
<%
  MyExpectedOutput = "This web site is cool"
  If MyExpectedOutput = "This web site is cool" Then
    Response.Write "Thanks for your kind words."
  End If
%>
```

You should see the following result:

```
Thanks for your kind words.
```

The If statement checks to see whether the `MyExpectedOutput` variable equals the desired value. If so, you thank the user. Keep in mind that when you compare two strings, every character is taken into account, even spaces. You can also set the conditions around embedded HTML using multiple blocks. You can arrange the example to look like this:

```
<%
  MyExpectedOutput = "This website is cool"
    If MyExpectedOutput = "This website is cool" Then
%>
Thanks for your kind words.
<%
  End If
%>
```

You should see the same results as the last example.

You can add the `Else` keyword to the statement to introduce another output if the expression does not meet your criteria. Create the following file and save it as if_then_else.asp:

```
<%
  MyExpectedOutput = "This website sucks."
    If MyExpectedOutput = "This website is cool" Then
      Response.Write "Thanks for your kind words."
    Else
      Response.Write "Hey, don't be so mean."
    End If
%>
```

You should see the following results:

```
Hey, don't be so mean.
```

The `If` statement checks to see whether the `MyExpectedOutput` variable equals the desired value—if not, you add a comment. Again, you can set the conditions around embedded HTML using multiple blocks like you did in the previous example:

```
<%
  MyExpectedOutput = "This website sucks"
    If MyExpectedOutput = "This website is cool" Then
%>
```

```
Thanks for your kind words.

<% Else %>

Hey, don't be so mean.

<%
  End If
%>
```

You should see the following result:

```
Hey, don't be so mean.
```

If. . .Then. . .ElseIf Statement

The If. . .Then. . .Else statement gives you the ability to provide two possible code continuations. If you need more than two, you could add another If. . .Then. . .Else statement, but the code would be in danger of becoming inefficient and sloppy. A better method is to use the ElseIf statement. It allows you to combine multiple If. . .Then. . .Else statements. Create the following file and save it as if_then_elseif.asp:

```
<%
  UserRating = 9
    If UserRating = 4 Then
      Response.Write "Why have you rated my website so low."

    ElseIf UserRating = 6 Then
      Response.Write "Cmon. You can do better than that."

    ElseIf UserRating = 9 Then
      Response.Write "Close, but I deserve better."

    ElseIf UserRating = 10 Then
      Response.Write "There you go!"

    End If
%>
```

You should see the following results:

```
Close, but I deserve better.
```

You can use an `Else` keyword for your last check in an `ElseIf` statement. It would act as the default program flow if none of the other conditions match. Be aware that if you use it, it must be the last statement, and it can never come before an `ElseIf`. The following example is OK:

```
<%
  UserRating = 9
    If UserRating = 4 Then
      Response.Write "Why have you rated my website so low."
    ElseIf UserRating = 6 Then
      Response.Write "Cmon. You can do better than that."

    ElseIf UserRating = 10 Then
      Response.Write "There you go!"

    Else
      Response.Write "I'm looking for a ten rating."

End If
%>
```

> **NOTE** *You can insert tags to help structure your* If *statements. On the ASP tab of the Insert toolbar, click the* if *button to insert* <% If Then %>; *the else button to insert* <% Else %>; *the elseif button to insert* <% ElseIf Then %>, *and the end button* <% End If %>.

Looping Logic

This type of logic can loop a block of code and have it execute multiple times while certain conditions are true or until they are met. For example, you may need to loop through records in a database to display them, or you may need to loop through variables until the last record is reached. There are several loop statements in VBScript that accomplish the same task. Let's go through a couple of the most commonly used ones.

Do...While Loop

This loop allows you to create a loop while a condition you specify is true. The `Do. . .While` loop takes the following form:

```
Do While your condition
  Code to be executed
Loop
```

Let's look at an example. Create the following file and save it as `do_loop.asp`:

```
<%
Dim intCount
intCount = 1

Do While intCount <= 15
  Response.Write intCount
  intCount = intCount + 1
Loop
%>
```

You should see the following results:

```
123456789101112131415
```

In the example, you looped the number 1 based on the condition that it is less than or equal to 15. Within the loop you printed the variable and incremented it by 1. The code continues to execute over and over, (printing the variable and then incrementing it by 1) until the condition becomes false.

While...Wend

Dreamweaver MX uses this loop in the `Repeat Region` server behavior for looping through database records. This loop works exactly like the `Do. . .While` loop. You can simply replace the `Do While` with `While` and the `Loop` with `Wend` in the example.

```
<%
Dim intCount
intCount = 1

While intCount <= 15
  Response.Write intCount
  intCount = intCount + 1
Wend
%>
```

See Chapter 7 for more information about `Repeat Region`.

Controlling the Flow of Your Programs

These are two cool features in ASP that allow you to control the flow of your programs. `Response.End` ends a web application immediately. Once the script engine hits it, no code after that line is executed. You would want to do this if, for example, you have a web application that streams a download to a user after payment. The application checks the database for the user's payment and if it is not found, you can automatically end the program so the rest of the script is not executed.

`Response.Redirect` works in the same manner except that instead of simply ending the program, it allows you to immediately redirect the browser to a specified URL. It's similar to `Response.End` in that no code is executed on the current page after it is processed.

Ending a Web Application Immediately

Let's try a few examples. Create the following file and save it as `check_password.asp`:

```
<%
  Password = "45gh4"
  UserInput = "45gh4"

    If UserInput <> Password Then
      Response.End
    Else
%>

Here is the very secret code only for users who knew the password:
<br><strong>The bird flew west when seeing the tarantula.</strong>

<%
  End If
%>
```

You should see the following results when viewing the page:

```
Here is the very secret code only for users who knew the password:
The bird flew west when seeing the tarantula.
```

This code set a password and checks it against the user input. It then specifies that if the two variables are not equal, end the code, or else continue and display the secret code.

You might be wondering how the user submitted the `UserInput` variable—you will learn about adding this kind of interactivity in the next section.

Change the `UserInput` password to make it deliberately incorrect and see what happens.

```
<%
  Password = "45gh4"
  UserInput = "12345"

    If UserInput <> Password Then
      Response.End
    Else
%>


Here is the very secret code only for users who knew the password:
<br /><b>The bird flew west when seeing the tarantula.</b>

<%
    End If
%>
```

When you view the page, it will be blank—the web application shut down because the password was incorrect. Isn't that cool!

Redirecting the Browser

`Response.Redirect` works the same way, but it redirects to another URL, after stopping code execution on the original page. Create the following file and save it as redirect_wrong_user.asp:

```
<%
  Password = "45gh4"
  UserInput = "12345"

    If UserInput <> Password Then
      Response.Redirect "http://www.google.com"
    Else
%>


Here is the very secret code only for users who knew the password:
<br><b>The bird flew west when seeing the tarantula.</b>

<%
    End If
%>
```

When you view the page, you should see that good ol' Google logo (as long as you are online, of course!). You can also redirect to another page within your own web site such as an error page or the index page. This is done by simply changing the URL specified in the `Response.Redirect` line.

Whatever you do, make sure you test your code—even a simple mistake can make a web application do the opposite of what you intended.

Applying Your ASP Knowledge

Thus far the web applications we've showed you have been very limited, but now you will finally see some practical ASP examples that allow users to interact and submit data to your web applications!

Cool Web Forms

Forms are pretty much the only way you can receive information from your users on your server. They are how users register, log into, and send feedback to your web site. The good news is that with your newfound knowledge of ASP and VBScript, forms become even more useful.

Your first question should be "How do we display information submitted by forms?" This is the key. If you know how to display it, you know how to retrieve it. And if you know how to retrieve it, you can do many things with it, as you will see in the later chapters.

Setting a Form's Method

The method of a form can be set to `get` or `post`. By default, a form's method is set to `get`, which appends the form fields to the URL as URL parameters (see the "URL Parameters" and "Retrieving URL Parameters" sections for a more in-depth explanation).

Using the `get` method makes things simpler because the values are easily seen in the Address bar, which also makes it easy to troubleshoot. However, be mindful that the client can also see these values, and the URLs are cached by the browser. This means that you should not use this method when submitting sensitive information. See the "Cookies (Not Made of Dough)" section for more on this.

The size of the values passed is restricted to the maximum length of characters allowed in the Address bar. This is different between browsers but you would not want to have more than 2,047 characters in the QueryString.

Using the `post` method submits the form field values in the HTTP header. This is the preferred method because the data submitted is not directly visible to the client. Another advantage is that you can send much larger bits of information using `post` than you could using `get`.

Retrieving Form Elements

`Request.Form` retrieves any form element submitted with a `post` method. Whenever you create a form element, you give it a name. For example, `<input type="text" name="username">` creates a text field named *username*. In order to display the value that was entered in this text field and submitted to the ASP, you need to use `Request.Form ("username")`. That username is contingent upon the name of the text field—if you change the name of that text field, you must change the name in the ASP code. They must match each other.

> **TIP** *Always make sure that the name of the form element and the value of the intended* `Request.Form` *match.*

Dummy Login Form

Now let's look at some code in action. You will create a dummy login form and display the username on the next page. Create the following files and display them in Code view, as shown in Figure 4-6 and Figure 4-7.

```
<!-- login_user.asp -->

<form name="form1" method="post" action="welcome_user.asp">

  username: <input type="text" name="username" /><br />
  password: <input type="text" name="password" /><br />
  <input type="submit" name="submit" value="submit" />

</form>
```

```
1  <%@LANGUAGE="VBSCRIPT" CODEPAGE="1252"%>
2  <!DOCTYPE html PUBLIC "-//W3C//DTD XHTML 1.0 Transitional//EN"
3  "http://www.w3.org/TR/xhtml1/DTD/xhtml1-transitional.dtd">
4  <html xmlns="http://www.w3.org/1999/xhtml">
5  <head>
6  <title>Login</title>
7  <meta http-equiv="Content-Type" content="text/html; charset=iso-8859-1" />
8  </head>
9
10 <body>
11 <form name="form1" method="post" action="welcome_user.asp">
12
13    username: <input type="text" name="username" /><br />
14    password: <input type="text" name="password" /><br />
15    <input type="submit" name="submit" value="submit" />
16
17 </form>
18
19 </body>
20 </html>
21
```

Figure 4-6. The code in DW Code view

```
<!-- welcome_user.asp -->

Welcome <strong><%=Request.Form("username")%></strong>!<br />
I know your password too but I won't display it ;)
```

```
1  <%@LANGUAGE="VBSCRIPT" CODEPAGE="1252"%>
2  <!DOCTYPE html PUBLIC "-//W3C//DTD XHTML 1.0 Transitional//EN"
3  "http://www.w3.org/TR/xhtml1/DTD/xhtml1-transitional.dtd">
4  <html xmlns="http://www.w3.org/1999/xhtml">
5  <head>
6  <title>Login</title>
7  <meta http-equiv="Content-Type" content="text/html; charset=iso-8859-1" />
8  </head>
9
10 <body>
11 Welcome <strong><%=Request.Form("username")%></strong>!<br />
12 I know your password too but I won't display it ;)
13
14
15 </body>
16 </html>
17
```

Figure 4-7. The code in DW Code view

If you access `login_user.asp` through your web server and enter your username as Rachel, you would see the following result on the `welcome_user.asp` page after clicking Submit:

```
Welcome Rachel!
I know your password too but I won't display it ;)
```

The `<%=Request.Form("username")%>` code in `welcome_user.asp` retrieves the value of the `<input type="text" name="username">` form element in the `login_user.asp` page. You can retrieve the other form elements on this page as well: ("password" and "submit") using `Request.Form("password")` and `Request.Form("submit")`.

Request.Form will only retrieve values of form elements that were directly submitted to it. In other words, you cannot display the form element values on a third page using `Request.Form` unless you pass the values from the second to the third page with another form that had the same default values as the first form.

Listbox Selection Form

You can also retrieve the values of other types of form elements such as chec boxes, listboxes, and other types. You will display the value selected from a listbox. Create the following files:

```
<!-- sex_selection.asp -->

<form name="form1" method="post" action="display_sex.asp">

  <select name="sex">
    <option>male</option>
    <option>female</option>
  </select>
  <input type="submit" name="submit" value="submit" />

</form>


<!-- display_sex.asp -->

You are <strong><%=Request.Form("sex")%></strong>


sex_selection.asp allows you to select your sex from a drop-down listbox,


and display_sex.asp displays the result.
```

Listbox Selection Form with Conditional Logic

You can also do some tricks utilizing your knowledge of conditional logic depending on what the user selects. You can change the code for the display_sex.asp to redirect to different pages depending on the user's gender. Let's change that page.

```
<!-- display_sex2.asp -->

<%
If Request.Form("sex") = "male" Then
    Response.Redirect "http://www.menshealth.com"
  ElseIf Request.Form("sex") = "female" Then
    Response.Redirect "http://www.ivillage.com"
  End If
%>
```

The code redirects the user to `http://www.menshealth.com` if the gender selection is male and `http://www.ivillage.com` if the gender selection is female. Because there are only two options, you could also use the following code:

```
<%
If Request.Form("sex") = "male" Then
    Response.Redirect "http://www.menshealth.com"
  Else
    Response.Redirect "http://www.ivillage.com"
  End If
%>
```

Instead of checking for both, you only check for the first. You know that if it doesn't equal the first option, it must equal the second. You will find other uses for these tactics in your own web development.

Check box Selection Form

Check boxes are also very useful—each check box that is in a checked state when the Submit button is pressed submits a value. This can come in handy when you want a user to make a simple selection. Create the following files:

```
<!-- send_note.asp -->

Send us a note!

<form name="form1" method="post" action="thank_you.asp">
```

```
  name: <input type="text" name="name" /><br />
  email: <input type="text" name="email" /><br />
  message:<br /><textarea name="message" rows="2" cols="20" wrap=hard>
</textarea><br />
  register for newsletter: <input type="checkbox" name="newsletter" value="1" />
  <br />
  <input type="submit" name="submit" value="submit" />

</form>

<!-- thank_you.asp -->

Thank you
<strong><%=Request.Form("name")%></strong>.<br />
You submitted the following message:
<strong><%=Request.Form("message")%></strong><p>

<% If Request.Form("newsletter") = 1 Then %>

You also signed up for our newsletter.

<% End If  %>
```

When send_note.asp is submitted, thank_you.asp displays the name and message. In addition, if the user does selects the check box, the value 1 will be submitted with its name newsletter, and the thank_you.asp page will display the following:

```
You also signed up for our newsletter.
```

In this section, you learned how to retrieve form elements submitted in a form via the post method with an ASP—the possibilities are endless. In the next three sections, you will learn how to submit form elements using the get method, and retrieve form elements from a URL parameter.

URL Parameters

Another way you can receive data from users is via the get method, using URL parameters. This can be used to pass data between pages. You can allow users to pass data or you can embed your own data to be passed in the source code via an href attribute. First, though, you may want to know what a URL parameter is. A URL parameter or QueryString, is any attribute and value passed after a question mark (?) attached to the end of a URL. Here's an example:

```
http://www.website.com/webpage.asp?name=rachel
```

The URL parameter in the URL is `name=rachel`.

Every URL parameter is made up of a name and a value just like any variable. The name of the URL parameter just shown is the name and the value of the URL parameter called `name is rachel`. Hence, this is also referred to as a **name/value pair**.

Multiple name/value pairs can be passed by adding an ampersand (&) between parameters. Here's an example:

```
http://www.website.com/webpage.asp?name=rachel&id=23
```

Retrieving URL Parameters

This is all well and good, but you want to know how to retrieve these URL parameters. It's simple and exactly like `Request.Form`, but you use `Request.QueryString` instead. For example, if the URL parameters `http://www.website.com/webpage.asp?id=23` were passed, you can display them using `Request.QueryString("id")`.

Create the following pages:

```
<!-- display_users.asp -->

<a href="get_id.asp?id=12">omar</a><br />
<a href="get_id.asp?id=15">rahim</a><br />
<a href="get_id.asp?id=145">michael</a><br />
<a href="get_id.asp?id=148">terry</a><br />

<!-- get_id.asp -->

Look at the URL Parameter in the address bar<br />
The ID you selected equals <strong><%=Request.QueryString("id")%></strong>.
```

Now when you click one of the links in `display_users.asp`, the ID value contained in the corresponding URL is retrieved and displayed by `get_id.asp`.

Submitting a Form

When you use the get method to submit a form, and the form fields are appended to the action page's URL as name/value pairs, the name sent will be the name of the form field, and its value will be the value entered or set for that particular form field. For example, let's look at a form with a text field named *name*, whose value has been set to *omar*, and a Submit button named *submit* that has a value set to *send*. If you submit this form to a page called thanks.asp, the URL will look like this after submission: `thanks.asp?name=rachel&submit=send`.

These values cannot be retrieved with `Request.Form`; rather they are retrieved like normal URL parameters are with `Request.QueryString`. For example, add the following to two new ASP files:

```
<!-- send_note2.asp -->

Send us a note!

<form name="form1" method="get" action="thank_you2.asp">



  id: <input type="text" name="id" /><br />
  name: <input type="text" name="name" /><br />
  <br />
  <input type="submit" name="submit" value="submit" />

</form>

<!-- thank_you2.asp -->

Thank you <strong><%=Request.QueryString("name")%></strong>.<br />
Your ID is: <strong><%=Request.QueryString("id")%></strong>
```

When the page is submitted, the form fields will be appended to the `QueryString` of the action page as URL parameters.

It's as simple as that. You change the value associated with your `Request.QueryString` depending on the URL parameter you want to display. If the URL parameter has an attribute called *name*, you can display its value with `Request.QueryString("name")`. URL parameters will be extremely important when you begin to display database records on your pages. You will usually need to pass that data to other pages.

Cookies (Not Made of Dough)

Whether you are an experienced web developer or simply an Internet enthusiast, you have no doubt heard about cookies. Cookies are simple text files that you can create and store on the client machine. They allow you to store simple data such as usernames, dates, and so on. The values of cookies can be created by the web application or they can accept parameters submitted by the user. However, they must be used with care.

Cookies are similar to the forms and URL parameters we discussed earlier—they allow you to maintain data across pages. When cookies are created, they are automatically stored in a specific folder in the user's hard drive, which cannot be changed—on Windows 2000 you can find this folder by going to C:/Documents and Settings/Administrator/Cookies. You will probably find dozens of cookies already stored there. Each cookie contains specific data stored by various web applications while you were using the Internet.

Creating and Retrieving Cookies

`Response.Cookies` is all you need to create a cookie. Simply name the cookie and give it a value. For example `Response.Cookies("MyCookie") = "Hello World"` creates a cookie called `MyCookie` with a value of `Hello World`. This example creates a specific value, but certainly you can store information entered by a user as the value if desired.

For example, if a user submits a form with a text field called *username*, you can store the value of that text field as the value of a cookie like so: `Response.Cookies("MyCookie") = Request.Form("username")`. This way you will have that data stored on the user's computer and you can retrieve it any time so long as it is not deleted.

After creating a cookie, you will want to retrieve it. `Request.Cookies` will retrieve any cookie you created, identifying it by name. For example, to retrieve the cookie named `MyCookie`, you would code the following: `Request.Cookies("MyCookie")`. How easy is that? If you want to output it on screen, you simply use `Response.Write Request.Cookies("MyCookie")`.

Let's look at an example to put this theory into practice. Create the following file:

```
<!-- my_first_cookie.asp -->

<%
Response.Cookies("username") = "rachel"
%>

<%=Request.Cookies("username") %>
```

You should see the following results:

```
rachel
```

You created a cookie named *username*, gave it a value of *rachel*, and displayed the cookie.

Now let's create some cookies based on what a user might submit in a form. You will use another dummy login form:

```
<!-- cookie_login.asp -->

<form name="form1" method="post" action="login_create_cookies.asp">

username: <input type="text" name="username" /><br />
password: <input type="text" name="password" /><br />
<input type="submit" name="submit" value="submit" />

</form>

<!-- login_create_cookies.asp -->

<%
Response.Cookies("userid") = Request.Form("username")
Response.Cookies("pwd") = Request.Form("password")
%>
userid cookie: <strong><%=Request.Cookies("userid") %></strong><br />
pwd cookie: <strong><%=Request.Cookies("pwd") %></strong>
```

After submitting the data, when you view the login_create_cookies.asp you should see the values you entered. You saw something similar before, but this time you didn't display them simply using Request.Form, rather, you stuffed the values into two cookies, and retrieved the values from there.

Note that now these cookies have been created, you can retrieve the data from any page without having to prompt the user again (until the cookies are deleted). This may come in handy if you wanted to, say, display the username across several pages.

Many web developers use ck to prefix cookies when naming them. For example: ckUserID, ckPassword, and so on.

Cookie Expiration

Cookies delete themselves once the user shuts down his or her browser if you do not specify an expiration date. This is fine if you only want the information for a single session, but you may want the information to be maintained for days, weeks, or even years. For example, you can specify a cookie named *userid* to expire after seven days like so: `Response.Cookies("userid").Expires = Date + 7.`

You can add expiration dates to your first cookie example in the `my_first_cookie.asp` page like so:

```
<%
  Response.Cookies("username") = "rachel"
  Response.Cookies("username").Expires = Date + 7
%>

<%=Request.Cookies("username") %>
```

You can increase the number of days you require from 7–365 or more. Still, be aware that a user can still delete cookies from his or her computer every so often.

Updating Cookies

You cannot create two cookies on the same computer with the same name, but you can update cookies by simply rewriting their values. See the following example:

```
<!-- rewrite_cookie.asp -->

<%
  Response.Cookies("ckRememberMe") = True
  Response.Cookies("ckRememberMe") = False
%>

<%=Request.Cookies("ckRememberMe") %>
```

If you view the page, you should see the following results:

```
False
```

You created a cookie called `ckRememberMe`, gave it a value of *true*, and then rewrote the value to *false*.

Deleting Cookies

You can delete cookies by simply giving them an empty string value. See the following example:

```
<!-- delete_cookie.asp -->

<%
  Response.Cookies("ckRememberMe") = True
  Response.Cookies("ckRememberMe") = ""
%>

<%=Request.Cookies("ckRememberMe") %>
```

Nothing should appear on the screen because the cookie does not exist. ASP doesn't throw an error when trying to retrieve a cookie that does not exist.

Cookies are useful and fun. They have many uses and can help web developers in many different situations—don't be afraid to use cookies if you see a good use for them in your web application.

A Word of Warning About the Use of Cookies

Never store any sensitive information, such as usernames and passwords, or heaven forbid, credit card details in a cookie. Because they are only unencrypted text stored in a file on a user's computer, any unscrupulous web users who can access the cookie's name could access the sensitive information any time.

Despite this, as long as you are wise in your use of cookies and heed these warnings, you should be fine—besides, cookies are beneficial to any web developer. They are quite handy for persisting data, and what's more, they do not take up server space like sessions (discussed later in this book) that are stored on the server. For more specific information see Netscape's legal notice on cookies at http://www.netscape.com/legal_notices/cookies.html.

Session Variables

Session variables provide another way to maintain state (information relevant to each user) across several pages within your web application. Once a user accesses a page on your site, memory is allocated on the web server for this user inside what is called a **session object**. Any variable stored in this session object is called a **session variable**. Session variables can be used to maintain state for the duration of a user's visit to the web site. You can store values into session variables that will be unique to each user (in the same way cookies are). Every user gets his or her own session when they access your web site.

Unlike cookies, sessions live on the server, not on the client's computer. They die if there is no request from the user to the server within a session timeout interval set either in IIS or an ASP page. In IIS, 20 minutes is the default timeout for sessions. This value can be increased or decreased by the web developer. You can change the default timeout from inside your web server program. For example, in Internet Services Manager:

1. Right-click Default Web Site.

2. Choose Properties from the shortcut menu.

3. Click the Home Directory tab.

4. Click the Configuration button.

5. Click the App Options tab.

6. Make sure the Enable Session State option is checked.

7. Set the Session timeout in minutes.

8. Click OK to exit the Application Configuration dialog box, and click OK again to exit the Properties dialog box.

You can also programmatically set the session timeout from within an ASP page by adding the following code at the top of your ASP page:

```
<% Session.Timeout = 10 %>
```

Creating and Retrieving Session Variables

Session variables are created just as easily as the other variables. You can write a value into a session variable with the following code:

```
Session("session_name") = "my value".
```

Retrieving session variables is very easy. You simply need to print out the session—for example `Response.Write Session("session_name")`.

Let's create an example similar to the cookie login, but instead of storing the values in cookies, you'll store them in session variables.

```
<!-- session_login.asp -->

<form name="form1" method="post" action="login_create_sessions.asp">

username: <input type="text" name="username" /><br />
password: <input type="text" name="password" /><br />
<input type="submit" name="submit" value="submit" />

</form>

<!-- login_create_sessions.asp -->

<%
  Session("userid") = Request.Form("username")
  Session("pwd") = Request.Form("password")
%>
userid session: <strong><%=Session("userid") %></strong><br />
pwd session: <strong><%=Session("pwd") %></strong>
```

Access `session_login.asp`, enter some values and submit the form. After submitting the data, when you view the `login_create_sessions.asp` you should see the values you entered.

Updating Session Variables

Session variables can be updated by simply rewriting the value, just like cookies. See the following example:

```
<!-- rewrite_session.asp -->

<%
  Session("svRememberMe") = True
  Session("svRememberMe") = False
%>

<%=Session("svRememberMe") %>
```

When viewing the page, you should see false.

Deleting Session Variables

You can destroy a particular session variable with `Session.Contents.Remove`. For example, the following code would destroy a session named `MM_Username`:

```
<% Session.Contents.Remove("MM_Username") %>
```

You can also destroy all values stored in the session object, which will destroy all sessions on the server that were set for the user, by using `Session.Abandon`. Use this with caution because it will delete all session variables associated with the user:

```
<% Session.Abandon %>
```

If you send the user to a page that contains this code, the user's sessions will be destroyed and memory will be freed. For example, if you create a page named `delete_sessions.asp` with the code just shown, access it, and then go back to your `rewrite_session.asp` page, you will find the sessions empty. You can also destroy the entire session object with the following code:

```
<% Session.Contents.RemoveAll %>
```

Note On Sessions

Because sessions can take up a lot of server memory, you should use them sparingly, especially if you are expecting a lot of users at your site. It can sometimes be difficult to know how long to set the timeout interval for. Setting the timeout interval too short while the session holds login information, for example, will force users to log in again if the system is idle for any length of time. On the other hand, setting the timeout interval too long will eat up server resources even if the user is no longer at your site.

Sessions will last according to their timeout scope. This means that if a user logs onto your site, therefore creating a session, but then leaves your site after one minute, that session will still last for 19 more minutes regardless, eating up your server memory (provided the time is set to its default value, or course). For this reason, the length of session timeouts should be kept short—anything over 25 minutes is way too much under normal circumstances. The key is using a balanced timeout interval and destroying the session in your ASP once you no longer need it. Don't let this scare you too much; as you become more experienced, you will know when and how to use them more efficiently.

Sessions can be problematic on certain older Windows servers, and because sessions are a type of cookie, they will not work if users have cookies turned off. You should test your application thoroughly on the live server to ensure that it is working as you expect in that environment and ensure that a user with no cookies is either able to use the site, or if the sessions or cookies are unavoidable, receives a message explaining that he or she will need to enable cookies for this site.

Environment Variables

Environment variables are pieces of information that the web server makes available to any program that requests them. These variables can offer very useful information such as the name of the web server or the user's IP address. You can then access these variables within your ASP script. Table 4-4 lists some of the more commonly used environment variables.

Table 4-4. Environment Variables

Environment Variable	Description
HTTP_REFERER	The URL of the page that sent the user to the current one
QUERY_STRING	The URL parameters following the (?) in the URL
REMOTE_HOST	The client's IP Address
SCRIPT_NAME	The URL of the current page
SERVER_NAME	The server hostname
URL	The URL of the ASP page (excluding the QueryString)

For more environment variables, visit http://www.aspfree.com/asp/
servervariables.asp.

You can retrieve a specific environment variable using the following syntax:

```
Request.ServerVariables("VariableName")
```

If you find it hard to remember the names of environment variables, Dreamweaver MX has a list of them in the ASP tab of the Insert Toolbar. To insert them, click the Server Variables button on the far left of the ASP Tab and the dialog box shown in Figure 4-8 appears.

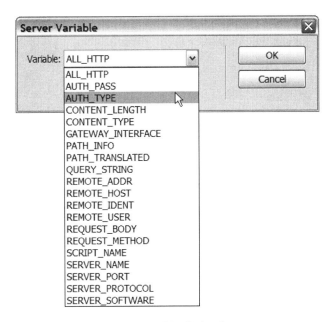

Figure 4-8. The Server Variable dialog box

Select the one that you want and click OK to insert the code in Code view.

```
Request.ServerVariables("REMOTE_USER")
```

If you simply want to Response.Write out that value, check the Wrap in <% %> check box and Dreamweaver will insert

```
<%= Request.ServerVariables("ALL_HTTP") %>
```

Create the following files to utilize some of the environment variables:

```
<!-- link_page.htm -->
```

```
<a href="http://localhost/env_variables.asp">link to env_variables.asp</a>
```

```
<!-- env_variables.asp -->
```

```
The URL of this page is: <strong><%=Request.ServerVariables("URL") %></strong>
<br />
Your IP address is: <strong><%=Request.ServerVariables("REMOTE_HOST") %>
</strong>
<br />
Go back to the page you came from:
<strong>
  <a href="<%=Request.ServerVariables("HTTP_REFERER") %>">
  <%=Request.ServerVariables("HTTP_REFERER") %></a>
</strong>
```

Environment variables are beneficial in that they can give you pertinent information. For example, you could put the user's IP address as the value of a hidden field in a feedback form so that you have the IP address of the submitter. This is helpful in identifying a particular user. If that user is, say, posting abusive or offensive messages on your site, you can use it to ban him or her from accessing the site anymore, by excluding their IP address.

Here is an example:

```
<!-- send_note3.asp -->
```

```
Send us a note!
```

```
<form name="form1" method="post" action="thank_you.asp">
```

```
name: <input type="text" name="name" /><br />
email: <input type="text" name="email" /><br />
message: <br><textarea name="message" rows=2 cols=20 wrap=hard></textarea><br />
register for newsletter: <input type="checkbox" name="newsletter" value="1">
<br />
<input type="submit" name="submit" value="submit" />

<input type="hidden" name="ipaddress" value="<%=Request.ServerVariables↵
("REMOTE_HOST") %>" />
</form>
```

When you run this page, view the HTML source code to see the form's hidden element value so you can see that your IP address is in fact being stored in the form ready to be submitted with the other fields.

Summary

You did it! You learned a lot in this chapter. You were introduced to the differences between static and dynamic web sites, and the most important aspects of creating ASP files with VBScript, such as

- Declaring variables

- Commenting code

- Conditional logic

- Built-in VBScript functions

- Web forms

- URL parameters

- Creating, updating, and deleting cookies

- Creating, updating, and deleting sessions

- Utilizing environment variables

The understanding of basic ASP principles you gained from this chapter will make things much easier for you when you begin to use Dreamweaver MX to generate ASP code for you. In Chapter 7, you will take a lengthy look at how to automate ASP code, using most of Dreamweaver MX's built-in Application behaviors. Before you do that however, you will learn the basics of connecting dynamic pages to databases.

Resources

The following list of links provides you with places to go if you want to read more about the subjects we have glossed over in this chapter. You don't need to know much about how the code works to build great dynamic web sites in Dreamweaver MX, as you will see in later chapters. However, it is highly recommended that you look into the code "beneath the hood" because it will increase your understanding of what's going on and give you more and greater flexibility.

- `http://www.w3schools.com/asp/`: Good ASP tutorial and reference guide suitable for beginners and more advanced developers

- `http://www.aspin.com`: An ASP scripts and resource index, good if you know what you are looking for

- `http://www.4guysfromrolla.com`: An excellent ASP resource web site with tutorials and FAQs for all levels of developer

- `http://www.devguru.com/Technologies/asp/quickref/asp_intro.html`: A good beginners guide to ASP

- `http://www.asptoday.com`: A site for the more advanced ASP developer

- `http://www.w3schools.com/vbscript/`: A useful VBScript tutorial suitable for beginners

- `http://www.devguru.com/Technologies/vbscript/quickref/vbscript_intro.html`: A beginners guide to VBScript

CHAPTER 5

Databases Overview

PEOPLE GENERALLY THINK that a database has to be created in a special piece of software such as Microsoft Access. However, a database could be defined as any store of data that is organized in a way that makes easy entry and retrieval possible. This means files created in Notepad or Microsoft Excel can be used as databases—although when they are used as such, we tend to refer to them as "datastores" to make it clear that they simply *store* data, they don't organize it.

Database applications provide a surrounding network of code for accessing the data—a flat text file, for instance, does not. If you want your database application to be easy to use (and let's face it, who doesn't?), two good choices are Microsoft Access 2000 and Microsoft SQL Server 2000.

How Do I Create a Database?

It is important to remember the difference between creating a database and creating the database content. When you create a database, you are creating the container in which your data can be stored. Only after you have created the container do you create the content.

In Microsoft Access

Microsoft Access 2000 offers a myriad of wizards and templates for you to choose from to get your job done. Creating your database is as simple as clicking the mouse button a few times and pressing a couple of keys.

1. Open Access 2000 to see the dialog box shown in Figure 5-1.

    This dialog box offers a few options. To open any existing database on your system, select the Open an existing file option and then either choose More Files or select a database from the list.

    You can also create a database by selecting the Access database wizards, pages, and projects option. This presents you with a choice of example databases to choose from, which might suit your particular needs (see Figure 5-2).

Figure 5-1. Create a blank Access database.

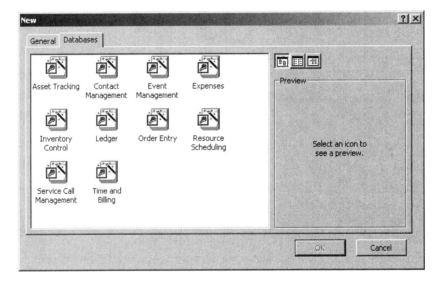

Figure 5-2. Example Access databases

2. You are going to create a database from scratch so click Cancel, select the Blank Access Database option, and click OK.

3. Name your database file and select the location to store it. (We named ours `webprodmx.mdb`—not to be confused with the `webprodmx_data` database used in the next chapter!) and store it in the My Databases folder in C:\databases\.

In Microsoft SQL Server

You will use Enterprise Manager to create the databases in SQL Server. This is one of SQL Server's main interfaces, but you could use the Query Analyzer to create your databases instead (using the SQL command CREATE DATABASE, for instance). In fact, SQL queries could be written into the Query Analyzer to perform everything you could think of with your database. However, although it is an extremely powerful tool, you're not going to use the Query Analyzer here because the benefits it offers are beyond your needs at this stage.

> **NOTE** *If you need to log on to your SQL Server, ensure that you are logged in as Administrator. By logging in as Administrator, any object that you create will be prefixed with* dbo. *to signify that the database owner is the owner of that object.*

1. Launch Enterprise Manager. When the Microsoft Management Console (MMC) opens, you will see two panes. The left pane is a tree view, as shown in Figure 5-3, and the right pane shows the contents of the left pane's selected element.

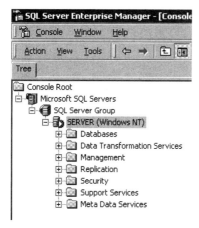

Figure 5-3. Tree view of database objects

2. Expand your tree view to look something like the one shown in Figure 5-3, right-click the Databases node, and select New Database from the context menu.

At a very basic level, all you need to do to create your SQL Server database is enter a name in the Name box on the General tab and click OK, which in many cases may be a perfectly adequate method.

It may not be adequate when your network administrator specifies the places where you must create all your files. In such a case, leaving the default locations of the data files and the transaction log files is not an option. To change the location of these files, you need to click each tab and use the ellipsis button (. . .) in the Location column to select the new storage location. You can also specify alternative names for the files here to replace the default database names, which were entered for you if you entered the database name on the first tab.

3. This shouldn't be an issue in this example, so simply enter webprodmx as the name for your new database, leave all the defaults in place, and click OK.

....

What SQL Server Does With Your Data

One of the main differences between Access and SQL Server is the way data is managed. Access uses a single file (the .mdb file) to store everything (the limitations of which will become apparent shortly), whereas SQL Server uses at least two files—a data file and a transaction log file.

Without getting very deep into the workings of SQL Server (which is beyond the scope of this book), what basically happens is that User1 logs into SQL Server and performs some actions on the data in a database. Those actions are written to a transaction log and applied to the data at a subsequent point. If anything goes wrong while User1 is interacting with the database that prevents User1's modifications from being completed successfully, the transaction will not be applied and the data will remain unaffected. This is called "transactional roll back."

SQL Server locks its data at the row level so that many users can use the same database—and even the same data—simultaneously. SQL Server also schedules multiple user access requests to that data. It does this by order of merit (depending on what action is to be performed on the data) and by the order in which those requests were originally made. This is known as "concurrency." (You can read more about this subject in Books Online. SQL Server's impressive help system, which can be found on the Microsoft SQL Server menu.)

Access, on the other hand, does not have this ability. Because it was designed for desktop use, Access locks its data at the database level so that only one user can access the database and modify the data at any one time. This may seem restricting (and it can be), but if your web traffic is low, this "one-user-at-a-time" principle shouldn't be noticeable. A web page uses a single database connection regardless of how many people are interacting with the site, so as far as the database is concerned, it's the same user making data requests each time.

This is one of the reasons why Access is widely used as a database manager for small web sites. Despite its limitations, it holds up remarkably well under small loads. If you're just learning or you expect very low web traffic on your web site (for example, if it's a personal web site), you might consider Access. That said, for anything resembling mainstream work for which you need good performance and reliability, you would be well advised to use a tool like SQL Server, which was designed for such work.

Expanding the Database node in the left pane of the SQL Server console displays your newly created database and its internal structure.

Preparing a SQL Server Database for Internet Use

The new SQL Server database contains eleven objects, two of which are pre-populated with data. When you click the webprodmx database under Databases in the left pane, the items associated with that database are listed on the right, as shown in Figure 5-4 (you can change this view by right-clicking the pane and selecting View).

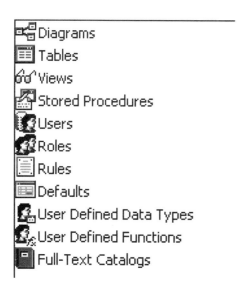

Figure 5-4. The database items

The Users object contains an item called dbo (Database Owner). The dbo item stores the database owner's account. For security reasons, you should create an account that has just enough access for each new user. This prevents the risk of accidental damage being done by someone with too many permissions. You can assign permissions on a new account manually, on an object-by-object basis, but it is often easier to simply assign a new account one of the predefined **roles** that SQL Server makes available. A role is an array of permissions that are pre-set for each database object, and each role represents one of a number of common database-related job roles. Roles are very useful if you are creating many user accounts.

> **NOTE** *To reduce clutter in the left pane, you may want to exclude from view all the system databases and objects. To do this, right-click the SQL Server name and select the Edit SQL Server Registration Properties option. On the resulting dialog box, deselect the Show system databases and system objects check box.*

You need to set up a special account in SQL Server in order for your web application to be able to talk to your database. This is the IUSR\MachineName account—the **Internet User** account. This account acts as an alias for all the traffic brought to the database from your web application.

Creating the IUSR Account in SQL Server

1. In the left pane of the SQL Server console, click Security, and then click the Logins node.

2. Right-click the right pane, which displays the current users of this database, and select New Login to display the dialog box shown in Figure 5-5.

3. Click the ellipsis button (. . .) next to the Name box to open the SQL Server Login Properties – New Login window. If it is not selected already, select your machine name from the List Names From drop-down menu. Scroll down the Names list until you find the IUSR_MACHINENAME login (with the name of your computer in place of MACHINENAME). Select it and click Add.

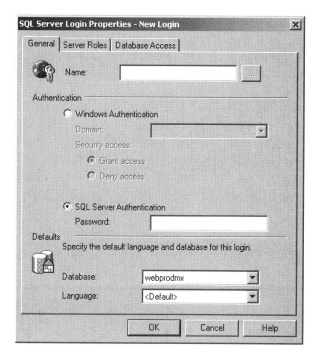

Figure 5-5. The New Login dialog box

4. Click OK and the dialog box will display the login details for IUSR. The name will be displayed as DOMAINNAME\IUSR_MACHINENAME (where your computer's domain appears instead of DOMAINNAME and the name of the machine replaces MACHINENAME).

5. You don't want this login to be domain-specific, however—you want people on the Internet to be able to use it, and they won't be logged in to our domain. To change this, select the SQL Server Authentication option to make this login an SQL Server authenticated login.

6. Enter a password.

7. Select webprodmx in the Database drop-down menu.

8. Click the Database Access tab. Scroll down the list until you can see webprodmx. Select the check box next to it and your new login details will be added to that database, as shown in Figure 5-6.

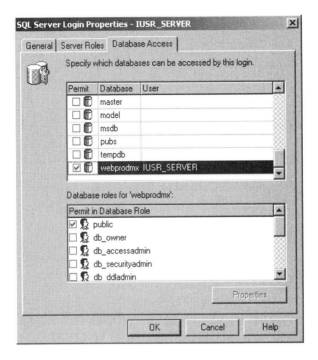

Figure 5-6. Selecting the database access

9. Click OK and your new Internet User login is created.

You can now set up a web site that can connect to this database. You will be doing exactly that later in this chapter, in the "Making The Connection" section.

Database Design

There is far more to good database design than just following a good naming convention. You could fill a whole book just by listing the dos and don'ts of database design—if fact someone did. Perhaps one of the best books you could buy on the subject is *Database Design For Mere Mortals* by Michael J. Hernandez (Addison-Wesley Publishing Co; ISBN: 0201694719).

We won't look at database design in great depth here, but we'll point out a couple of things that you should consider when designing your database—if only to save you from headaches later on!

Object Naming Conventions

SQL has a number of reserved keywords that must be avoided at all costs when creating names for your database objects and their properties. For a complete list, launch Books Online, go to the Index tab, enter **keywords reserved for SQL Server**, and click Display.

Using a good naming convention can help you understand what is going on when you use your database later on, or when you return to a project you wrote months ago.

For example, say you have a few database tables named as follows:

- `tbl_Categories`

- `tbl_Books`

- `tbl_Users`

It wouldn't take a genius to figure out that `tbl_Categories` is a good place to look if you wanted to view the categories. Naming things logically makes it easy to quickly assess what an object contains and what it should be used for. This is especially useful when accessing these objects from external programs such as Dreamweaver MX 2004.

In the example just shown, we prefixed each table name with `tbl_`, which is short for Table. We do this so that we know it's a table and not a view, stored procedure, or any other database object. For views, we use a prefix of `view_`, for stored procedures, we use a prefix of `sp`. Note that we do not use an underscore after the `sp` prefix because SQL Server uses that prefix for its own internal system stored procedures. If you were to adopt the `sp_` convention yourself, there's the danger that you'd give one of your own stored procedures the same name as a system stored procedure. If that happened SQL Server would run the system-stored procedure instead of your own—possibly causing untold damage to your database.

Table column names are another area that can cause serious problems if you are not careful. For example, if you want to include a column that stores dates in a table, you couldn't call that column `Date` because "Date" is a reserved word in SQL Server. Instead you could call the column, for example, `U_Date` instead (`U_` signifying that it belongs to the `Users` table): this avoids any naming conflicts and the column name still makes sense.

Do not use spaces in object and property names. All the examples in this book use the underscore character in place of spaces. You could also use the capitalization method in which the first letter of each new word is capitalized instead of being separated with underscores. For example, the `tbl_Categories` object would be written as `tblBooksInCategories`.

Creating Tables

A table structure defines the order and sequence in which data is stored and retrieved from your database. Each entry consists of a **record**, which you can think of as a horizontal row containing data in a series of columns, known as **fields**. Each field stores equivalent items of data for each record. It is common practice (and one that we will adopt from here on) to make the first field a unique identifier for the record it belongs to: known as a **primary key**. This field will be useful when you begin to build relationships between the tables you have created.

Table 5-1 summarizes table structure with two imaginary records.

Table 5-1. Table Structure

Primary Key	Field 1	Field 2	Field 3	Field 4
1	Value for field 1	Value for field 2	Value for field 3	Value for field 4
2	Value for field 1	Value for field 2	Value for field 3	Value for field 4

Of course, you could store all the data for a given record in exactly the same form, and if you were dealing with a comma-delimited text file, that would be exactly what you would do. However, the values in each field of a record are almost always different, depending on what each field is supposed to store, so the use of **data types** (such as integer or date) can greatly improve the efficiency of your database and help prevent inappropriate data types from being entered in a given field.

Let's say you want to create a table called tbl_Users that stores users details. In it, you will have the following fields:

- A primary key, which you'll call UserID

- The user's first name, which you'll call FirstName

- The user's last name, which you'll call LastName

- The user's email address, which you'll call EmailAddress

- The user's access group, which you'll call AccessGroup

- The date the user record was created, which you'll call DateCreated

Access doesn't give you as much information about the data types as SQL Server does, but setting the correct data types for each field and determining how much space each one can take up will help you maintain the integrity of the data, save storage space, and even help to speed up data access.

Data types are set at table level, so let's now take a look at the process of creating a table and the different data types that can be stored in the fields within it. We'll look at Access first.

Creating Tables Using Access

1. Open your empty database, select Tables in the left column of the database window, click New, and select Design View from the dialog box. (You could also have double-clicked the Create Table in Design View icon in the Tables window.)

    Table Design view opens, as shown in Figure 5-7.

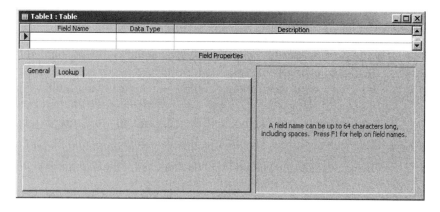

Figure 5-7. Table Design view

There are three values that you can assign to each field.

-   **Name**: Text that identifies a given field within a table

-   **Data type**: A very general class of data into which the data falls, such as Number or Currency

-   **Description**: Text that tells you what a given field holds

2. Click inside the Data Type box for the top field and click the down arrow to see a list of the general data types that Access recognizes. Select a general data type, and in the Field Properties dialog box, select Format (for most of the general types) or Field Size (in the case of Number data types). Click the down arrow that appears to see all the subtypes you can assign to your data. For instance, the subtypes of a Number data type are

- Byte

- Integer

- Long Integer

- Single

- Double

- Replication ID

- Decimal

If you've done any programming before, you may be familiar with the concept of using different data types to optimize how your data is stored and handled within your code. If not, don't worry, you can play around with the different data types and field lengths at your leisure—most of them are fairly easy to grasp—and you won't need any expertise in this for the simple table we're about to create. If you would like a full explanation of any and all possible data types available to you in SQL Server, open Books Online (SQL Servers help system) and on the Contents tab, expand the Transact SQL Reference, scroll down, and click the Data Types book.

Let's now take a look at creating that tbl_Users table in Access.

3. To create the primary key, in the first Field Name box in Design view, type **UserID**. Give it a data type of Autonumber: Access ensures that the value created for each record is unique. The field size is set as Long Integer by default, so leave it like that.

4. Click the gray square to the left of your field name to highlight the entire row. Right-click the selection and click Primary Key. A small key icon appears in the gray square to the right of your field name. This signifies that Access will now treat this field as the primary key for this table. To maintain integrity, Access only allows you to assign this property to one field in a table at any one time.

5. Move down to the next field and name it **FirstName**. Give it a data type of Text and increase the field size (the number of individual characters) to 100. Always aim to make a field no bigger than the maximum size of value you expect it to ever have to hold.

6. Name the next field **LastName** and give it a field type of Text and a field size of 100.

7. Name the next field **EmailAddress** and give it a field type of Text and a field size of 255.

8. Name the next field **AccessGroup**, and give it a field type of Text and a field size of 20.

9. Name the next field **DateCreated** and give it a field type of Date/Time.

10. Name the last field **Included** and give it a field type of Yes/No.

11. Save your newly created table by clicking File ➤ Save As, and entering **tbl_Users** as your new table's name.

You can now view your table in Datasheet view by selecting View ➤ Datasheet View.

Creating a Table in SQL Server

1. Select the webprodmx database under Databases in the left pane. In the right pane, right-click the Tables icon and select New Table. The New Table dialog box opens, as shown in Figure 5-8.

2. This should be fairly clear: enter the field name in the Field Name column, click the Data Type column, and click the down arrow that appears to see a list of all the types of data types that SQL Server supports. Unlike Access, SQL Server does not have general data types that break down into more specific subtypes, but it has a great many more actual types. This reflects the fact that SQL Server is optimized for fast data retrieval and efficiency of storage.

3. If you refer back to the example table, tbl_Users, you'll recall that it has a primary key field named UserID. As shown in Figure 5-9, in the New Table dialog box, give this record a data type of int and set the Identity box in the Columns tab to Yes.

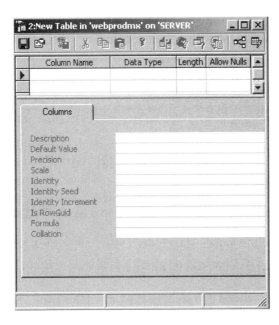

Figure 5-8. The New Table dialog box

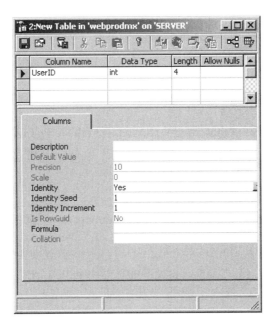

Figure 5-9. Setting the Identity column

SQL Server's built-in primary key data type is named Identity. When the first record is created, the Identity field defaults to the Identity Seed, or starting point. This means that the first record is given a primary key of 1 and each successive record will have a primary key incremented by 1, as prescribed by the Identity Increment. This is fine for our purposes, but SQL Server can customize things in even more detail.

Because you selected an int data type, which occupies four bytes by default, you can't change the value in the Length column. If you had selected a Text data type, you could set its field size and thus, how much of the total storage space this field will use for each record. As you saw in Access, the decision about how big a field should be must be made with care. An int can store up to about 2 billion values, which may seem like overkill (even if we *were* designing for Amazon.com!), but remember that any value stored here can never be used again, and customers will come and go. Using an int for a field of this kind is appropriate, especially because the next smallest size available is tinyint, which can only store up to 256 different values.

Now you will create the other fields: `FirstName`, `LastName`, `EmailAddress`, `Password`, `AccessGroup`, `DateCreated`, and `Included`. For normal fields like this, you can permit the value to be a Null. Null is an unknown value; it contains nothing. The use of a `null` explicitly stores the fact that no value was entered here. You can also specify a default value in the Columns tab, which is the value that is entered in this field if no other value is provided.

4. Give the `FirstName` and `LastName` fields the char data type and a field size of 100. You may think this is too much, but there are some long names out there! A char data type has a fixed length, which is to say it always holds 100 characters even if the users name is simply John Smith: the rest of the field would be filled up with spaces. (This may sound very inefficient but using fixed-length fields allows SQL Server to search for and retrieve values much faster because it does not have to check for the end of each field all the time.) Make sure you uncheck the Allow Nulls column and don't bother entering any default values because neither of these options are appropriate for these two fields.

5. Give the `EmailAddress` field a char data type and a field size of 250 characters. Give the `Password` field a char data type and a field size of 50. Give the `AccessGroup` field a char data type and a field size of 20. Make the default value of this field `User` so that as new users sign up, they are automatically added to the User access group.

6. Give the `DateCreated` field a Date/Time data type. In the Default Value field, type **getdate()** so that the current date is inserted automatically when a new record is created.

7. Give the `Included` field a bit data type. Set its default value to 1 so that all new entries are included automatically by default.

    Your finished New Table dialog box should look like Figure 5-10.

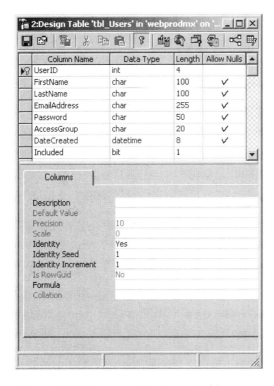

Figure 5-10. The completed users table

8. Save this table by clicking the Save button in the top left of this dialog box, and name it **tbl_Users**. Close the dialog box and click the Tables icon in the right pane. Your new `tbl_Users` table is listed in the resulting display.

Now let's create the `tbl_Categories` and `tbl_Books` tables that you will use for the examples in this book. The column names and data types for the `tbl_Categories` table are shown in Table 5-2. The column names and data types for the `tbl_Books` table are shown in Table 5-3.

Table 5-2. tbl_Categories

Column Name	Data Type	Length	Allow Nulls
CategoryID	integer	4	No
Category	char	30	No

Set CategoryID as the primary key in this table.

Table 5-3. tbl_Books

Column Name	Data Type	Length	Allow Nulls
BookID	integer	4	No
BookTitle	char	30	No
BookAuthorFirstName	char	50	No
BookAuthorLastName	char	50	No
BookPrice	smallmoney	4	No
BookISBN	char	20	No
BookPageCount	int	4	No
BookImage	char	50	Yes
CategoryID	int	4	No
DateAdded	datetime	8	No

Set BookID as the primary key in this table. As you did earlier, type **getdate**() in the DateAdded field so that it is automatically filled with the current date when you add new records.

Relational Databases and Referential Integrity

Relational databases allow you to store lots of information in a structured and organized way, without needing to store multiple copies of the same data. The use of primary keys is crucial to how this is achieved.

For example, say you have a web site in which one book could feasibly be stored in several categories. You could have one record for the same book for category that it is in, but that's a lot of repetition. Fortunately, thanks to relational databases, you can split the information into related tables.

- The tbl_Books table has one record per book

- The tbl_Categories table has one record per category

You can set up a relationship to show how an entry in tbl_Books relates to an entry in tbl_Categories. The relationship is created using the value of CategoryID, the primary key from tbl_Categories. This is known as a **foreign key**. A foreign key is simply a primary key from one table recorded as a field within another table.

Like a leash connects a dog to its owner, the foreign key in tbl_Books table ties the book records to the category in which they belong. You will probably have several records with the same CategoryID in the tbl_Books table. For example, if you have three books in one category, there would be one record created in tbl_Categories and three records created in tbl_Books.

Let's see how this is done.

Creating a Relationship in Access

1. To create a relationship in Access, click the Relationships button on the toolbar, as shown in Figure 5-11.

Figure 5-11. The Relationships button on the Access toolbar

Access displays a large blank gray canvas onto which you need to add the tables you want to relate to each other.

2. To relate the tbl_Books table to the tbl_Categories table, right-click the screen and select Show Table from the context menu. From the dialog box, select tbl_Books and click Add. You should also add tbl_Categories to the relationships layout.

3. In the list of columns, drag the tbl_Categories object to the CategoryID field in the tbl_Books object. After you drop the tbl_Categories object, the Edit Relationships dialog box appears in which you can specify the details of this relationship, as shown in Figure 5-12.

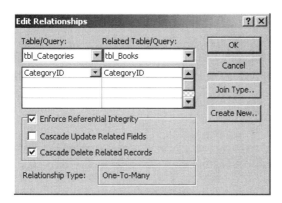

Figure 5-12. The details of the relationship

You want to set up a **one-to-many** relationship between tbl_Categories and tbl_Books, and the columns that have the related data in them are both called CategoryID. They don't have to have the same name, though; they just have to contain the same data and be stored using the same data type.

As in Figure 5-12, you also want to specify Cascade Delete Related Records in the referential integrity area so that if a record is deleted from the tbl_Categories table, all the related records from my tbl_Books table will be deleted as well.

4. Click Create to create the relationship and a black line appears between the two tables to signify the relationship. Notice that at one end of the line there is a 1 and at the other end there is an infinity symbol (which looks like a sideways 8). These visually signify the one-to-many relationship you have created between these two tables, as shown in Figure 5-13.

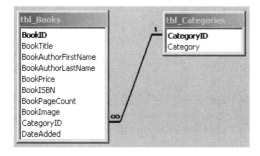

Figure 5-13. A one-to-many relationship

Creating a Relationship in SQL Server

As ever with SQL Server, there is more than one way to achieve your objective. To visually create your relationships, click Manage Relationships on the toolbar in Table Design view and use the resulting dialog box. Or, to create a Database Diagram, follow these steps.

1. In the left pane of Enterprise Manager, expand the webprodmx database, and then click the Diagrams object.

2. Right-click the right pane and select New Database Diagram from the context menu to launch the Create Database Diagram Wizard. Click Next.

3. To select the tables to add to your diagram, click them and click the Add button between the left and right lists. If you select the Add Related Tables Automatically option, any related tables will automatically be added. You can also specify how many levels of related tables it should add automatically. The default is 1. You want to add tbl_Books and tbl_Categories to the diagram, so select them and click Add to put them into the list on the right, as shown in Figure 5-14.

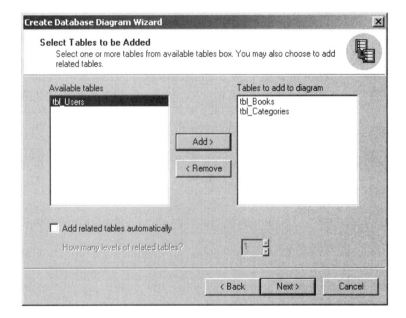

Figure 5-14. Selecting the tables to be added to the diagram

4. Click Next to check the details then click Finish if everything looks OK (if you made a mistake, click Back to go back and correct it). SQL Server generates a basic diagram for you.

5. Once again, drag the `tbl_Categories` object to the `CategoryID` field in the `tbl_Books` object. A dotted line appears between the objects as you drag. When you release the mouse button, the Create Relationship dialog box appears in which you can specify the details of this relationship, as shown in Figure 5-15.

Figure 5-15. The Create Relationship dialog box

One of the very useful options here is the Check existing data on creation check box. This allows you to ensure that any data already in these tables conforms to this relationship. If you know it doesn't, make sure this check box is left unchecked; otherwise SQL Server will throw an error and the relationship will not be created. When creating relationships between empty tables, it does not matter if you leave it checked, of course.

If you plan to use this database in a replication environment (a collection of databases that synchronize their content at predefined intervals), select the second check box to specify that this relationship should be enforced. We are not going to use replication in this book, so clear that box also.

6. Finally, clear the Cascade Update option because it won't affect this relationship in this instance. You cannot change the CategoryID value for a record in your tbl_Categories table because it is the Identity value, which is a read-only value. Therefore, Cascade Update for this relationship isn't possible.

7. Click OK to create the relationship.

   A line with a gold key at one end and an infinity symbol at the other visually signifies the one-to-many relationship you have created between these two tables, as shown in Figure 5-16.

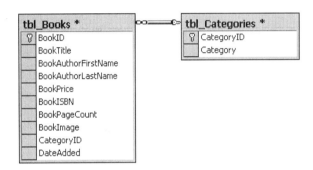

Figure 5-16. A one-to-many relationship

8. Save the diagram. You can accept the default name of Diagram 1, although a descriptive name may help you in the future if you create many diagrams in your database.

When you save your diagram, some behind-the-scenes modifications need to be applied to the tables involved in it to ensure that the relationships you just specified will be adhered to. Click Yes to allow these changes to be saved.

SQL Server Views and Access Queries

Views and **queries** are ideal ways to bring together the data you retrieve from the tables in your database.

Using views and queries allow you to store some of the SQL work within your database instead of having the entire SQL statement passed to the database from your web page. This means that to change the data displayed on a page, you might only need to modify the code in your database, rather than editing the SQL in your web page.

SQL queries can get very complex quite quickly in large projects, so we use views or queries to gather the data we want before using a simple `select` statement to grab all those records in the web page. We may even pass a filtering parameter into the view to narrow down the recordset even further. The beauty of doing it this way is that the complex SQL statement stays in the database and the run-time performance of the queries can be increased (your web pages will load faster).

Let's depart from the simple database example for a moment in order to illustrate this point. Let's say you want to view sales of items from a web site by seeing who bought products and how much they spent in total. You don't need to know what they bought or where they live right now, you only want to see the crucial data: their name and their total purchase amount.

To generate the recordset for a web page to show this data in Dreamweaver MX, you could open the Recordset Builder, switch to Advanced view, and build the following statement:

```
SELECT dbo.tbl_Customer_Orders.OrderID, dbo.tbl_Customer_Orders.PostalFullName,
       SUM(dbo.tbl_Customer_Order_Details.TotalCost)
AS TotalPurchaseCost
FROM dbo.tbl_Customer_Orders INNER JOIN dbo.tbl_Customer_Order_Details
ON dbo.tbl_Customer_Orders.OrderID = dbo.tbl_Customer_Order_Details.OrderID
GROUP BY dbo.tbl_Customer_Orders.OrderID, dbo.tbl_Customer_Orders.PostalFullName
```

The Recordset Builder will help you create this SQL statement, but it won't be able to do it all, so you will have to add some code by hand. As we've said before, it's often easier to get visual tools to do the job for you. We will look at how to use the Simple Recordset Builder and the Advanced Recordset Builder later in this chapter.

A simpler way to do this is to create a view called `view_Purchase_Totals` in SQL Server, or a query in Access to house the SQL code just shown, and then use the Dreamweaver MX Recordset Builder to build a recordset with the following code:

```
SELECT * FROM view_Purchase_Totals
```

We know which method we prefer!

Views and queries become even more useful when you need to gather data from larger numbers of tables. Using a view or query to select records from a single table may offer some benefits if the table is large and you are selecting most of the columns, but if it's a small table, the benefits are often much less.

Simple SQL

Later in this chapter, you will see just how easy Dreamweaver MX 2004 makes building SQL statements to create recordsets for your web pages. To give you a fuller understanding of this creation process and the final SQL code that it produces, let's have a quick primer in some simple SQL.

Many of the SQL statements you will see here can be created in Dreamweaver MX 2004's Simple Recordset Builder, but when you need to specify more than one criterion in your statement, you'll need to use the Advanced Recordset Builder.

SQL Server uses a strict naming convention for its objects. If you have programmed a language that uses dot notation before, you will recognize this. If not, it really is quite logical.

To reference an object in SQL Server, you use the following standard:

```
databaseowner.objectname
```

For example:

```
dbo.tbl_Books
```

> **NOTE** *Access doesn't need this extra information, nor would it understand it if you used it. The reason is that Access doesn't use the ownership metaphor or permissions principles that SQL Server does: Access is intended as a single-user database manager. SQL Server ensures that only the people with the relevant permissions can perform actions on the database objects, but in Access, it's a free-for-all!*

The following examples use the table object, `tbl_Users`, and assume that the owner of the database objects in SQL Server is dbo.

Selecting All Records from a Table

In Access, the following is probably the simplest SQL statement there is:

```
SELECT * FROM tbl_Users
```

In SQL Server, the following is probably the simplest SQL statement:

```
SELECT * FROM dbo.tbl_Users
```

This statement is an instruction to select all the records contained in tbl_Users. In this example, the asterisk (*) means all columns. This is not to be confused with the mathematical notation that uses the same asterisk symbol to signify the multiplication operator.

Selecting All Records That Meet One Criterion

This is almost as easy as the first example, but there are a couple of crucial rules to bear in mind. You are going to use a similar statement to the one just shown, but you only want to return records that contain a specific value in the specified column. You use the keyword WHERE to specify this.

In Access

```
SELECT * FROM tbl_Users WHERE EmailAddress = 'value'
```

In SQL Server

```
SELECT * FROM dbo.tbl_Users WHERE EmailAddress = 'value'
```

Strikingly similar aren't they?

The statement is an instruction to select all the records contained in tbl_Users for which the value contained in the EmailAddress column matches the value specified (in place of value).

There is a SQL statement regarding the data type of the column that stores the value you are trying to match. In the example just shown, the EmailAddress column has a text-based data type, which means that the value you're going to compare with the value in that column needs to be enclosed in single quotation marks. If it had been a numeric column, the single quotes would not have been used.

To illustrate this point, the following SQL code will show you the correct way to use a numeric value in the value area of this statement.

In Access:

```
SELECT * FROM tbl_Users WHERE UserID = value
```

In SQL Server:

```
SELECT * FROM dbo.tbl_Users WHERE UserID = value
```

This statement is an instruction to select all the records contained in tbl_Users for which the value contained in the UserID column matches the value specified (in place of value).

The UserID in your database is a numeric value, therefore the comparison value needs to be numeric too. By removing the single quotes from around the value, the SQL statement becomes valid. If you left the single quotes around the value and tried to execute the statement, you would get a data type mismatch error because the SQL will see that you are trying to compare a non-numeric value to the value contained in a numeric column.

Bearing these facts in mind, let's quickly step through a couple of increasingly complex, yet still very straightforward, examples.

Selecting All Records That Meet Several Criteria

The AND keyword allows you to create SQL statements that specify that more than one criteria must be met in order to return any results.

In Access:

```
SELECT * FROM tbl_Users WHERE FirstName = 'Rob' AND LastName = 'Turnbull'
```

In SQL Server:

```
SELECT * FROM dbo.tbl_Users WHERE FirstName = 'Rob' AND LastName = 'Turnbull'
```

This statement is an instruction to select all the records contained in tbl_Users for which the value contained in the FirstName column matches Rob AND the value contained in the LastName column matches Turnbull.

Selecting Records That Meet One or More of Several Criteria

The OR keyword allows you to create SQL statements that specify that one or more criteria of *either* of the specified criteria must be met in order to return any results.

In Access:

```
SELECT * FROM tbl_Users WHERE FirstName = 'value' OR LastName = 'anothervalue'
```

In SQL Server:

```
SELECT * FROM dbo.tbl_Users WHERE FirstName = 'value' OR LastName = 'anothervalue'
```

This statement is an instruction to select all columns for all the records contained in `tbl_Users` for which the value contained in the `FirstName` column matches the value specified (in place of `value`), `OR` the value contained in the `LastName` column matches the value specified (in place of `anothervalue`).

If you were to build a slightly more complex SQL statement that utilized the `OR` keyword and the `AND` keyword, you would be well advised to use parentheses to encapsulate the `OR` criteria. If you don't do this, you may get erroneous results. The following Access-based examples will explain this. To use this example in SQL Server, just add `dbo.` in front of the table name.

```
SELECT *
FROM tbl_Users
WHERE (FirstName = 'value' OR LastName = 'anothervalue')
AND AccessGroup = 'yetanothervalue'
```

This would correctly return all columns for all records from the `tbl_Users` table that meet the criteria of having a matching `FirstName` value `OR` a matching `LastName` value `AND` also have a matching `AccessGroup` value. Compare it with the following, which could return incorrect results:

```
SELECT *
FROM tbl_Users
WHERE FirstName = 'value' OR LastName = 'anothervalue'
AND AccessGroup = 'yetanothervalue'
```

Here, the SQL might be saying what the first example said, or it might be interpreted as an instruction to return all records from the `tbl_Logins` table that meet the criteria of having a matching `FirstName` value `AND` also having a matching `AccessGroup` value `OR` a matching `LastName` value. If you say the whole statement out loud with a big emphasis on the `OR` keyword, you'll understand the point we're making.

Basically, the more complex your SQL statements become, the more careful you will have to be in creating them.

Useful SQL Keywords

There are far too many SQL keywords to cover them all. However, a quick glance at some of the more commonly used ones might help you understand how to achieve the results you are after. To see all the SQL keywords, check out Books Online.

COUNT

If you want to count how many user records are stored in your tbl_Users table, for example, you could use the COUNT keyword in the following way.

In Access:

```
SELECT COUNT(UserID) AS TotalUsers FROM tbl_Users
```

In SQL Server:

```
SELECT COUNT(UserID) AS TotalUsers FROM dbo.tbl_Users
```

This illustrates two very useful SQL keywords: COUNT and AS.

The COUNT(UserID) section counts how many rows there are in the table tbl_Users, whereas the AS TotalUsers section returns the COUNT value to an alias column called TotalUsers. TotalUsers doesn't exist as a column in your database but you are declaring it as an alias by using the AS keyword.

SUM

If you want to add the values of several rows (such as a total value of all the books' prices in a particular category), you could use the SUM keyword in your SQL statement as in the following example.

In Access:

```
SELECT SUM(BookPrice) AS GrandTotal FROM tbl_Books WHERE CategoryID = 2
```

In SQL Server:

```
SELECT SUM(BookPrice) AS GrandTotal FROM dbo.tbl_Books WHERE CategoryID = 2
```

The SUM(BookPrice) section adds all the rows contained in the table tbl_Books that match the WHERE criteria and returns a single row contained in a column called GrandTotal using the alias keyword AS. In this example, the rows that match must have an CategoryID of 2.

TOP

The TOP keyword is very useful if you want to specify that only a certain number of rows should be returned to your recordset. Obtaining exactly the right amount of data you require and nothing more is good for performance reasons.

For example, if you had a table that contained hundreds of thousands of rows of data and you knew that over 10,000 of those rows match your specific WHERE criteria but you only wanted to view a sample of those records rather than all of them, the TOP keyword can arrange that for you.

All you need to decide is how many records you want to retrieve. Let's say that we want 100. Here's what you'd do.

In Access:

```
SELECT TOP 100 * FROM tbl_Books WHERE CategoryID = 2
```

In SQL Server:

```
SELECT TOP 100 * FROM dbo.tbl_Books WHERE CategoryID = 2
```

The process this statement goes through is fairly straightforward. It filters the table tbl_Books with the criteria specified (CategoryID must equal 2) and from that resultset, it selects the first (TOP) 100 records.

You'll notice the * immediately after the 100 in the statement. This signifies which columns of the table we want returned. We could have specified one or more column names here to narrow down even further the data that is returned, but we wanted all of the columns, so we used *.

That's all well and good but what if you didn't want the top 100 records? Say you wanted to view the last 100 books added to your database between two dates. To do that, you could either specify the dates in your SQL statement using the BETWEEN keyword, or you could use the ORDER BY keyword. We will look at both of these in turn.

BETWEEN

The BETWEEN statement has a lot of uses and just a couple of simple stipulations in how it is used. Let's look at an example of BETWEEN in use and then break it down to see what's going on.

In Access:

```
SELECT TOP 100 *
FROM tbl_Books
WHERE CategoryID = 2
AND DateAdded BETWEEN #01 September 2003# AND #31 September 2003#
```

In SQL Server:

```
SELECT TOP 100 *
FROM dbo.tbl_Books
WHERE CategoryID = 2
AND DateAdded BETWEEN '01 SEPTEMBER 2003' AND '31 SEPTEMBER 2003'
```

You want to SELECT all columns of data for the TOP 100 records that are returned that match the criteria specified. In this case, you specify that CategoryID is 2 and the DateAdded column must contain a date that is BETWEEN the dates of the 1st and the 31st of September 2003, inclusive.

There are a couple of things that you need to keep an eye out for when using BETWEEN.

- The statement must specify inclusive values

- The statement must be compared to the same data type

In the example just shown, the DateAdded column has a Date data type so the first and second values must be date values also.

For a more in-depth look at dates and how they are used in SQL, see the "Going on a DATE" section later in this chapter.

ORDER BY

ORDER BY is a powerful keyword that you can use to order the way your records are returned to you. You might want them in the order in which they were entered into the database, using the primary key value, which is usually a sequential number for each row. You might want to specify multiple columns by which to order your data. The way in which that data would be returned to you is dependent on the order in which you specify the columns in the ORDER BY statement.

A couple of examples will help to illustrate this powerful keyword.

In Access:

```
SELECT TOP 100 *
FROM tbl_Books
WHERE CategoryID = 2
AND DateAdded BETWEEN #01 SEPTEMBER 2003#
AND #31 SEPTEMBER 2003#

ORDER BY CategoryID, BookPrice
```

In SQL Server:

```
SELECT TOP 100 *
FROM dbo.tbl_Books
WHERE CategoryID = 2
AND DateAdded BETWEEN '01 SEPTEMBER 2003'
AND '31 SEPTEMBER 2003'

ORDER BY CategoryID, BookPrice
```

Using the BETWEEN example, we added the ORDER BY keyword so that all the results returned that meet the criteria specified will be ordered by their CategoryID and then by their BookPrice.

This means that the books that match the overall statements criteria will be returned with the cheapest book in the first category listed first, up to the most expensive book in the first category, then the cheapest book from the second category up to the most expensive book from the second category, and so on until all the matching records have been sorted. Then the TOP 100 books *from that set* will be retrieved.

You can also specify the direction in which a sort order is used, either from the smallest value to the largest, or from the largest value to the smallest. This is achieved by using the ASC or DESC keywords (short for ASCending and DESCending). The default sort order is ascending; you can use it in your SQL statements but it is not necessary unless you are specifying more than one sort order.

To sort the previous example so that the most expensive books are listed first and the cheapest are listed last within each category, with the categories in ascending order, add the ASC and DESC keywords to the statement, as in the following example.

In Access:

```
SELECT TOP 100 *
FROM tbl_Books
WHERE CategoryID = 2
AND DateAdded BETWEEN #01 SEPTEMBER 2003#
AND #31 SEPTEMBER 2003#
ORDER BY CategoryID ASC, BookPrice DESC
```

In SQL Server:

```
SELECT TOP 100 *
FROM dbo.tbl_Books
WHERE CategoryID = 2
AND DateAdded BETWEEN '01 SEPTEMBER 2003'
AND '31 SEPTEMBER 2003'
ORDER BY CategoryID ASC, BookPrice DESC
```

IN

The IN keyword is useful for those times when you might have several criteria that you want to use as a filter on your data.

You could write a long WHERE clause that uses many OR statements, or you could write a much shorter WHERE clause that uses the IN statement. The following examples illustrate this point.

First let's look at solving this problem by using the OR keyword.

In Access:

```
SELECT BookTitle, CategoryID, BookImage, BookPrice
FROM tbl_Books
WHERE CategoryID = 1
OR CategoryID = 2
OR CategoryID = 3
OR CategoryID = 4
OR CategoryID = 5
```

In SQL Server:

```
SELECT BookTitle, CategoryID, BookImage, BookPrice
FROM dbo.tbl_Books
WHERE CategoryID = 1
OR CategoryID = 2
OR CategoryID = 3
OR CategoryID = 4
OR CategoryID = 5
```

Now let's use the IN keyword. You specify the values to compare against the column within parentheses.

In Access:

```
SELECT BookTitle, CategoryID, BookImage, BookPrice
FROM tbl_Books
WHERE CategoryID IN (1,2,3,4,5)
```

In SQL Server:

```
SELECT BookTitle, CategoryID, BookImage, BookPrice
FROM dbo.tbl_Books
WHERE CategoryID IN (1,2,3,4,5)
```

If the data type that you are comparing a value against is not numeric, it requires single quotes around it. The example doesn't use them because the CategoryID column is a numeric column.

GROUP BY

The GROUP BY keyword groups identical values in a column in your resultset. In this regard, it is quite similar to the ORDER BY keyword. It differs in the data that is not allowed to be specified in the overall SQL statement. For example, in Access you cannot include a memo field in a GROUP BY clause. In SQL Server, you cannot include a text field.

The data is sorted first in the order of the columns specified in the GROUP BY statement, then in an ascending order, row by row, unless you specify an ORDER BY as well.

For example, in the `tbl_Books` table you might have many books that share the same category and you might want to return a resultset that groups the results by category and then by price, as in the `ORDER BY` example. `ORDER BY` allows you to return any and all columns of data. `GROUP BY` must look at the data first to see if a grouping is allowed on the data required, and unfortunately, not all data types can be grouped. For example, a memo field in Access or a text field in SQL Server cannot be returned in a `GROUP BY` statement unless they are being used as an expression of criteria to be met (that is, you want all the records in which the description column is not empty).

A valid `GROUP BY` statement might be created as follows.

In Access:

```
SELECT TOP 100 BookTitle, CategoryID, BookImage, BookPrice
FROM tbl_Books
GROUP BY CategoryID, BookTitle, BookPrice
```

In SQL Server:

```
SELECT TOP 100 BookTitle, CategoryID, BookImage, BookPrice
FROM dbo.tbl_Books
GROUP BY CategoryID, BookTitle, BookPrice
```

You can see that you have to specify the columns that you want to be returned by this statement. You cannot use the * wildcard to return all columns because you cannot include all the columns of this table in a `GROUP BY` clause.

The following example shows the use of the `GROUP BY` statement in conjunction with the use of a `WHERE` clause.

In Access:

```
SELECT TOP 100 BookTitle, CategoryID, BookImage, BookPrice
FROM tbl_Books
WHERE (BookTitle IS NOT NULL)
GROUP BY CategoryID, BookTitle, BookPrice
```

In SQL Server:

```
SELECT TOP 100 BookTitle, CategoryID, BookImage, BookPrice
FROM dbo.tbl_Books
WHERE (BookTitle IS NOT NULL)
GROUP BY CategoryID, BookTitle, BookPrice
```

You still select the same columns as before but the results will be filtered to show only records that have a value that is NOT NULL in the BookTitle column.

The use of the NOT keyword comes into play here. It is used to reverse the logic of the statement that contains it. In this case it is used to reverse the normal IS NULL statement by specifying IS NOT NULL so that all records that have a BookTitle will be returned.

DISTINCT

DISTINCT is used to prevent duplicate rows from being returned to the resultset.

If you absolutely must have a resultset that contains at least one unique value on every row, DISTINCT can be the answer. However, it isn't always necessary to use DISTINCT because you generally return the primary key value of each record in your query. If the need arises for a resultset that doesn't include the primary key value, DISTINCT ensures that no duplicate records are returned.

The following is an example of using the DISTINCT keyword.

In Access:

```
SELECT DISTINCT BookAuthorFirstName, BookAuthorLastName FROM tbl_Books
```

In SQL Server:

```
SELECT DISTINCT BookAuthorFirstName, BookAuthorLastName FROM dbo.tbl_Books
```

This selects all the individual first names and last names of the authors from the BookAuthorFirstName and BookAuthorLastName columns in the tbl_Books table. You may have hundreds of rows of books in that table, and some of them were written by the same author. This example will return each author name only once; regardless of how many times that author name is stored in the database.

Going on a DATE

Dates are notoriously awkward—this, of course, refers to a date as a type of data and not that person you've been having occasional late night drinks with! If you live anywhere outside of the countries that follow the US date format, you can find yourself in all sorts of trouble when storing dates in your database.

In the examples used for the BETWEEN keyword earlier in this chapter, you specified the date in a manner that leaves no ambiguity over how the date should be read. However, 01/09/2004 could mean the first of September or the ninth of January, depending on where you are in the world.

Access and SQL Server always try to store the date in the U.S. format, Month, Date, and Year. If they come across a date that cannot be stored this way, such as 17/09/2004, that date is converted into the Month, Date, and Year format. To save yourself a lot of trouble, just use non-ambiguous dates like 01 September 2004.

When using dates in your SQL statements, such as when searching for matching items that occur between two dates that you specify, remember the following strict rules about how each database application requires that dates are presented.

- Access requires the date value be wrapped in pound symbols, that is
  `#01 September 2003#`

- SQL Server requires the date value be wrapped in single quotes, that is
  `'01 September 2003'`

Making the Connection

To be able to use data on your web pages, you need to tell your web application where to look for that data. (Chapter 6 includes a recap on using these connection types in the context of a real web application.)

There are two ways of doing this. You can either tell Dreamweaver MX that a System DSN (Data Source Name) has been set up on your computer and you want to use that, or you can define a custom connection string that encapsulates all the information required to connect to the data source, including where the database is and security information needed to access the data. We will concentrate on using a System DSN.

There are no real advantages to be had in using one method over the other. It might simply come down to your hosts not allowing you to create a system DSN on their servers. If this is the case, you would need to use a custom connection string, known as a DSN-less connection.

This can all be done from Dreamweaver MX 2004 but it's just as easy to set it up from your operating system—use the same method outlined as follows.

Setting Up a DSN to an Access Database

1. Open the Data Sources (ODBC) administrator on your computer.

2. Click the System DSN tab then click Add.

3. Select Microsoft Access Driver (*.mdb) from the list and click Finish.

4. Enter the name of this DSN. We're going to call ours `DSNwebprodmxAccess`.

5. Leave the description field empty unless you really want to enter something in there. It's not necessary for this to work.

6. Click Select to select the location of your database. Use the dialog box to find the database and select it. Click OK and the full path to your database will be now shown above the Select button. Ours is C:\databases\webprodmx\webprodmx.mdb.

7. Click OK twice to close the dialog boxes.

Your DSN is set up and ready to use.

Setting Up a DSN to a SQL Server Database

1. Open the Data Sources (ODBC) administrator on your computer.

2. Click the System DSN tab then click Add.

3. Scroll the list to the bottom, select SQL Server and click Finish.

4. For the name, we're going to call ours DSNwebprodmxSQL.

5. Either type the name of your SQL Server into the Server drop-down menu or click your server to select it, and then click Next.

6. If you've followed this chapter from the start, the next few screens are all filled in for you. The database is already set to webprodmx because that is what you set it to when you created your login in SQL Server. Leave the other settings as they are. Click Next and then click Finish.

7. Click Test Data Source and if all is well, you should see a screen that contains the words Tests Completed Successfully.

8. Click OK twice to get back to the original DSN screen, where you will see your newly created DSN in the list.

9. Click OK to close this screen.

Connecting to Dreamweaver MX 2004

The final step for connecting your web site to the database is defining a connection in Dreamweaver MX 2004 that will use the DSN that you just set up. This connection is stored in a Connections folder in your site definition and will be referenced on every page that you create that needs to talk to the database. The beauty of doing it this way is that if your connection details change for some reason, you will only need to change one connection file to bring your entire site up to date, rather than modifying every single page by hand.

1. To define your connection, open the Databases panel in the Application panel group. Click the plus sign (+) button and select Data Source Name (DSN) from the pop-up menu.

2. In the dialog box, name this connection and select which DSN on your computer that it should use. Then provide the username and password that the DSN needs to authenticate itself with in the database, if required. (In the Access examples, we didn't set a username or a password so these can be left blank. In the SQL Server example, we had to specify the username but we left the password blank.)

3. For Access databases, fill out the dialog box as shown in Figure 5-17 and click OK.

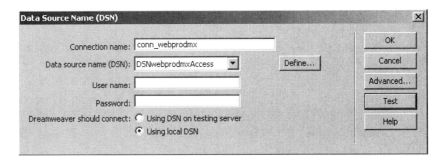

Figure 5-17. The Data Source Name dialog box for Access

4. For SQL Server databases, fill out the dialog box as shown in Figure 5-18 and click OK.

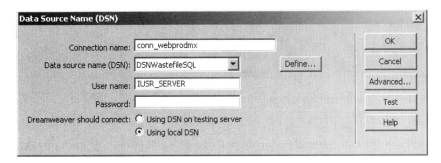

Figure 5-18. The Data Source Name dialog box for SQL Server

Once your connection file has been created within your site, you can start to build recordsets.

> **NOTE** *If you start to build a recordset before a connection file has been created for your site, the connections drop-down menu in the recordset dialog box will be empty. You can create the connection by clicking the Define button next to the connections drop-down menu and following the steps just outlined.*

The Simple Recordset Builder

The Simple Recordset Builder allows you to build a SQL statement to request data from your database. You won't always need to specify a WHERE clause in your SQL statement but if you do, the Simple Recordset Builder allows you to specify a single WHERE clause. If that is not enough for your purposes, you will need to use the Advanced Recordset Builder. We'll get to the Advanced Recordset Builder in the next section.

There are only a few preparatory steps you need to follow to be able to use dynamic data on a web page. The first thing to do in Dreamweaver MX is to set up a site definition in which you are going to build your web application. After you have created your site definition, you will create a new page. You will specify that this page is a dynamic page and which server-side scripting language you are going to use. See Chapter 6 for further information on all the steps mentioned here.

Once you have created a page to which you can add data, the Bindings panel in the Application panel group tells you that you need to create a recordset this, as seen in Figure 5-19.

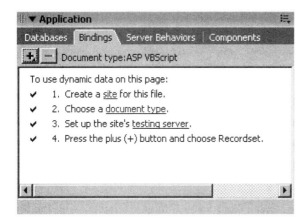

Figure 5-19. Bindings panel of the Application panel group

1. To build a recordset using the Simple Recordset Builder, click the plus sign (+) button in either the Bindings panel or the Server Behaviors panel and select Recordset (Query) from the pop-up menu. It is the first option on the menu, as shown in Figure 5-20.

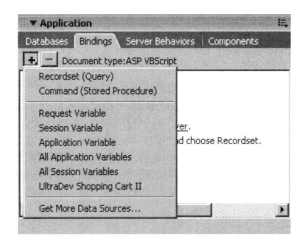

Figure 5-20. The recordset menu option

2. The Simple Recordset Builder interface appears in which you can define what data you want to retrieve from the database. To retrieve the whole of the tbl_Books table, complete the dialog box in the way shown in Figure 5-21.

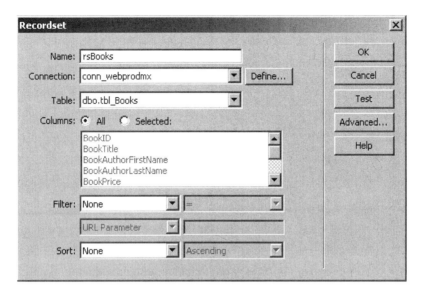

Figure 5-21. The completed Simple Recordset dialog box

The Simple Recordset Builder also allows you to specify a single WHERE clause and a single ORDER BY clause.

To illustrate just how easy this is, let's apply a filter to the CategoryID column and specify that the category must equal 2. We'll also set an ORDER BY clause to sort these records by their price starting with the cheapest.

3. To do this, select CategoryID from the Filter drop-down menu and select the equality operator (=) from the drop-down menu. Then select Entered Value from the list below the Filter drop-down menu and in the text box to the right, type **2**. In the Sort drop-down menu, select BookPrice and in the bottom right drop-down menu, select Ascending. You should now have something that looks like Figure 5-22.

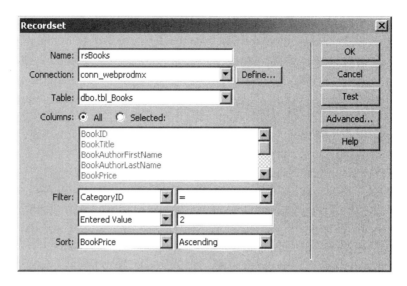

Figure 5-22. The completed Simple Recordset dialog box with Sort option

When you click OK, the recordset is created and added to the Bindings panel. If you click the plus sign icon next to the recordset name, you can see all the columns of the `tbl_Books` table and you could start adding these pieces of data to your web page, as shown in Figure 5-23.

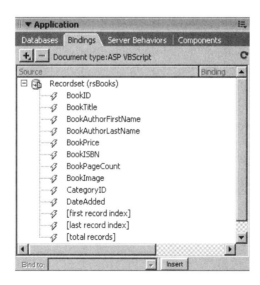

Figure 5-23. A recordset listed in the Bindings panel

Not only did this retrieve all the columns from the `tbl_Books` table, it also added three extra items. They are [first record index], [last record index], and [total records].

These three elements are useful for signposting data. For example, if you create a search results page that displays 10 results per page, you could include these three elements on the page to indicate, for example, that the user is currently looking at records 1 to 10 of 73 records. In this example, the 1 is produced from [first record index], the 10 is produced from [last record index] and the 73 is produced from [total records]. If you used a link to get the next page of records (next 10), the first two signposts would change to "Currently viewing 11 to 20 of 73 records."

To make this simple recordset a lot more flexible and far more useful for a web page, instead of specifying that the `CategoryID` must be 2, you can make it use a parameter that your web page must pass to this recordset to use as the filter.

4. Open the Recordset dialog box for this recordset again by double-clicking the recordset name in the Bindings panel. Where you previously selected Entered Value from the drop-down menu, select URL Parameter. Where you previously entered 2 in the text box, type **catID**. This will be the name of the parameter that this recordset will use, as shown in Figure 5-24.

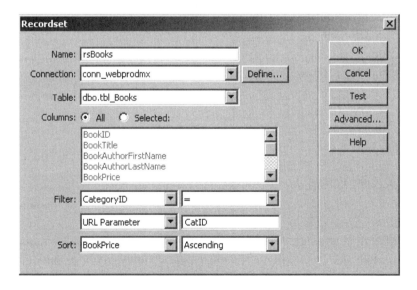

Figure 5-24. The completed Simple Recordset dialog box with filter applied

If this recordset were on an actual web page that displayed data, and you browsed to that page specifying a URL parameter of catID=2, the recordset would be filtered to show only books with a CategoryID equal to 2. If the URL parameter were catID=3, only books with a CategoryID equal to 3 would be shown.

Easy, flexible, and powerful—what more could you want?

The Advanced Recordset Builder

The Advanced Recordset Builder is the place to build those recordsets that require more detail than can be offered by the Simple Recordset Builder.

Once you know how to work it, creating simple or advanced recordsets in the Advanced Recordset Builder is limited only by your knowledge of SQL. The basic layout of the SQL statement is put into place as you click through the building process. After that, you must dive into the code and enter the final details. Don't worry; it's easier than it sounds.

You'll build the same recordset you built with the Simple Recordset Builder but this time you'll add an extra parameter into the mix to illustrate the power that the Advanced Recordset Builder affords you.

1. Start the same way as before, click the plus sign (+) button in either the Bindings panel or the Server Behaviors panel and select Recordset (Query) from the pop-up menu. On the right side of the Simple Recordset Builder dialog box, press the Advanced button to switch to the Advanced Recordset Builder.

   > **NOTE** *When you build a recordset and click OK, the dialog box you used to build that recordset is the one you'll see the next time you go to build a recordset.*

   Now you will see the empty Advanced Recordset Builder in which you are going to build your SQL statement.

2. Name the recordset. We're going to call ours rsBooks again.

   Now you need to select the database connection so that you can view the database objects in the Database Items window at the bottom of this dialog box. If you were to click the plus sign (+) icons next to the three items in there, Tables, Views, and Stored Procedures before you selected your connection, they will contain nothing. Once you have selected your connection, they will be populated with your database objects and you can build your SQL statement.

3. Select your connection from the Connections drop-down menu.

4. In the Database Items window of this dialog box, click the plus sign (+) icon next to Tables and a listing of all the tables in your database will be displayed. Click the plus sign (+) icon next to tbl_Books and the list will be updated to show all the columns of the tbl_Books table.

5. Ordinarily, you would click the table name to highlight it and then click the SELECT button to the right of the Database Items window to start creating your SQL statement. However, here's a little shortcut: you want to select all the columns for all the records in this table whose CategoryID value that matches your criteria, so the quick way to generate the SQL statement for this is to click the CategoryID column and click the WHERE button to the right of the Database Items window.

    The SQL window shows the beginnings of your SQL statement, as shown in Figure 5-25.

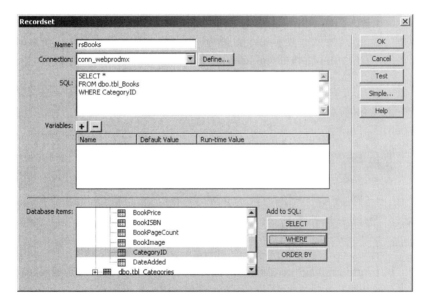

Figure 5-25. The Advanced Recordset dialog box

You now have an incomplete WHERE statement that if left as it stands would make this recordset fail. You need to define what that CategoryID should equal.

6. Click to place the cursor after `CategoryID` in the SQL window and type

   = varCatID

   You have total control over the naming of your variables. We chose to give ours meaningful names so we will have an idea what the content is, and to prefix them with *var* to remind ourselves that it is a variable.

   You know this variable is going to contain a numeric value so you don't use single quotes around the variable name. If you were using a text-based column to filter on, the variable name would have to be wrapped in single quotes to identify it as such.

7. Now you need to define what value `varCatID` should pass to this SQL statement. You do this using the Variables window below the SQL window. Click the plus sign (+) icon above the Variables window. A new variable line is added to the Variables window that you are going to fill in with the following details:

   - Click the Name column of this new variable line and type **varCatID**

   - Click the Default Value column (or press Tab) and type **0**

   - Click the Run-Time Value column (or press Tab again) and type **Request("catid")**

   In the SQL statement in the SQL window, you said that the column `CategoryID` should equal the value contained in the variable called `varCatID`.

   The Default Value you supplied serves two purposes. First, it allows you to test your completed SQL statement to make sure that you are getting the results that you expect, and second, when the page is used in a live environment, it acts as the actual variable value if the `catid` URL parameter doesn't exist.

   The Run-Time Value column is where you specify what should be used as the actual value to filter this recordset. As previously mentioned, if this parameter doesn't exist, the default value will be used to filter the recordset. We used a default value of 0 to ensure that the recordset will be empty if the `catid` parameter does not exist. You may want to use a default value of an existing `CategoryID` to ensure that this recordset always contains data.

8. In the Simple Recordset example, you added a sort order to your records that returns the cheapest first. To accomplish this, select BookPrice in the Database Items window and click the ORDER BY button to the right. As previously discussed, ORDER BY defaults to ascending so we don't need to add that unless we are adding more than one ORDER BY clause.

The finished Advanced Recordset should look like Figure 5-26.

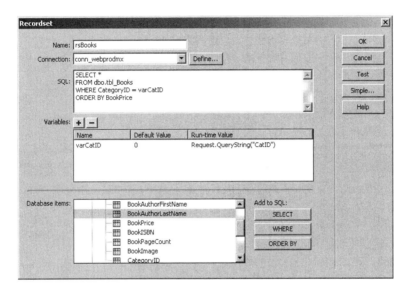

Figure 5-26. The completed Advanced Recordset dialog box

9. Click OK to close the dialog box and create the recordset.

Hopefully you can see the advantages of using the Advanced Recordset Builder over using the Simple Recordset Builder. You can use multiple parameters in your statements, and you can write your SQL statement directly in the SQL window by hand.

Using Commands

At some point in your web site development you will no doubt want to add, edit, or delete data from your database. In Dreamweaver MX 2004 there are two ways you can do any of these actions. The first, and perhaps most common way is to use the standard Insert, Update, and Delete server behaviors, which you can read more about in the next chapter.

The other way is to use a **command**. Commands can be created to perform the same database operations as their server behavior counterparts with the addition of being able to utilize **stored procedures** (more on those in the next section of this chapter).

You might prefer to use commands over server behaviors if you are comfortable writing syntactically correct SQL statements by hand or even if you just have an understanding of the correct formation of SQL. You will find the Command interface very much like the Recordset Builder interface.

If you need to have more than one of the same database interactions on the same page, you will need to use one command per database interaction. For instance, you might want to insert a new record into your database that needs to be split over two tables. You could set up two commands on a page to do this for you. The server behavior versions of these database interactions can only be included on your web page once.

Perhaps the major benefit of commands over server behaviors is the amount of code produced. Server behaviors tend to produce bulky code because they need to cater for a lot of different scenarios, commands produce a very small amount of code while maintaining adaptability.

The following examples introduce you to each of the commands available to you with the exception of the Stored Procedure Command, which is covered later.

The creation process of each of these commands begins in exactly the same way.

NOTE *Your command will be listed in, and therefore editable from, the Server Behaviors panel no matter in which panel you create it.*

1. Click the plus sign (+) button in either the Bindings panel or the Server Behaviors panel and select Command from the pop-up menu. You will see the Command dialog box, which is shown in Figure 5-27.

2. All commands are given a default name but it's not too descriptive. You can name the command whatever you like in the top-left box of the dialog box.

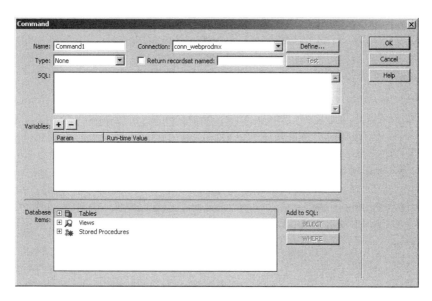

Figure 5-27. The Command dialog box

Inserting a Record

This Insert command will add a new book record to your database. We are going to call ours cmdInsertBook.

The connection is selected because we already set up a connection for this site. If your connection is not selected, you will need to set up a connection before continuing, which you can do by clicking the Define button in this dialog box or you can follow the steps outlined in "Making the Connection," earlier in this chapter.

1. In the Type drop-down menu, select Insert because this is an INSERT command (easy, isn't it?). Immediately after you select Insert from the list, the basic INSERT statement is added to the SQL window. All you are going to do is populate this statement with the relevant information. You can ignore the check box next to Return Recordset Named because this is only used for stored procedures and even then, only if you actually return a recordset from the stored procedure.

    The buttons in the lower-right of the dialog box, under the Add to SQL: heading, change to reflect the type of statement you are building. For the INSERT statement only one of the two buttons is active and it is called COLUMN.

2. In this case, you want to insert only certain pieces of information into the tbl_Books table and in all likelihood, those pieces of information would have been submitted from a form on the previous page. With this in mind, select the columns you are inserting your data into from tbl_Books in the Database Items window and then click the COLUMN button.

3. Select BookTitle and click COLUMN. The SQL window is updated to reflect your selection.

4. Select BookAuthorFirstName and click COLUMN.

5. Do the same for BookAuthorLastName, BookPrice, BookISBN, BookPageCount, BookImage, and CategoryID.

   The SQL window should now read as follows:

   ```
   INSERT INTO dbo.tbl_Books
   (BookTitle, BookAuthorFirstName, BookAuthorLastName, BookPrice,
   BookISBN, BookPageCount, BookImage, CategoryID)
   VALUES ( )
   ```

   Now you must tell it what values to insert into the specified columns. An important point to note is that you cannot mix up the items between lists; they must be in the exact same order. In other words, the order in which you specify the items in the INSERT INTO line must be the same order in which you specify the items in the VALUES line.

   To get values into this INSERT command from a fictitious form on the previous page, you need to Request that information and use variable placeholders in the values listing, as follows.

6. Click inside the parentheses after Values and enter the following string of variable names, each separated by a comma. Don't forget, text-based values need to be surrounded by single quotes and numeric values do not.

   ```
   'varBookTitle','varBookAuthorFirstName','varBookAuthorLastName',
   varBookPrice, 'varBookISBN','varBookPageContent',
   'varBookImage',varCategoryID
   ```

   Now you need to define where these variables are going to get their information. This example assumes that you are getting your information from a form on the previous page and that the form elements were named as shown in the Request parts of the following details.

7. Click the plus sign (+) button above the Variables window, click the Name column, and type **varBookTitle**. Tab to the Run-Time Value column and type **Request("BookTitle")**.

8. Add another variable line for `varBookAuthorFirstName` with the Run-Time Value of **Request("BookAuthorFirstName")**.

9. Add another variable line for `varBookAuthorLastName` with the Run-Time Value of **Request("BookAuthorLastName")**.

10. Add another variable line for `varBookPrice` with the Run-Time Value of **Request("BookPrice")**.

11. Add another variable line for `varBookISBN` with the Run-Time Value of **Request("BookISBN")**.

12. Do the same for `varBookPageCount` with a Run-Time Value of **Request("BookPageCount")**.

13. Once again for `varBookImage` with a Run-Time Value of **Request("BookImage")**.

14. Once more for `varCategoryID` with a Run-Time Value of **Request("CategoryID")**.

Your Command dialog box should now look as shown in Figure 5-28.

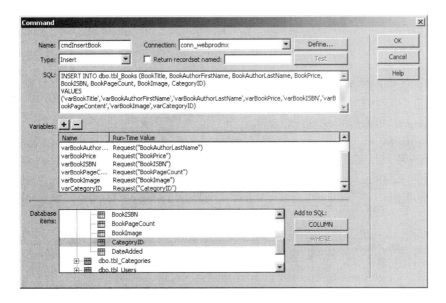

Figure 5-28. The completed Command dialog box

15. Click OK and your command is applied to the page.

Now when the form on the previous page submits its information to this page, it will be inserted into the database.

Updating a Record

This UPDATE command allows you to update a file name stored in the BookImage column of a record (for instance, the one you just inserted with the INSERT command).

1. With the Command dialog box open, name this command cmdUpdateBook and select Update from the Type drop-down menu. Your connection should already be selected in the Connection drop-down menu. The two buttons in the Add to SQL area are labeled SET and WHERE because that's the syntax of the UPDATE statement.

2. In the Database Items window, expand the Tables listing and then expand the tbl_Books table. Click to highlight the BookImage column and click SET. Your SQL window is updated to show the following SQL code. (This example is using SQL Server, the Access version of this would be the same but without the dbo. prefix on the table name.)

   ```
   UPDATE dbo.tbl_Books
   SET BookImage
   WHERE
   ```

3. Type = **'varBookImage'** after BookImage to tell it what value BookImage should be set to and identify which record this statement should be applied to. The SET line of the SQL window will now read as follows:

   ```
   SET BookImage  = 'varBookImage'
   ```

4. varBookImage is a variable that will get its Run-Time Value from a field called BookImage, which we will assume has been submitted from the previous page. Click the plus sign (+) button above the Variables window and add **varBookImage** as the variable name and **Request("BookImage")** as the Run-Time Value. The only thing left to do is to make sure that you are going to update the right record in your database.

5. To do this, use the ID number of the record, which will also have been passed through to this page from the previous page. Click BookID in the Database Items window and then click WHERE. Click the SQL window after BookID and add **= varBookID**. You now need to add that variable to

the variables list, so click the plus sign (+) button above the Variables window again and on the new variable line, set the variable name to **varBookID** and the Run-Time Value to **Request("BookID")**.

Your finished update Command dialog box should look as shown in Figure 5-29.

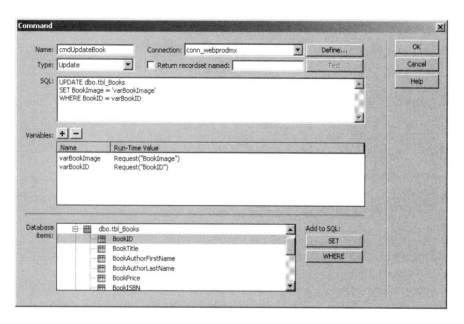

Figure 5-29. The completed update Command dialog box

Updating Multiple Records (Simple Example)

You might want to be able to update more than one user at a time. Let's say you have a page that displays all your web site users and a check box for each one. This example explains how to do this.

1. With the Command dialog box open, name this command cmdUpdateMultiUsers and select Update from the Type drop-down menu (your connection should already be selected in the Connection drop-down menu). Expand the Tables listing in the Database Items window, expand the tbl_Users table, highlight Included, and click SET.

   Your SQL window should now look like this.

   ```
   UPDATE dbo.tbl_Users
   SET Included
   WHERE
   ```

2. Now type **= 0** after Included. This column of the database is binary so a 1 (SQL Server) or –1 (Access) in this column means that the record is included—a zero means it is excluded.

3. Now you need to specify which records to update. You will use the IN keyword in this case (see "Useful SQL Keywords," earlier in this chapter for further information). In the Database Items window, click UserID and then click WHERE. UserID is added to the SQL window. Click in the SQL window to place the cursor after UserID and type the following:

```
IN (varUserID)
```

Your SQL should now look like this.

```
UPDATE dbo.tbl_Users
SET Included = 0
WHERE UserID IN (varUserID)
```

All you need to do now is add the varUserID to the Variables window.

4. Click the plus sign (+) button above the Variables window and enter **varUserID** in the Name column. In the Run-Time Value column, type **Request("UserID")**.

Your finished multiple update Command dialog should look as shown in Figure 5-30.

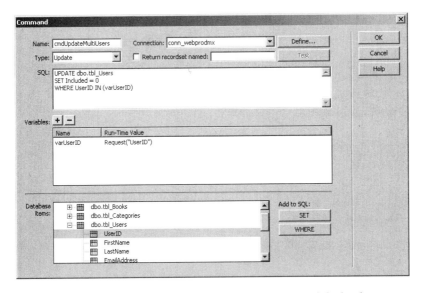

Figure 5-30. The completed multiple-update Command dialog box

Now when multiple check boxes are selected on the page that submits to this page, a list of user IDs will be delivered in a comma-delimited string and all the records that match one of those user IDs will have their Included column updated to contain a 0. These users can no longer login—as long as the correct logic is in place to assure that the Included column is used, of course!

Deleting a Record

Deleting records is sometimes a necessary step for keeping your database up to date. The following example shows you how passing the ID number of a book record to a DELETE command will delete that book.

1. With the Command dialog box open, give the command a name of **cmdDeleteRecord** and select Delete from the Type drop-down menu. Your connection should already be selected in the Connection drop-down menu. The shortcut detailed in other commands doesn't work for the DELETE command, you have to specifically click the table name in the Database Objects window and click the DELETE button to add the table name to the SQL.

2. Expand the tbl_Books table in the Database Objects window and click the BookID column. Click WHERE to add this column to the SQL window.

   Your SQL window should look like this.

   ```
   DELETE FROM dbo.tbl_Books
   WHERE BookID
   ```

3. Place the cursor after BookID and type = **varBookID**.

4. Add the variable to the Variables window by clicking the plus sign (+) button above it. In the Name column, type **varBookID** and set the Run-Time Value to **Request("BookID")**.

   Your final Command dialog box should look as shown in Figure 5-31.

5. Click OK to apply this command to the page. When this page is passed the ID number of a record in the BookID parameter, that record will be deleted.

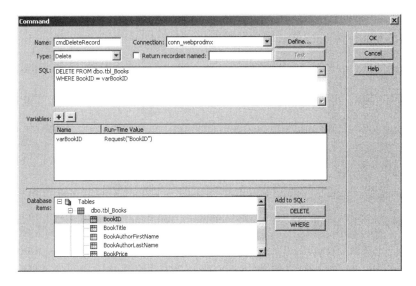

Figure 5-31. The completed delete Command dialog box

Deleting Multiple Records (Simple Example)

It is also not uncommon to need to delete multiple records. You could delete them one at a time, but if you need to delete lots of records, it can get very time consuming. Instead you can create a command to delete multiple records, as shown in the following example.

1. With the Command dialog box open, give the command a name of **cmdDeleteMultiBooks** and select Delete from the Type drop-down menu. Your connection should already be selected in the Connection drop-down menu. In the Database Items window, select the table that you are deleting the books from, in this case it is tbl_Books, and click the DELETE button. Then click the BookID column and click the WHERE button.

   Your SQL window should now look like this.

   ```
   DELETE FROM dbo.tbl_Books
   WHERE BookID
   ```

2. Place the cursor after BookID and type: **IN (varBookID)**.

3. Click the plus sign (+) button above the Variables window to add a new variable line. Click in the Name column and type **varBookID**. Tab to the Run-Time Value column and type **Request("BookID")**.

Your final Command dialog should look as shown in Figure 5-32.

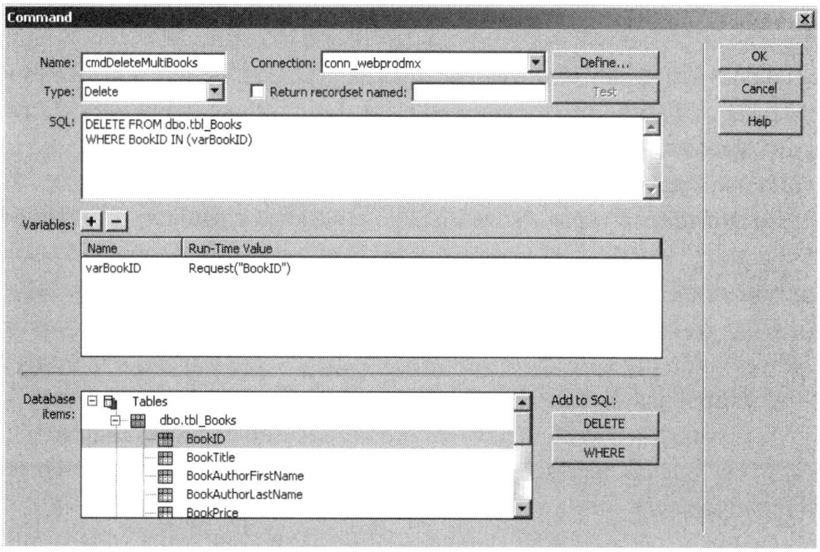

Figure 5-32. The ompleted multiple-delete Command dialog box

4. Click OK to apply this command to the page. When this page passes the ID number of one or more records in the BookID parameter, those records will be deleted. You can pass a comma-delimited string of numbers into this command and it will delete each record whose ID is contained in that string.

Stored Procedures

Stored procedures are precompiled SQL statements that are stored in the database—Access doesn't support them, but SQL Server does. They have the benefit of being much faster to execute than a standard piece of SQL code because they are compiled the first time they are executed. They are also modular in design so they can be reused from various web pages without you needing to re-create the SQL statements contained within the stored procedure each time.

Where they show their real power is in their ability to utilize parameters. You can define parameters within your SQL statement and then pass values into the stored procedure for use in the SQL statement.

An example of how stored procedures are used is if you needed to perform a repetitive task such as inserting multiple rows of data into a database table. Ordinarily, you might create a web page to manually feed each record into the database one at a time. With a stored procedure and the right piece of coding, you could pass a file to a web page, have that page loop through each line of the file, and then pass each line to the stored procedure through the use of parameters, which would insert each row of data into your database tables according to your SQL statements.

To take that example a stage further, let's suppose you have two related tables in your database, `tblUsers` and `tblUserDetails`. Now suppose that all the code on your web page was in place to take the contents of a text file and pass those contents, line by line, to a command that had been programmed to pass a single line of information to a stored procedure in your database. That command would have been set up to use a variable for each piece of information on that line.

You would then need to have a stored procedure in your database that could accept the data being passed in the variables from this command and insert it into your two tables.

On top of all that, because the two tables are related, you need to grab the primary key value after a new record has been inserted into `tblUsers` to use in `tblUserDetails` as that record's foreign key.

A stored procedure to do exactly that could be coded like this:

```
CREATE PROCEDURE dbo.spAddUser(
@UName nvarchar(100),
@UEmail nvarchar(250),
@UUsername nvarchar(100) = NULL,
@UPassword nvarchar(100) = NULL,
@DAddress1 nvarchar(100) = NULL,
@DAddress2 nvarchar(100) = NULL,
@DAddress3 nvarchar(100) = NULL,
@DTown nvarchar(100) = NULL,
@DCounty nvarchar(50) = NULL,
@DCountry nvarchar(50) = NULL,
@DPostcode nvarchar(20) = NULL,
@DPhone nvarchar(20) = NULL,
@DFax nvarchar(20) = NULL,
@DWebAddress nvarchar(250) = NULL,
@DDescription nvarchar(1000) = NULL)
AS
Declare @NewID Int
INSERT INTO dbo.tblUsers(UName, UEmail, UUsername, UPassword)
VALUES(@UName, @UEmail, @UUsername, @UPassword)
```

```
SELECT @NewID = SCOPE_IDENTITY()
INSERT INTO dbo.tblUserDetails(UserID, Address1, Address2, Address3,
Town, County, Country, Postcode, Phone, Fax, WebAddress, DDescription)
VALUES(@NewID, @DAddress1, @DAddress2, @DAddress3, @DTown,
@DCounty, @DCountry, @DPostcode, @DPhone, @DFax, @DWebAddress,
@DDescription)
GO
```

Starting from the top, you tell SQL Server that you want to create a stored procedure called spAddUser. You then set about defining all the parameters that you are going to use in this stored procedure, assigning them the correct data type for the data that they are going to hold and specifying NULL against those values that are allowed to store NULL values. These parameters will get their values passed to them from the command that is calling this stored procedure. You then say what you would like to create this stored procedure AS, which is where the SQL statements come into play. You declare a local variable called NewID, which is going to store the primary key value from the first table. That value is an integer and so the variable is declared as an integer.

The next line takes the first four values passed to the stored procedure and inserts them into the tblUsers table. Then the local variable called NewID is assigned the value of the last created identity value, which is the primary key value from the first table. The rest of the details passed from the command to this stored procedure are then inserted, along with the NewID value, into the second related table.

> **NOTE** SCOPE_IDENTITY() *is an internal SQL Server 2000 variable that stores the last identity value created and is specific to the connection that created it. This ensures that no incorrect identity numbers can be passed between users of the database if they both insert data at the same time.*

The final statement GO tells SQL Server to execute this batch of SQL statements.

In order for your web application to be able to use this stored procedure, you're going to have to grant the Exec permission to your IUSR account, which you can do from the Stored Procedure Properties window. You can either right-click the Stored Procedure Name then select Properties from the context menu, or you can simply double-click the Stored Procedure name. Then click the Permissions button in the top-right corner of the Properties dialog box and click the Exec column for the IUSR user. Click OK to close the dialog boxes.

The Stored Procedure Command

This brings us neatly to the command that we haven't yet covered—the Stored Procedure command. It is a little different than the other commands but it's still fairly easy to understand.

1. Open the Command dialog box by selecting Command from the Bindings or the Server Behaviors panel. In the Name box, type **cmdSPInsert** and select Stored Procedure from the Type drop-down menu.

2. In the Database Items window, expand the Stored Procedures node to view all stored procedures in your database that you have permission to use. If your list is empty, you will need to close the Command dialog box, assign the Exec permission to your stored procedure, and then start creating your command again.

3. Select the stored procedure called dbo.spAddUser and then click the PROCEDURE button to the right. Your stored procedure is added to the SQL window and all of its parameters are added to the Variables window, which has suddenly grown a few extra columns. Most of the details are filled in for you but you should feel free to change anything that you need to. In our case, we do not want to return any values so all these variables should have their Direction column value set to IN because they are to be fed IN to the stored procedure.

4. Specify the length of each item in the Length column. These should be the same as the lengths declared in your stored procedure after the data type declaration of each parameter.

   The need to specify a default value depends entirely upon your web application—if you are certain that all values that need to be passed to the stored procedure will actually be passed, you can leave the Default Value column blank. If not, a value in this column might be a good idea. If, as in our example, your Stored procedure can accept NULL values in some of its columns, default values will not be necessary for those columns. In our example, only the name and the e-mail address are definitely required by your stored procedure and a default value for those would probably be a bad idea. So to get around that you would make sure that they contained a value by using form validation on the page that submits the data.

The final column to fix is the Run-Time Value column. This is the important one and works in exactly the same way as the Run-Time Value columns for all the previous examples of command usage—you set each parameter's run-time value to the place it should look for its data. As previously mentioned, this column has already been filled in, but in all likelihood it will be wrong because it uses the parameter names you used as its guess. You should check them all carefully before continuing.

5. Click OK in the Command dialog box to apply it to your page.

The following line is part of the code automatically generated for you by Dreamweaver MX 2004:

```
cmdSPInsert.Prepared = true
```

The `Prepared` property of a command, when set to `true`, means that it will be compiled when first run. This benefits you in terms of the speed at which your application will perform if you plan to use the same command object several times. If you plan to use it only once, it may slow your application slightly because of the delay caused by compilation.

Most databases support prepared commands but if yours does not, it may return an error if you try to send a prepared command to it. SQL Server does support them so you won't encounter this problem using this database.

Summary

This chapter introduced the basics of the SQL language and gave you a few pointers on database design. Hopefully we prompted a few ideas of the possibilities available to you when working with commands and stored procedures by detailing some simple examples and explaining their usage.

When it comes to using the power of SQL, this chapter only touched the surface—we heartily recommend that you seek out a good book solely dedicated to the subject of SQL to take your knowledge to the next level.

With careful planning and good database design, the knowledge you have gained from this chapter can take you a long way in your web application development projects.

CHAPTER 6

The Application Panel

NOW THAT YOU ARE FAMILIAR with ASP/VBScript coding and database structures, you can delve into the fabulous server behavior features Dreamweaver MX 2004 has to offer. In this chapter, we will introduce you to the Application panel and explain what each behavior can do.

It is wrong to think that each server behavior does only one thing. On the contrary, with a few exceptions (such as Log In User), each server behavior can have multiple uses for many different kinds of web applications. The behaviors are generic blocks of code that can be used in various aspects of your web applications.

It is important to know when and how to use the Application panel. We will look at full-blown applications in later chapters; here we will concentrate on the following areas:

- **Databases/Connections**: How Dreamweaver connects to databases via Data Source Names or Custom Connection Strings

- **Bindings**: How to bind data to pages via recordsets, application variables, request variables, and session variables

- **Server behaviors**: How to add these are prewritten pieces of server-side code to your applications

Connections

Before you can utilize your database within your ASP web applications, you need to create a connection from the ASP page to your database. Fortunately Dreamweaver MX 2004 makes it simple for you. There are two ways you can create a connection to your database: **Data Source Name (DSN)** or **Custom Connection String** (often referred to as a "DSN-less connection").

Before you can create connections you must make sure the PC that hosts the database and serves the connection has the appropriate data access drivers (Microsoft Data Access Components—MDAC) installed. Look for driver details in the following places:

- **Windows 95, 98, or NT**: Go to Start ➤ Settings ➤ Control Panel ➤ ODBC Data Sources (32-bit)

- **Windows 2000**: Go to Start ➤ Settings ➤ Control Panel ➤ Administrative Tools ➤ Data Sources (ODBC), and click the Drivers tab

- **Windows XP**: Go to Start ➤ Control Panel ➤ Performance and Maintenance ➤ Administrative Tools ➤ Data Sources (ODBC), and click the Drivers tab

If you see the ODBC icons, the appropriate drivers should already be installed. These drivers are usually installed as standard, but if you find yourself without the right drivers you can download the latest ones from `http://www.microsoft.com/data/download.htm`.

Custom Connection String

The connection string is simply a string of variables that contain information about connecting to the database, such as the provider type, physical location of the database on the server, and username and passwords if any. You can choose between two provider types—an **ODBC (Open Database Connectivity)** and an **OLE DB** provider. The providers allow you to make a connection between your application and your database by specifying the database driver and database location. The string must then be embedded in every page that will retrieve database records. When you give Dreamweaver MX 2004 the string you want to use, it creates a separate folder called Connections with a file named after your connection. Whenever you create a recordset, Dreamweaver MX 2004 includes the string at the top of your page by default so you don't have to worry about adding the connection string yourself (recordsets are discussed in the next section).

The connection string syntax varies, depending on the provider and database you use. Because Access and SQL Server are the two database types most often used with ASP, we will show the syntax for both of them for both the ODBC and OLE DB providers.

ODBC

Setting up an ODBC connection to Access and to SQL Server is done using the following connection strings.

Access:

```
Driver={Microsoft Access Driver↵
 (*.mdb)};Dbq=C:\folder_name\dbname.mdb;Uid=username;Pwd=password;
```

SQL Server:

```
Driver={SQL Server};Server=server_name;Database=dbname;Uid=username;Pwd=password;
```

OLE DB

Setting up an OLE DB connection to Access and to SQL Server is done using the following connection strings.

Access:

```
Provider=Microsoft.Jet.OLEDB.4.0;Data Source=c:\folder_name\dbname.mdb;↵
User Id=username;Password=password;
```

SQL Server:

```
Provider=SQLOLEDB;Data Source=machine_name;↵
Initial Catalog=dbname;User ID=username;Password=password;
```

The strings should be written in one line. If you are not protecting your database with a username and password, leave out the following part of the ODBC string:

```
Uid=username;Pwd=password;
```

Or in the OLE DB string, leave out the following:

```
User ID=username;Password=password;.
```

Password-Protected Access Database

As you may know, you can set a password for an Access database through Access tools. For **ODBC** connection strings, if you set a password on an Access database, you can leave out `Uid=username;` out and simply fill in the password. Here is an example:

```
Driver={Microsoft Access Driver (*.mdb)};Dbq=C:\folder_name\dbname.mdb;Pwd=123456;
```

For **OLE DB** connection strings, if you set a password on an Access database, you need to manipulate the string a bit. You should replace `User ID=username;` `Password=password;` with: `Jet OLEDB:Database Password=12345`. Here is an example:

```
Provider=Microsoft.Jet.OLEDB.4.0;Data Source=c:\folder_name\dbname.mdb;↵
Jet OLEDB:Database Password=123456;
```

> **TIP** *Many web developers have performed tests to compare the providers and it turns out that the OLE DB provider is recommended as being a faster connection than ODBC.*

For more connection strings, go to `http://www.dwteam.com/articles/ado/`.
Your database should be located above the wwwroot because if it resides below the wwwroot folder, it will be available to viewers of your web site. Anyone who knows the name and location of the database can attempt to download it! If it resides above the wwwroot directory, you can retrieve the physical path to the database by using the code `Server.MapPath`. You should know the name of your database and the folder it resides in. You can create a file containing a line of ASP similar to the following within the wwwroot of your site to display the physical path to the database:

```
<!-- display_dbpath.asp -->
```

```
<%=Server.Mappath("folder_with_database\webprodmx.mdb") %>
```

Connect to a Database

Before you add a connection, you must open a page.

1. Create a new dynamic ASP web page and save it as **categories.asp** in your webprodmx_files directory. The file will now be associated with your webprodmx site (save all future files in this site).

2. You can create a connection to a database using a custom connection string by writing the appropriate string in the field of the custom connection string dialog box. Click the plus sign (+) under the Databases tab from the Application panel. Click the Custom Connection String option, as seen in Figure 6-1.

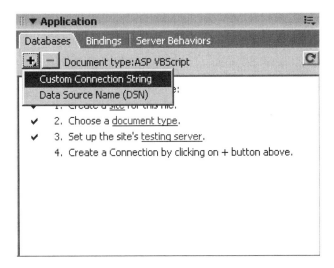

Figure 6-1. The Custom Connection String menu option

You should then see the dialog box shown in Figure 6-2.

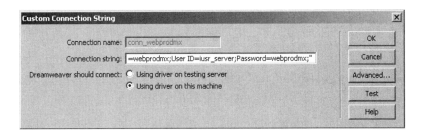

Figure 6-2. The Custom Connection String dialog box

3. Here you must enter a name for your connection and the custom connection string in the appropriate fields. Name your connection **conn_webprodmx**, and enter the appropriate string (shown in Figure 6-2), making sure that you adjust the database location and ID and password as needed. In this instance, you created a connection string to your SQL Server database.

4. Test your connection by clicking the Test button. If it is successful you will see the alert box shown in Figure 6-3.

Figure 6-3. Connection created successfully

5. Click OK, and then click OK in the Custom Connection String dialog box. If everything was successful you should see your connection added in the panel space under the Databases tab.

The connection is then added to the connections list underneath the Databases tab. If you expand the connection listing and its sub elements by clicking the plus sign (+) next to them, you will see your database tables, views, and stored procedures, as shown in Figure 6-4.

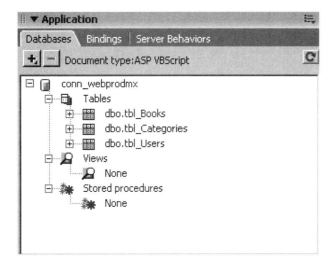

Figure 6-4. The Databases panel of the Application panel group

You can create connections to different databases for the same site, but one usually suffices because all your data will most likely be stored in one database. Creating a connection to your database is the *first* thing you need to do when preparing a database-driven web application. Until then, none of the other ASP application behaviors will be made available.

System Data Source Name

Although a custom connection string is a faster connection, it requires you to know some detailed information about the database you are connecting to, such as the physical path of the database on the server, and that data is not always readily available. The next best thing is to simply create a DSN, which is a pointer to a system data source you set up in the ODBC manager on the server. Once you set one up on the server, you only need to know the DSN name and the username/ password (if any) in order to create the connection. The connection string is simply DSN=dsn_name. Dreamweaver MX 2004 generates this string for you as it does custom connection strings.

For further information on how to set up a System DSN for an Access or a SQL Server database, refer to the "Making the Connection" section in Chapter 5.

Bindings

The Bindings panel of the Applications panel group holds dynamic content that you can bind to your pages as you build them. For example, any recordsets you create are listed in the Server Behaviors panel and the Bindings panel. If you double-click a recordset in either of those panels, you can edit its content. See the "Server Behaviors" section of this chapter for more on recordsets.

Recordsets are not the only dynamic content you can store in the Bindings panel; you can also store other dynamic text such as request variables, session variables, and application variables. Request variables include cookies, query strings, form variables, and environment variables. (If you need a refresher on request and session variables, see Chapter 4.)

Bear in mind that the Bindings area does *not* create the variables for you. It simply allows you to store the dynamic variables you have already created so that you can access them easily. For example, the Log In server behavior creates a session variable named MM_Username that holds the username of a successful login. You can then add MM_Username to the bindings area so you can use it with ease on any documents you create.

Request Variables

Now let's test some dynamic variables and store them in the Bindings tab so you can get a feel for how this all works. To start, you will look at request variables.

Creating Request Variables

1. Create a new ASP web page and save it as **create_request_variables.asp**. Add the following code to the body of your page:

    ```
    <p>
    <a href="create_request_variables.asp?age=30&name=rob">create query_string
    parameters</a></p>
    ```

2. When this link is clicked, two parameters are passed through the query string: age and name. Store these variables in the Bindings area by selecting Bindings, then Request Variables (this can be found in the menu underneath the plus sign (+) button). Select Request.QueryString from the Type menu and type **age** in the Name field. Click OK. You will now see the QueryString.age variable listed under Request in the Bindings window.

3. Follow the same steps to add the name parameter (as shown in Figure 6-5) and it will be added to the Request list.

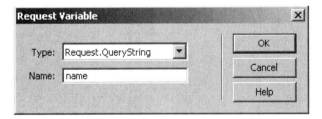

Figure 6-5. Creating a request variable

Now you can start using and reusing your dynamic variables wherever you want. You can drag them from the Bindings window to anywhere you like in your document, and Dreamweaver MX 2004 will generate the ASP code to display the variables. For example, if you drag one instance of each variable you just created into create_request_variables.asp, your code will now look like this.

```
<p>
<a href="create_request_variables.asp?age=30&name=rob">create query_string
parameters</a></p>
<p><%= Request.QueryString("name") %></p>
<p><%= Request.QueryString("age") %></p>
```

Now if you load your page in a browser and click the hyperlink, the values of the parameters should appear wherever you placed them on your page, as shown in Figure 6-6.

Figure 6-6. Viewing the page in a browser

4. Go back to the code. Create a form and place a text field and a hidden field inside the form. In Design view, select the text field and from Bindings, select the name query string variable. Click the Insert button at the bottom of the Bindings window to bind the name query string variable as the value of the <textfield> element. Do the same to bind the age query string variable to the hidden field. When this page is viewed live and the parameters are passed through the query string, the text field and hidden form elements will be populated with the query string variables.

This tactic may be used to maintain state between pages by passing data held as query string variables inside a form. Of course, instead of the form, you could create another hyperlink and simply pass the current parameters to a second page. These methods are often used to pass data from page to page. Remember, unlike sessions and cookies, parameters passed through a query string or from a form cannot be retrieved on a page unless they are passed from a prior page—or the same page, if it submits to itself.

Dreamweaver MX 2004 makes it easy to reuse the dynamic query string variables on pages throughout your site. After adding them to Bindings, you can simply drag them from the Bindings window. Henceforth instead of typing `<%=Request.QueryString("parameter_name") %>` when you click the Request Variable option from Bindings, you see that there are other request variable types besides query strings. You can store those request variables in the Bindings window just as you have with query strings.

Creating Request Form Fields

1. On the same page, create a horizontal rule underneath the previous code, and then insert the following code:

   ```
   <form name="form2" method="post" action="create_request_variables.asp">
   <p>Username: <input name="username" type="text" id="username" /></p>
   <p>Password: <input name="password" type="password" id="password" /></p>
   <p><input type="submit" name="Submit" value="Submit" /></p>
   </form>
   ```

2. Select Bindings, and then Request Variables. In the pop-up box that appears, select Request.Form from the Type menu and type **username** in the Name field. Click OK. You will then see the `Form.username` variable listed under Request in the Bindings window. Follow the same steps to also add the `password` form field to the Request list.

   As with the other variables, you can now call these variables anywhere you want in your page by dragging them from the Bindings window onto your page or into your code. When you enter values into your form and submit it, the values appear wherever you placed the variables.

Creating Request Cookies

1. On the same page, insert a horizontal rule below the form you just created. In Code view, add the following code above the opening `<html>` tag:

   ```
   <% Response.Cookies("ckHello") = "Hello" %>
   ```

2. In the same manner as before, select Bindings, click Request Variables, choose Request.Cookie from the Type menu, and type **ckHello** in the Name field. If you now drag the `ckHello` variable underneath the last horizontal rule you added, and view your page through a browser, the cookie variable should be displayed because the cookie is created when the page is parsed by the server.

Creating Request Server Variables

1. On the same page, insert a horizontal rule below the dynamic cookie variable you just created.

2. In the same manner as before, bring up the Request Variables pop-up box. Select Request.ServerVariable from the Type menu and type **remote_host** in the Name field. Click OK and drag the remote_host variable from the Bindings window onto your page. Press F12 to view the page in your default browser, and the remote_host value should be displayed.

Creating Session Variables

You can also store session variables in the Bindings window. Of course, you have to create one first.

1. Create a new dynamic ASP web page and save it as **create_session.asp**. In Code view, add the following code above the opening <html> tag:

```
<% Session("svSayGoodbye") = "Goodbye" %>
```

2. Select Bindings and then Session Variable. Type **svSayGoodbye** in the Name field and click OK. The variable should be listed under a Session heading in the Bindings window. Drag the svSayGoodbye variable onto your page or into your code as you did before with the request variables.

3. View the page in a browser, and the session variable should be displayed as the session gets created when the page is parsed by the server.

The Bindings area is useful timesaving feature of Dreamweaver MX 2004—use it as much as you can. It organizes your dynamic variables and keeps them accessible as you build documents. Another good reason to use it is that you won't have to remember the names of the dynamic variables after you have created them! Once you create a dynamic variable, always add it to the Bindings window for easy access to its value.

Server Behaviors

All the prebuilt ASP code blocks that help you build your web applications (except of a few that are located on the Application Objects tab) are located on the Server Behaviors tab. The first server behavior we will cover is the Recordset Server Behavior.

Recordset (Query)

The Recordset Server Behavior creates a recordset, which is a subset of database records. A recordset is the object that sends a SQL query to a database, which then returns the data requested. The recordset is a part of the ADO (ActiveX Data Objects) set of objects that Microsoft created to make it easier to access data stored in a wide variety of database sources. Fortunately, you do not need to know the ASP syntax to create a recordset object. In fact, you do not even have to know the SQL, but if you've worked through Chapter 5, you should be familiar with it.

You will now create a simple recordset from the database. Once you create your recordset, you will be able to drag the records onto your page.

1. Let's retrieve the list of categories stored in the table named tbl_Categories. Create a new ASP page and call it **categories.asp**. Now, from the Bindings or Server Behaviors tab, click the plus sign (+) and select Recordset (Query), and you should see the pop-up box shown in Figure 6-7.

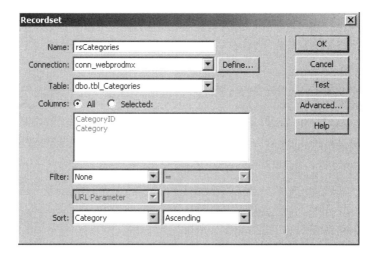

Figure 6-7. The simple Recordset dialog box

2. Name your recordset **rsCategories** (it is common to prefix recordset names with "rs").

3. Select the connection you will be using (use the one you created earlier).

4. Select the tbl_categories table, and select both fields.

5. To sort the records in alphabetical order, from the first Sort drop-down menu, select the Category column; from the second Sort drop-down menu, select Ascending.

> **TIP** *For future reference, only select the columns that you need. Retrieving columns that will not be used only slows down the execution time.*

6. Click the Test button, and Dreamweaver MX 2004 will send the query to the database to test it. If successful, a box should pop up showing you all the records retrieved for that query.

7. Click OK in the test box and click the Advanced button to look at the SQL Dreamweaver MX 2004 generated. You could have typed this in yourself, but it has been done for you. Switch back to Simple mode and click OK.

8. Click the Bindings tab from the Application panel and you will see that the records are now available for your page, displayed in expandable tree form.

9. On your page, create a table with two rows and two columns with 50 percent width. Drag the appropriate fields from Bindings into each table column, respectively; it should look something like Figure 6-8 in Design view.

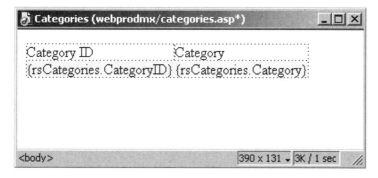

Figure 6-8. Design view of the bindings on the page

10. View categories.asp through a browser. As long as your database contains some data, you should see something similar to Figure 6-9.

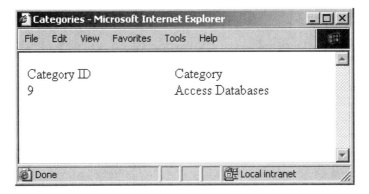

Figure 6-9. Viewing the page in a browser

You may wonder why the first record is the only one showing—in the next section, you will find out why and learn how to display the rest of the records.

Repeat Region

Although your recordset retrieves all the records from your categories table, it will not automatically display all the records. When you try to display the database columns, ASP displays the first record retrieved (in the order your SQL statement specifies if it uses an ORDER BY clause). In order to display all records in the table, you must loop through the records. Fortunately, there is a server behavior that does this for us, called Repeat Region. This server behavior generates the ASP code necessary to loop through your records. Now that you have dragged the variables onto your page, you must add a Repeat Region behavior to the row of the table that contains the dynamic data.

1.   Select the area that we want repeated by placing your cursor in the second row of the table and clicking the <tr> tag on the Quick Tag Selector bar at the foot of the page. This will highlight the second row of the table. You could also drag the mouse pointer through that row until the required table cells are highlighted. Click the plus sign (+) from the Server Behaviors tab and select Repeat Region. Select All records and click OK to apply the Repeat Region to the page, as shown in Figure 6-10.

Figure 6-10. The Repeat Region dialog box

2. View the page in your browser, and it should look something like Figure 6-11.

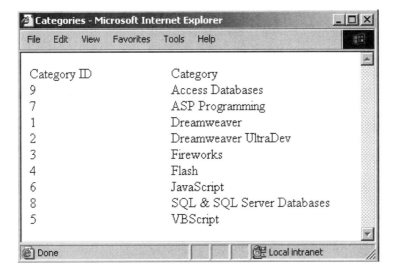

Figure 6-11. Viewing the page in a browser

You displayed your categories dynamically from your database. You created a recordset to retrieve the records, and then you created an HTML table and placed the dynamic text into the table columns, adding a repeat region behavior to display all the records.

It didn't take too long to do this, but Dreamweaver MX 2004 has another feature that can save you even more time! Go to Insert ➤ Application Objects. The **Dynamic Table Object** icon is under the Application tab in the Insert bar. Using it, you can re-create the page you just created but in two steps. Let's do that now.

3. Create a new dynamic ASP web page and save it as **dynamic_table.asp**. You must create the same recordset you created in the first example (hint: you can copy and paste recordsets between pages in the Bindings panel or the Server Behaviors panel).

4. Place your mouse pointer in the document where you want to insert your dynamic table and select Insert ➤ Application Objects ➤ Dynamic Data ➤ Dynamic Table. Or just click the icon on the Insert bar in the Application section. The pop-up box shown in Figure 6-12 will appear.

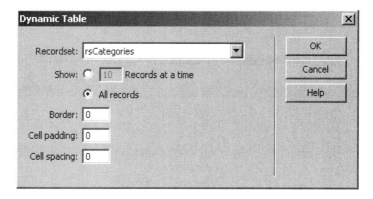

Figure 6-12. The Dynamic Table dialog box

5. Select the recordset you created, select the All Records radio button, set your table settings for border cell padding and cell spacing sizes, and click OK. What do you see? The same table you created in the first example. Dreamweaver MX 2004 generates the table, adds the dynamic fields from the recordset, and finally adds a repeat region all in one simple dialog box!

Go to Detail Page

This behavior usually consists of two pages: the Master page and the Detail page. This is based on the one-to-many table relationship, that is, two tables for which the primary key of a record in one table is stored as a foreign key in a second table that contains additional information associated with that record. You can retrieve information from both tables as long as you have the key (if you need a refresher on this, please review Chapter 5).

You can also use the Go to Detail Page server behavior to retrieve different numbers of columns from the same table on different pages. For example, you might display minimal information about records on your master page, but display more information when you click through to the details page. You pass the primary key onto a detail page, open the same recordset, but retrieve more columns than those retrieved on the master page.

In your `webprodmx` database, the `tbl_Categories` and `tbl_Books` tables have a one-to-many relationship—the primary key of the `tbl_Categories` table is stored as a foreign key in the `tbl_Books` table. The schema is set up like this so that each book is associated with a particular category. In a real-world web application, you would display the categories on a master page and pass the primary key ID of a selected record to a detail page that displays the books associated with that ID.

Master Page

You already have a working master page that displays the categories from your database named `categories.asp`. You need to adjust it so that each category links to a detail page passing the unique ID of the record (which will be the primary key: `CategoryID`) as a `QueryString` parameter.

1. Make a new copy of `categories.asp` and call it **categories2.asp**. Highlight the `category` dynamic text within the HTML table, select Server Behaviors, click the plus sign (+), and click Go to Detail Page. Fill in the fields in the Go to Detail Page dialog box as shown in Figure 6-13.

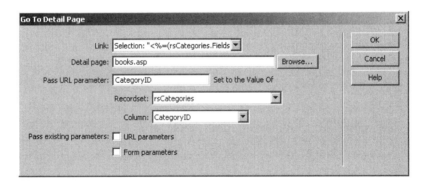

Figure 6-13. The Go to Detail Page dialog box

2. You will create the Detail page next, so type **books.asp** in that field. By default, the URL Parameters passed should be the `CategoryID`. You can change the name of the URL Parameter, but it's easier to name the URL Parameter after the database column name. You could also change the Column selector to pass a different column as the URL Parameter, but you will usually pass the primary key of the table because this is the unique key. Make sure Recordset and Column are set to `rsCategories` and `CategoryID`, respectively.

3. Leave the check boxes for Pass Existing Parameters cleared because you have no existing URL parameters or form parameters that you want to pass to the books.asp. If there were, you could pass them along with the CategoryID URL Parameter you are passing here. Click OK and the category dynamic text in your table on the page will turn into a hyperlink.

Before you create the detail page (books.asp) let's have a look at categories2.asp in a browser to see what has happened. If you hover your mouse over the category hyperlinks, you will see that each one has its own URL—see the status bar at the bottom of the browser window shown in Figure 6-14.

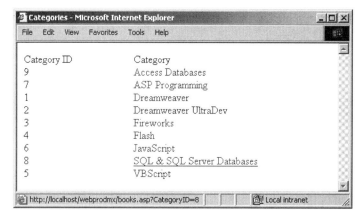

Figure 6-14. Showing the status bar text when mousing over a link

Now you just need to create books.asp. However, before you do that, let's look at an alternative way to generate your dynamic links.

An Alternative Way to Generate a Master Page

Instead of using the Go to Detail Page behavior here, you could manually generate the action of passing a URL Parameter to a detail page.

1. Make another copy of categories.asp and call it **categories3.asp**.

2. Highlight the category dynamic text as before, but this time go down to the Properties window and select the little yellow folder to the right of the Link field. The dialog box shown in Figure 6-15 is displayed.

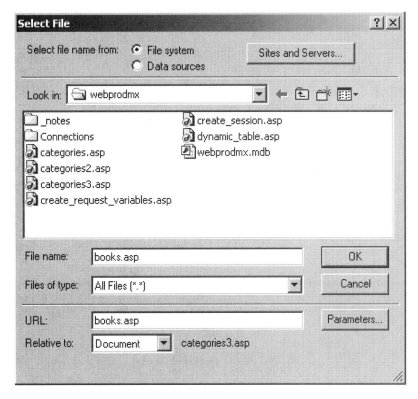

Figure 6-15. Selecting a file to link to

3. Type **books.asp** as the file name and click the Parameters button to see
    something like Figure 6-16.

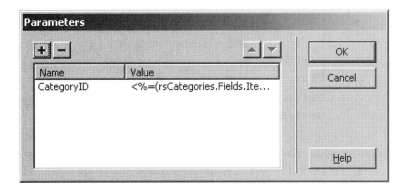

Figure 6-16. The Parameters dialog box

4. Under Name, enter the name of your URL Parameter, **CategoryID**. To pull
    the appropriate values out of your database and place them in the Value
    field, click the lightning bolt icon to the right of the field. The Dynamic
    Data dialog box appears, as shown in Figure 6-17.

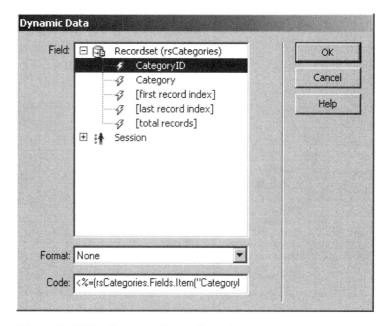

Figure 6-17. The Dynamic Data dialog box

5. Expand the rsCategories recordset, select the CategoryID column, and
    click OK. Click OK again to close the Parameters dialog box, and hit OK a
    third time to close the File Select dialog box.

Now if you look at the Link field in the Properties window, you should see that
it has been filled in with something like
`books.asp?CategoryID=<%=(rsCategories.Fields.Item("CategoryID").Value)%>`. You
should also notice that your hyperlink has been created on your page, the same as
when we used the Go to Detail Page earlier.

You can pass URL parameters using either method. The Go to Detail Page
behavior is nice because it saves time but it has a shortcoming—you cannot pass
more than one URL Parameter. For example, you might want to pass the Category
name as a URL Parameter along with the CategoryID. When you do it manually, you
have the option of adding multiple Parameters.

Now let's create the books.asp detail page.

Detail Page

You must now create a recordset that opens the `tbl_Books` table and filters it using the CategoryID passed as a URL Parameter.

1. Create a new dynamic ASP page and save it as **books.asp**.

2. Select Server Behaviors ➤+ ➤ Recordset, and switch to Advanced mode when the dialog box appears. Name your recordset **rsBooks** and select the `conn_webprodmx` connection from the menu. Enter the following SQL in the space provided:

```
SELECT BookID, BookTitle, BookAuthorFirstName,
BookAuthorLastName, BookPrice, BookImage
FROM dbo.tbl_Books
WHERE CategoryID = varCategoryID
ORDER BY BookTitle
```

> **NOTE** *When creating SQL queries, you can utilize the SELECT, WHERE, and ORDER BY buttons to quickly add the desired statement. For example, if you want to build a* SELECT *statement, simply expand the database tree until you can see all the fields in the table, click each field you want to select, and press the SELECT button. The fields will be added to the* SELECT *statement in the SQL query.*

If you are using an Access database, you should not use dbo. in front of the table name in your SQL statement.

3. Click the plus sign (+) button to add a variable. Enter the name as **varCategoryID**, the Default Value as **0**, and the run-time value as **Request.QueryString("CategoryID")**. The variables area gives you the ability to list the names and values to represent dynamic variables you may use in your SQL. Dreamweaver MX 2004 will then simply use a variable named `varCategoryID` in the SQL to represent the dynamic URL Parameter variable `Request.QueryString("CategoryID")`.

TIP *When you add your own variable in the list make sure it matches the variable in the SQL exactly, otherwise the code will throw an error when executed live. For example,* varCategoryID *in the SQL must match* varCategoryID *in the variable list. To make sure you've got it right, click the Test button. If there is an error, you'll get a warning message.*

The dialog box should now look like Figure 6-18.

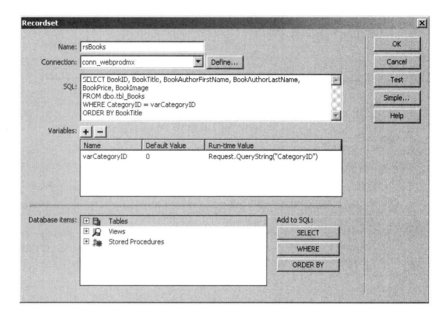

Figure 6-18. The completed Advanced Recordset dialog box

You are retrieving six columns from your books table—BookID, BookTitle, BookAuthorFirstName, BookAuthorLastName, BookPrice, and BookImage. Also, you want to list the books in alphabetical order by title. You filtered your recordset to retrieve only the records whose CategoryID is equal to the CategoryID URL Parameter passed from the previous page.

varCategoryID is the name of the variable in your recordset that will contain the value of the URL Parameter. You can name this variable anything you like.

4. As a quick test, replace the default value of your variable, which is cur-
    rently set to 0 (zero), with a number that will return results—let's say 5.
    Click Test—you should see the results appear in a new dialog box. This
    test simulates a passed URL Parameter. In the real-world application, the
    ID will be passed in the query string. Click OK to leave the test box, and
    OK again to submit your recordset, but don't forget to reset your default
    value back from 5 to 0.

Using Dynamic Images

1. In your document, create a table with two rows and two columns. Add
    headings into the columns of the first row, such as **Book cover** and **Book
    details**. Place your mouse pointer in the second row of the left column
    and choose Image from the Insert menu. The dialog box shown in
    Figure 6-19 will appear.

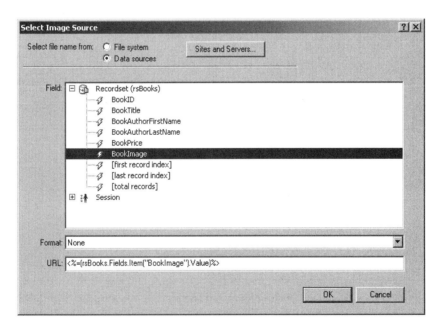

Figure 6-19. The Select Image Source dialog box

2. Select the Data Sources option. You will see all the recordsets you created for this particular page—there should only be one currently—rsBooks. Expand the tree for this recordset, and select the database column that holds the URL path to the image—BookImage. Click OK.

   Dreamweaver MX 2004 adds an image placeholder for the dynamic image to your page. When the page is viewed live, the appropriate image will appear (as long as you have the images in your site to display them!). In the case of this exercise, the book images are stored in a bookimages folder inside the media folder of your site so you can prefix the dynamic name of the image source with this path to ensure that the images are displayed. The link will look like this:

   ```
   media/bookimages/<%=(rsBooks.Fields.Item("BookImage").Value)%>
   ```

3. Place your cursor in the second row of the right column and from the Bindings panel. Drag BookTitle, BookAuthorFirstName, BookAuthorLastName, and BookPrice into the column. Format the text as you like.

4. Highlight BookPrice on your page, and in the Bindings panel you should see this field highlighted. Click the down arrow to the right of it and you will see the formatting options shown in Figure 6-20 (you may have to scroll the Application panel to the right).

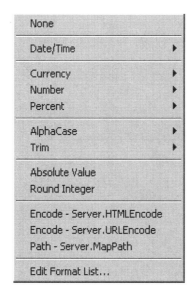

Figure 6-20. The Formatting Options menu

5. Select Currency ➤ Default. This will format the text as currency, using a VBScript built-in function. (See Chapter 5 for a refresher on VBScript built-in functions.)

6. To add a repeat region so that all the records will be displayed, select the entire second row of the table, select <tr> from the Quick Tag Selector bar of the document window, and select Server Behaviors ➤ Repeat Region. Choose the rsBooks recordset from the recordset menu and display all the records. Click OK. You might also want to add a link back to the master page somewhere on your detail page, for example, above the table.

7. Load the categories3.asp page in your browser and click the Dreamweaver link. You should be taken to the detail page (books.asp) and it should display a list of the books associated with that category (ours looks like Figure 6-21).

Figure 6-21. Viewing the books page in a browser

Isn't that cool? You didn't have to manually create that long list of books with static HTML and you won't have to update it manually either—Dreamweaver MX 2004 generates the ASP that generates the HTML for you! All you have to do now to display new information through your web application is to add new records to your tbl_Books table.

NOTE *You can manually add a record to the database in Access or SQL Server, or you could create an online content management system for yourself to make it easier to update your records at any time. You will learn more about this type of thing in the sections on the Insert, Update, and Delete behaviors later in this chapter.*

In case you have a category that doesn't have any books in it, you can make the book details page user-friendlier by utilizing the Show If Recordset Is Empty server behavior. We will explain this server behavior in the "Show Region" section, later in this chapter, but before we get to that, let's play with this page even more using some other cool server behaviors.

Recordset Paging

So far, you displayed your categories dynamically. When a category is clicked, the user is shown a complete list of all books associated with that category. At the moment, you only have a few different records to display—but what about in the future, when you want to display lots more? And when you add thumbnail images, they will increase the page loading time even further, so it will eventually become unmanageable to display all the records for each category every time on just one page.

To keep your pages manageable for the end users and to keep the page loading time down, you can employ the Recordset Paging server behaviors. This loads only a few of the total number of records for the selected category at a time.

Displaying a Few Records at a Time

Let's make some adjustments to the books.asp page by only allowing a maximum of four records to be displayed at a time. Before you go any further you have to edit your Repeat Region. Double-click the Repeat Region behavior in the Server Behaviors list on the Application panel. This will re-open the dialog box that sets your Repeat Region parameters. Select the option to show a specified number of records at a time and enter **4** in the text box, as shown in Figure 6-22. Click OK to close the dialog box and update the code.

Figure 6-22. The Repeat Region dialog box

Moving to Previous Record

1. Right-click the current top row of the table and select Table ➤ Insert Row from the context menu. You'll use this to house your links for the record-set paging.

2. Place your mouse pointer in the left cell of this new first row and select Server Behaviors ➤ + ➤ Recordset Paging ➤ Move to Previous Record, which should display the dialog box shown in Figure 6-23.

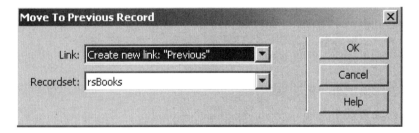

Figure 6-23. The Move to Previous Record dialog box

3. Leave the value for the Link field the way it is; it will create the text for you. Make sure the rsBooks recordset is selected in the Recordset field and click OK. The Previous link will be added to your page where you put your mouse pointer.

Moving to Next Record

1. Place your cursor in the right cell of the new first row and select Server
    Behaviors ➤ + ➤ Recordset Paging ➤ Move to Next Record, and click OK.
    A Next hyperlink will be added to the cell.

    Before you view the page in your browser, let's use an Application Object
    called the **Recordset Navigation Status**. This object creates a display of
    how many records exist and how many are being displayed currently. It
    shows the user where he or she is in the context of all the records collec-
    tively. Before you add it, let's make some room for it by adding another
    new row above the row that contains the Previous and Next links.

2. Place your cursor in the current first row, right-click and select Table ➤
    Insert Row.

3. Place your mouse pointer in the second column of the new first row.
    To add the object to your page, select Insert ➤ Application Objects ➤
    Recordset Navigation Status, and click OK on the dialog box that appears.
    (It should have the correct recordset already selected. If your page has
    more than one recordset on it, make sure you select the correct recordset.)
    Now when you view the books.asp page in a browser you should see some-
    thing like Figure 6-24.

Figure 6-24. Viewing the page with paging options applied

Although the page looks great, there is one slight problem—did you notice it? When you get to the detail page, the Previous hyperlink is displayed even though there are no previous records (when records 1-4 are displayed). In addition, when you click the Next hyperlink and get to the last page of records, the Next hyperlink is still displayed.

You want the Previous link to show only if you are *not* at the first record, and the Next link to show only if you are *not* at the last record. Dreamweaver MX 2004 has another group of server behaviors that do this for you! They can be found under Server Behaviors ➤ + ➤ Show Region.

Show Region

Show Region server behaviors allow you to show regions of your document based on a condition. In the example application, you'll utilize two of these to remedy the issue of displaying links that you don't want to appear.

Show Region If Not First Record

1. Highlight the Previous hyperlink that was generated by the Move to Previous Record behavior.

2. Select Server Behaviors ➤ + ➤ Show Region ➤ Show Region If Not First Record, and click OK the box that appears.

Show Region If Not Last Record

1. Highlight the Next hyperlink that was generated by the Move to Next Record behavior. Select Server Behaviors ➤ + ➤ Show Region ➤ Show Region If Not Last Record, and click OK in the box that appears.

2. Now view the books.asp page in a browser, and you should see that the Previous hyperlink does not appear until you move away from the first group of records. Similarly, the Next hyperlink does not appear when you get to the last group of records.

Recordset Navigation Bar

Think about how many steps it took to implement the recordset Paging—you had to work with four different server behaviors: Move to Previous Record, Move to Next Record, Show Region If Not First Record, and Show Region If Not Last Record.

Brace yourself. . .you could've done this in one step using the Recordset Navigation Bar object! It is found under Insert ➤ Application Objects. This object utilizes the same server behaviors you used before, but selecting it inserts fully functional First, Previous, Next, and Last hyperlinks instantly.

> **NOTE** *Dreamweaver MX 2004 has some other application objects that save you extra steps, as we will show you later. However, you should use and understand the server behaviors individually before using the additional timesaving application objects.*

Now let's continue our look at the Show Region behaviors.

Show Region If Recordset Is Empty

There may be some instances in which a recordset comes up empty, meaning it has retrieved no records based on the query. In this case, you would most likely want to display a message to the user. For example, you might display, "Sorry, no records found. Please go back and select another category." Without further ado, let's do that now. You'll add the text first.

1. Add a new row above the other rows in your table, place your mouse pointer in the second column of this row and type your message. Highlight the row by selecting the `<tr>` tag from the page status bar while your mouse pointer is in the row.

2. Select Server Behaviors ➤ + ➤ Show Region ➤ Show Region If Recordset Is Empty.

Of course, you only want to show the rest of this table if the recordset is not empty, so let's add that server behavior to the page.

Show Region If Recordset Is Not Empty

1. Return to your document in Dreamweaver MX 2004 and highlight the remaining rows of the table.

2. Select Server Behaviors ➤ + ➤ Show Region ➤ Show Region If Recordset Is Not Empty. Now if you view the page in a browser, the rest of the table should not be displayed when the recordset on the detail page is empty.

> **TIP** *If you get an error about not allowing overlapping server behaviors when applying this second server behavior, don't worry—you can work around it. Make your selection again and go into Code view. You will see that the selection doesn't quite capture all of the repeat region code, which is why the problem occurs. Manually select all the required table rows and make sure that all of your repeat region code is highlighted too. Then you can apply the server behavior to the page. But wait, that's still not the end of the problem…bizarrely, Dreamweaver MX 2004 puts the closing piece of code from the Show Region if Recordset is not Empty server behavior before the closing repeat region code! To resolve this issue, simply cut and paste that line of code after the end of the repeat region code. Phew!*

Let's create a web application with Dreamweaver MX 2004 that will allow you to insert, update, and delete database records.

Insert Record

The Insert Record behavior is found under Server Behaviors. This behavior creates all the code necessary to insert a record into your database. The only thing you need to do is create an HTML form. Each column is parallel with a form field except the `AutoNumber` column, which is automatically generated by the database, and the `DateEntered` column, as that is automatically filled by your database when you add new records.

You will insert a new category into your `tbl_Categories` table. There are only two columns in this table and one of them is an Identity column so you will only need to insert into one column using one form field. A single text field will be fine for this task.

1. Create a new page called **insert_category.asp** and save it to your site. Add a form tag to the page and in the Properties inspector for the form, set the form action to `insert_category.asp` (this page will submit to itself).

2. Inside the form, add a table that has two columns and three rows and is 400 pixels wide. In the first row type the text, **Add Category**. Type the text **category:** in the left column of the second row.

3. Insert a text field in the right column of the second row by placing your mouse pointer there and selecting Insert ➤ Form Objects ➤ Text Field. Name the text field **category** and enter a value of 30 in the Max Chars field in the Properties inspector. You do this to make sure that no more than the maximum number of characters allowed in your column in the database can be entered on this form. You could get an error from this page if you try to submit more data than the database allows.

4. Insert a button in the third row, second column (below the text field), and change the label of the button to **Insert Category**. The form should now look something like Figure 6-25.

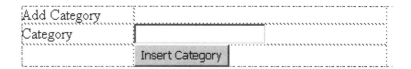

Figure 6-25. The form in Design view

> **TIP** *Giving form fields that insert data into database columns the same name as the database columns themselves makes it easier to recognize which form fields send data to which database columns. It also allows the Dreamweaver MX 2004 Insert Record server behavior to automatically associate the form fields with their respective database columns without you having to do so manually.*

5. Now that you have created your form you can add the Insert Record behavior. Select Server Behaviors ➤ + ➤ Insert Record, and the Insert Record dialog box will appear.

6. In the Insert Record dialog box, select the `conn_webprodmx` connection from the Connection menu. Then select the `tbl_Categories` table to insert the form values into. Browse to or type **categories3.asp** in the After Inserting, Go To field. This is the page to which you redirect after the insertion takes place.

7. Select the correct form in your document that holds the Insert Record form. By default it will be named Form1 unless you change the name yourself. You gave the form field the same name as the database field, so Dreamweaver MX 2004 chooses the text field named category to be the source of data to be inserted into the Category database table. (If they do not have the same name, you can make the association manually by changing the text in the Form Elements field.)

8. The category should be submitted as Text (see the Submit As field), as shown in Figure 6-26.

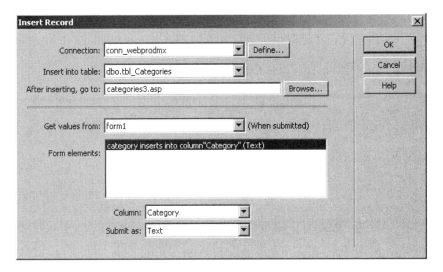

Figure 6-26. The completed Insert Record dialog box

9. Click OK to add the server behavior to the page.

10. View your insert_category.asp page in a browser, type a name for a new category in the form field, and click Submit. The new category should automatically appear in the Categories list. It will also automatically be placed in the list alphabetically. Hover your mouse pointer over the new category and look at the status bar; you will see its new ID number that was generated by the database. Click the new category to go to the books.asp page; you should receive the message, "Sorry, no records found" because you have not added any books under this category yet.

You now know how to insert records into your database online. Before we move onto the Update Record server behavior, let's try to insert records into the tbl_Books table for your new category.

Using the Record Insertion Form Wizard

You may be wondering how you will know the category ID of the specific category for the book you are adding. There are different ways of finding this information but the best option is to create a recordset to retrieve the categories from the database and bind them to a select list in your form. It is very important that the category ID is inserted properly because it is how the books are associated with their respective categories.

1. Create a new page called **insert_books.asp**, type **Insert Book** onto the page, and save it to your site.

2. To build a recordset to retrieve your categories from the database, click Bindings ➤ + ➤ Recordset (query) and build a recordset that uses the following SQL:

```
SELECT CategoryID, Category
FROM dbo.tbl_Categories
ORDER BY Category
```

3. Click OK to add the recordset to your page.

4. Click Insert ➤ Application Objects ➤ Insert Record ➤ Record Insertion Form Wizard. Alternatively, select the Application part of the Insert bar and click the Record Insertion Form Wizard icon, as shown in Figure 6-27.

Figure 6-27. The Record Insertion Form Wizard menu option

5. Select the `conn_webprodmx` connection from the connections menu and then make sure the `dbo.tbl_books` table is selected as the table into which the data will be inserted. For the purposes of this example, you will redirect to `categories3.asp` so you can test that your book was inserted.

6. Now to set up the form fields. You need to remove the `BookID` column from this wizard because it is the Identity column and is automatically generated for you by the database. Highlight that row and click the minus sign (–) button next to the words Form fields. Scroll down to the bottom of the fields list and remove the DateAdded column also—this column is automatically filed in by the database too.

7. Scroll back to the top of the list and click `BookTitle`: in the Label column. Add a space in the Label field so that *Book* and *Title* are two words.

8. Change the other labels as follows:

    *   `BookAuthorFirstName` becomes Author First Name

    *   `BookAuthorLastName` becomes Author Last Name

    *   `BookPrice` becomes Price

    *   `BookISBN` becomes ISBN

    *   `BookPageCount` becomes Page Count

    *   `BookImage` becomes Image Name

    *   CategoryID becomes Category

9. While you have the `CategoryID` column selected, you have some changes to make. You want to use a select list, populated by your `rsCategories` recordset, to insert the Category ID in to the database. Click Display as list and select Menu. Then click the Menu Properties button that appears after you select Menu from the list. The Menu properties dialog opens.

10. Select Populate menu items from database and change the Label value to Category. The value should be set to CategoryID. Click OK. The wizard is now complete and should look something like Figure 6-28.

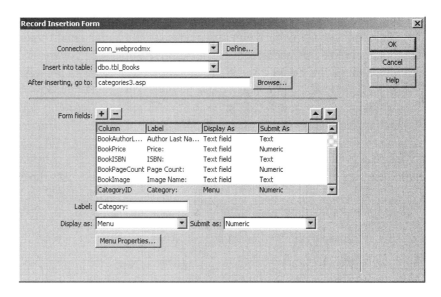

Figure 6-28. The completed Record Insertion Form dialog box

11. Click OK to apply the code to the page. The wizard adds a form tag, builds a table that it centers on the page, adds your modified labels to it, adds the form elements, builds a dynamic list menu for the categories, and adds a Submit button with Insert Record as the label.

12. Set the alignment of that table to Default by selecting it and selecting Default from the Align menu in the Properties inspector. Then save the page.

You can now test the page and add a book if you like. Notice that the categories menu is in alphabetical order. One thing to note is the image name field. This simple page doesn't allow you to upload images, so if you enter an image name in the form, make sure that the image exists on your web server; otherwise you'll end up with a broken image placeholder on your page.

Your insert book page should look something like Figure 6-29 in the browser window.

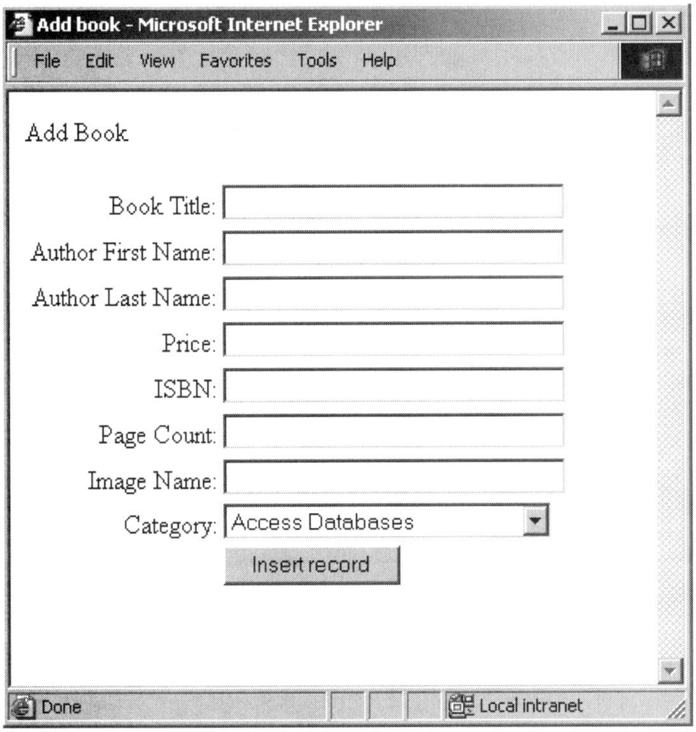

Figure 6-29. Viewing the Insert form in a browser

Creating this form was easy. It could have taken a lot longer if you had done it manually by creating all the individual elements yourself. Thanks to Dreamweaver MX 2004 and its Record Insertion Form Wizard, it was a breeze!

Now that you know how to insert records, let's update them!

Update Record

Unlike inserting records, when you update a record you need to retrieve the record you want to update first—that is, you need to *find* it, *open* it, and then you can *update* it. The Update Record server behavior will do the third part, but it will not automatically find and open the record. This means that you always need to create a recordset before you use the Update Record server behavior.

You will build a recordset that filters the tbl_Books table using the BookID value that is passed to your update_book.asp page.

1. Open your books.asp page and add the text **update** within the repeat region besides the other dynamic text. It will be repeated beside each record when the page is viewed live. Turn the update text into a hyperlink that points to a page called update_book.asp, which you are just about to create.

   You want to pass the BookID as a URL Parameter. You already know how to do this. You could use the Go to Detail Page behavior or manually add it from the Link dialog box. Let's do it manually.

2. Select the link and click the yellow folder beside the Link field from the Properties inspector to display the Select File dialog box.

3. Enter **update_book.asp** as the file name.

4. Click the Parameters button to open the Parameters dialog box.

5. Add a new URL Parameter by clicking the plus sign (+) button and name it BookID.

6. Click the Value field, and click the lightning bolt to the right of it. In the Dynamic Data dialog box that appears, select the BookID column from your rsBooks recordset.

7. Click OK in all the dialog boxes to close them. View the updated categories3.asp page in a browser, and click a category to go to the books.asp page. Hover your mouse pointer over each of the update hyperlinks and you'll notice that the appropriate BookID is attached to the end of each URL.

   Now let's create your update_book.asp page.

8. Create a new ASP web page and save it as **update_book.asp**. Create a new recordset called **rsUpdateBook**, making sure the conn_webprodmx connection is chosen. Enter the following SQL in the SQL box:

   ```
   SELECT BookID, BookTitle, BookAuthorFirstName, BookAuthorLastName,
   BookPrice, BookISBN, BookPageCount, BookImage, CategoryID
   FROM dbo.tbl_Books
   WHERE BookID = varBookID
   ```

9. Add a new variable. Enter **varBookID** as its name, enter **0** for the default value, and enter **Request.QueryString("BookID")** as its run-time value.

10. Click OK. This recordset will retrieve the book information from your tbl_Books table with the book ID equal to that passed in the URL Parameter.

    You also need the same Categories recordset that you had on your Insert record page. You can either re-create it here, or simply copy it from the insert_books.asp page and paste it onto this one.

    As a reminder, the SQL for your categories recordset is

    ```
    SELECT CategoryID, Category
    FROM dbo.tbl_Categories
    ORDER BY Category
    ```

    As with the Insert Record behavior, you need to create a form that reflects the database columns and table you want to update. To do this, you will use another of Dreamweaver MX 2004's timesaving Objects—the Record Update Form Wizard.

11. Select Insert ➤ Application Objects ➤ Update Record ➤ Record Update Form Wizard, or click the icon on the Insert bar in the Application section.

12. In the Record Update Form dialog box, select the conn_webprodmx connection, select tbl_Books as the table to update, select rsUpdateBook recordset, choose BookID as the unique key column, and redirect to categories3.asp after updating, as shown in Figure 6-30.

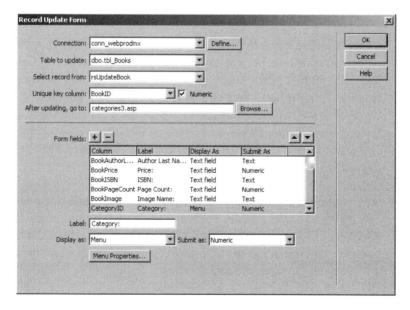

Figure 6-30. The completed Record Update Form Wizard

13. Remove BookID and DateAdded from the list of form fields like you did with the Insert Form Wizard.

14. Go through the same renaming of the labels as you did on the Insert form. Here they are again:

    - `BookTitle` becomes Book Title

    - `BookAuthorFirstName` becomes Author First Name

    - `BookAuthorLastName` becomes Author Last Name

    - `BookPrice` becomes Price

    - `BookISBN` becomes ISBN

    - `BookPageCount` becomes Page Count

    - `BookImage` becomes Image Name

    - `CategoryID` becomes Category

    With Category still selected, you have some changes to make. You want to use a select list, populated by your `rsCategories` recordset, to update the Category ID in the database. You might not want to change the category, but if you do, this list makes it as easy as possible to do so.

15. Click the Display as list and select Menu. Click the Menu Properties button that appears after you select Menu from the list. The Menu Properties dialog box opens.

16. Select Populate menu items from database and make sure that the correct recordset, `rsCategories`, is selected. Change the Label value to **Category**. The value should be set to CategoryID. Finally, check that the correct value is set in the Select value equal to field. You want your Category list on the web page to automatically select the book's current value when the page loads, and this value comes from the `rsUpdateBooks` recordset, `CategoryID` column. Click OK to close all the dialog boxes. The Update Record form is created in your document.

17. Save your page and upload it to your web server for testing. Open `categories3.asp` and press F12 to browse the page. When you click a category, you will go to the `books.asp` page that displays the books in that category. Each book has the update link you added; click the update link and test your new `update_books.asp` page.

Delete Record

The Delete Record server behavior works in a very similar way to the Update Record server behavior in that you need to retrieve the record from the database before deleting it. This is a long-winded way of deleting a record but it is good if you need to see the record details you are about to delete before deleting them. What we will demonstrate here is a faster, cleaner way to achieve the same goal. It requires the use of a simple extension that Massimo Foti made available free of charge from his web site (http://www.massimocorner.com).

1. Select the Dreamweaver section and then the Behaviors section and scroll down the page until you see Confirm Message 1.0. Click to download the extension and then double-click the downloaded file on your computer to install it into Dreamweaver MX 2004.

    You will need to restart Dreamweaver if you install the extension while Dreamweaver is running.

2. Open your books.asp page and add a delete hyperlink that links to a page called delete_book.asp (you will create this new page shortly). Pass the BookID from the rsBooks recordset as a URL Parameter, as you've done before.

    That completed link should look like this.

    ```
    delete_book.asp?BookID=<%=(rsBooks.Fields.Item("BookID").Value)%>
    ```

3. Select the link on the page and apply the Confirm Message behavior. In the Tag panel, Click Behaviors ➤ + ➤ Massimocorner ➤ Confirm Message. In the dialog box that appears, remove the current message, type **Are you sure?**, and click OK to add the behavior to the page. This will prevent you from accidentally deleting records if you click the delete link by accident.

4. Create a new ASP web page and save it as **delete_book.asp**.

5. You're going to add a delete command and a piece of code to redirect users after the delete has taken place. Click Server Behaviors ➤ + ➤ Command and in the dialog box, type **cmdDeleteBook** as the name of this command. Make sure your connection, conn_webprodmx, is shown in the Connection list and then select Delete from the Type list.

6. Expand the Tables node in the Database items window and then expand the tbl_Books table within it. With tbl_Books selected, click the Delete button, select BookID, and click the WHERE button.

Your SQL window should now contain the following SQL:

```
DELETE FROM dbo.tbl_Books
WHERE BookID
```

7. Place your mouse pointer after BookID in the SQL window and type **= varBookID**. Then click the plus sign (+) button above the Variables window to add a variable. Click the Name column and type **varBookID**, and then click the Run-Time Value column and type **Request.QueryString("BookID")**.

   Your Command dialog box should now look like Figure 6-31.

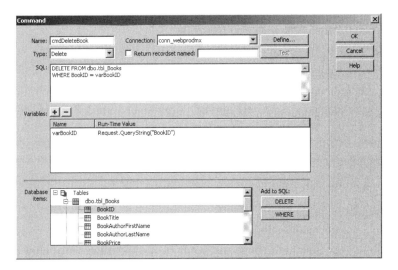

Figure 6-31. The completed Delete Command dialog box

8. Click OK to add the command to your page.

9. Switch to Code view. You will never actually see this page displayed so you can delete all the HTML tags from the page leaving only your ASP code on it. The last thing you need to add to the page is the code to redirect after the deletion has taken place. To do this, place the mouse pointer after the closing ASP tag of the command and add the following piece of code:

```
<%
Response.Redirect("categories3.asp")
%>
```

This code will redirect users to categories3.asp after the record is deleted. You could, of course, redirect to another page if you like, but for this example, this works nicely.

10. Load `categories3.asp` into your browser (select it in the site window and press F12 to preview it), click a category, and then click the delete link next to a book. The confirmation message pops up. If you cancel it, nothing happens but if you click OK, your record will be deleted and you will return to the categories list.

You have completed a fairly simple web application that allows you to view and update a book database via the web. You can insert categories or books, and update and delete books. However, as your pages currently stand, anyone who browses them can perform all the tasks that only an administrator should be allowed to perform. To remedy this, you can extend your application to include a facility for users to login and then add a little code to show or hide those buttons that most users shouldn't see.

User Authentication

The User Authentication group of server behaviors contains four server behaviors that make creating a login extremely easy. Once you have a login set up, you will be able to restrict access to pages or to parts of pages. Let's create a login page using these server behaviors.

Log In User

This server behavior generates the required code that will open a table, verify a user, and redirect him or her to the specified page. All you have to do is create the login form. The Log In User behavior also creates one session by default and an optional second one. The session created by default holds the username of the person logging in—called `MM_Username`. The optional second one will set a session for the column that holds an access level. The session is called `MM_UserAuthorization`.

Login In User authenticates the user by checking to see if the values submitted in the login form match the specified `username` and `password` columns. In this example, you will use the EmailAddress column as the `username`.

1. Create a login form by inserting an empty form in the document. Rename the form **login**, and insert a table that has three rows and two columns inside the form, and that is approximately 300 pixels wide.

2. Type the text **Username:** in the left column of the first row and **Password:** in the left column of the second row. Insert text fields in the first and second rows of the right-hand column. Name the username text field

username and set its maxchars value to 250 because your usernames are email addresses and that's the maximum number of characters your email address column allows.

3. Set the password text field **password** with a maxchars value of 50. Select the password text field and in the Properties inspector, change the Type to Password. This will make sure that asterisks replace the characters typed in that field. This will keep the password hidden even while logging in.

4. Insert a button in the bottom row of the right column and change the label of the button to **Login**. The form should now look like Figure 6-32.

Figure 6-32. The Login form viewed in a browser

5. Add the Log In User behavior by selecting Server Behaviors ➤ + ➤ User Authentication ➤ Log In User. Fill in the resulting dialog box so it looks exactly as shown in Figure 6-33.

As you can see, we selected `access_group` as the column to Get Level From—this will make the behavior create the optional session variable we talked about earlier called `MM_UserAuthorization`. It will hold the value of the `access_group` column when a user logs in successfully. You can then restrict access to pages or elements of pages using this session variable. You could restrict access based solely on username and password, but that could make for hard work in the real world. Click OK to apply the server behavior to the page.

The Login page is half completed at this stage, but is completed enough to test it. However before you test it in a browser, select Bindings ➤ Session Variable, type **MM_Username**, and click OK. You will now see the session available under Bindings. This makes it easier for you to add the code `Session("MM_Username")` to any of your other pages because once you add a session variable to the Bindings panel, it is available to all the pages in your site. Do the same for the `MM_UserAuthorization` session variable.

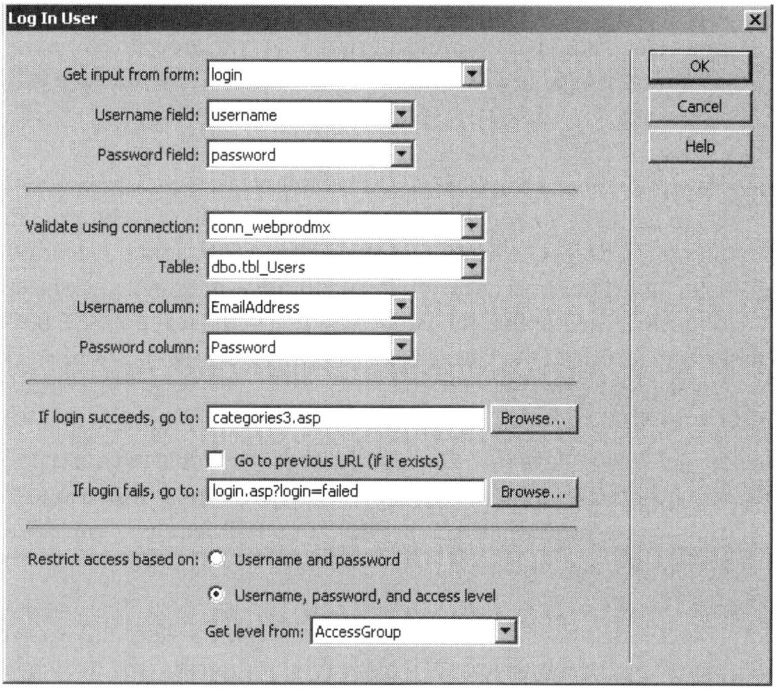

Figure 6-33. The Log In User dialog box

6.   The final element that you need to add to this page is a message that tells
     the user that his or her login failed. To do this, add a new row to the top of
     the current table and in the cell on the right, type **Login failed, please retry**.

     This table row should only be displayed if the user fails to login. You don't
     want to show it when the page first loads. To do this, you need to wrap the
     table row in some conditional code. When you applied the Log In User
     server behavior to the page, the page to which the user will be redirected
     if the login fails had a URL Parameter on the end of it that looked like this.

```
login.asp?login=failed
```

     You will use that parameter to conditionally show the table row that tells
     users that their login failed. The code you need to use to do that will be
     wrapped around the entire table row, the final code is as follows:

```
<% If Request.QueryString("login") = "failed" Then %>
  <tr>
    <td> </td>
    <td>Login failed, please retry </td>
  </tr>
<% End If %>
```

The login.asp page is finished! You can test it now to see the "login failed" message in action by submitting data that you know doesn't exist in your database. The page will submit and the login failure message will be displayed.

7. Now you will add a couple of extra elements to your categories3.asp page. Open it and at the top of the page, add a two row, one column table. In the first row type the text, **Welcome username!** Highlight the username text, select the MM_Username session from Bindings, and then click Insert at the bottom of the Application Panel. The username text on the page should be replaced with the code <%=Session("MM_Username")%> (look in Code view to see this).

8. If you already have some data in the tbl_Users table in your database, you can now test your login properly. If not, add some so you can test it. Make sure to give yourself an AccessGroup of Administrator—you'll find out why in just a moment.

9. Load the login.asp page into your browser by pressing F12 with the page focused in Dreamweaver MX 2004. Type your username (which is your email address in this case) and your password and click the Login button. The form is submitted and if you logged in successfully, the categories3.asp page will display your username after the word Welcome at the top of the page.

10. The second row of the table you added to categories3.asp is for a link to the insert_category.asp page. Type **Add a category** in that table row, select the text, and make it a link to the insert_category.asp page using the Properties inspector.

   Now you can add some code to show or hide this table row depending on whether the user's access level is allowed to see it.

11. Select the table row by placing the mouse pointer in the row and clicking the <tr> tag on the Quick Tag Selector bar. Now go into Code view and your selection should be highlighted in the code. Wrap that selection in an IF statement that will compare the user's MM_UserAuthorization value to one you have predetermined should be allowed to see this table row. The code should look like this when completed.

```
<% If TRIM(Session("MM_UserAuthorization")) = "Administrator" Then %>
  <tr>
    <td><a href="insert_category.asp">Add a category</a> </td>
  </tr>
<% End If %>
```

This says that if the user's `MM_UserAuthorization` value is equal to Administrator, you will display this table row. We use the VBScript TRIM function to ensure that no extra characters or spaces in the session variable are compared to the specified value.

If you change your access level in the database to User and log in again, you will not see the Add a category link.

Log Out User

Forget server behaviors for a second—what does Log In User do? It authenticates a username and password against the `tbl_Users` table, creates either one or two session variables, and populates them with the relevant data. The session variables are the key here as they give you the opportunity to personalize the user's experience as long as you have a unique identifier for the user, which in this case is the username.

On this note, logging a user out is nothing more than simply clearing the session variables. You can clear all session variables by using `Session.Abandon`, or if you are running IIS5 or higher, you can use `Session.Contents.Remove(key)` where the key is the name of the session variable to be removed. This allows you to remove specified session variables as opposed to the whole lot at once.

The Log Out User behavior takes care of this for you. It clears the `MM_Username` session and if you restricted access based on username, password, and access level when applying the Log In User behavior, it adds the code to clear the `MM_UserAuthorization` session too. It also gives you two options: you can log a user out but keep him or her on the same page, or log a user out and redirect him or her to another page. Let's do it using the redirect method.

1. Open `categories3.asp` and place the mouse pointer at the end of the Welcome username text. Add a space and then type **Logout**. Select the Logout text and click Server Behaviors ➤ + ➤ User Authentication ➤ Log Out User. The dialog box shown in Figure 6-34 appears.

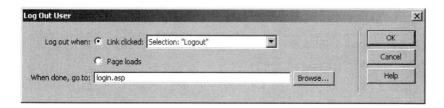

Figure 6-34. The Log Out User dialog box

2. Type (or browse to) `login.asp` in the "When done, go to" field, and click OK to apply this server behavior to your page.

   You are using the Link Clicked method in this scenario but if you created a page specifically for the purposes of logging a user out, you could apply this server behavior to that page and choose the Log out when: Page loads option so that this code would run when the page loads.

3. Save your page and upload it to your web server for testing. When you click the Logout link on the `categories3.asp` page, you will be logged out and redirected back to the `login.asp` page automatically.

Restrict Access to Page

Now that you have the login pages working and various elements are shown or hidden based on your `AccessGroup` value stored in the `MM_UserAuthorization` session variable, you can restrict access to entire pages based on that value.

Some sites have no need for access levels. For example, if all users have access to the same information, there is no point. However, it is good to learn this concept because it is often needed. You use the `AccessGroup` column to simply give each a user a level of power. "Administrator" signifies a user who should have full site access, whereas "User" should not have access to certain site functions, such as inserting, updating, and deleting categories or books. Let's add this server behavior to your insert, update, and delete pages now.

1. Open the `insert_books.asp` page and select Server Behaviors ➤ + ➤ User Authentication ➤ Restrict Access to Page to display the dialog box shown in Figure 6-35.

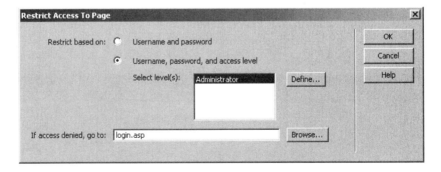

Figure 6-35. The Restrict Access to Page dialog box

2. Select the Username, Password, and Access Level option. Click the Define button to open the Define Access Levels dialog box and type **Administrator** to add it to the list. Click OK to go back to the main Server Behavior interface. Type **login.asp** in the If access denied, go to field and click OK to apply the server behavior to the page.

   Now this page will only allow access to those who have an access group of Administrator. If a user who is not an Administrator tries to get to this page, he or she will be redirected to the login.asp page.

3. Save this completed page and upload it to your webserver.

4. Open the delete_book.asp page and repeat steps 1–3. One notable exception is that you won't have to define the access levels every time—now that you added the Administrator level to the list, it will always appear in the list for this site.

5. Add the same server behavior to the update_books.asp page.

Now that you have restricted access to your pages let's test it. Load your categories3.asp page and try to edit or delete a book. You will be redirected to the login.asp page if you don't have an access group of Administrator.

You have now safeguarded the administrative options of your site by giving access to them to administrators only, all with a few server behaviors.

Check New Username

The last of the four User Authentication server behaviors is called Check New Username, which rather unsurprisingly, checks with the database to make sure the new username is unique before allowing it to be added. Let's create one last new page add_user.asp for this chapter.

1. Use the Record Insertion Form Wizard to build a page and name it **add_user.asp**. Open the Record Insertion Form Wizard by clicking Insert ➤ Application Objects ➤ Insert Record ➤ Record Insertion Form Wizard. Alternatively, select the Application part of the Insert bar and click the Record Insertion Form Wizard icon.

2. Select conn_webprodmx as your connection, select dbo.tbl_Users as the table, and type **login.asp** as the page to redirect to after the insertion has taken place. Remove the UserID, DateCreated, and Included columns from the Form fields list because they are all dealt with automatically by the

database. Next, label the remaining items (add a space to some of them) to the following:

- `FirstName` becomes First Name

- `LastName` becomes Last Name

- `EmailAddress` becomes Email Address

- `AccessGroup` becomes Access Group

3. With Access Group selected, choose Menu from the Display as list and click the Menu Properties button. You are only going to add two levels in this example but you could add as many as would suit your needs.

4. In the Menu Properties dialog box, leave the default selection of Populate menu items: Manually selected. Click to select Item1 that is already in the list and type Administrator in the Label and Value boxes below the list of items. Click the plus sign (+) button to add another item to the list and type **User** in the Label and Value boxes for this item. Click OK to close the Menu Properties dialog box. Your completed Record Insertion Form Wizard should look like Figure 6-36.

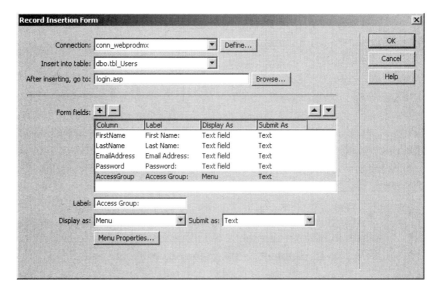

Figure 6-36. The complete Record Insertion Form Wizard

5. Click OK to apply the code to the page. If you're not a fan of centered tables, select the table on the page and set its Align property in the Properties inspector to Default.

6. Now all you need to do is add the Check New Username server behavior to the page. Click Server Behaviors ➤ + ➤ User Authentication ➤ + ➤ Check New Username to display the dialog shown in Figure 6-37.

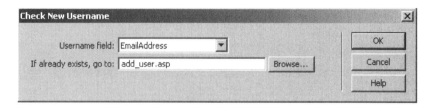

Figure 6-37. The Check New Username dialog box

This server behavior checks that the value submitted as a username does not already exist in the database. If it does exist, you will be redirected to the page specified. In this example, you will be redirected to add_user.asp. The server behavior also creates a URL Parameter called *requsername* that you can use if you want to—and you want to!

7. Right-click the Email Address row of the table and select Table ➤ Insert Row to add a row above it. In the new row, type **Username already exists**. Select the entire row and go into Code view to add some conditional logic to the page. Your selected table row needs to be wrapped in an IF statement, which will look like this.

```
<% If Request.QueryString("requsername") <> "" Then %>
  <tr valign="baseline">
    <td nowrap align="right"> </td>
    <td>Username already exists</td>
  </tr>
<% End If %>
```

Now when a username is submitted that already exists in the database, that table row will be displayed on the form.

8. That's all there is to it. Save your page and upload it to your webserver for testing.

Summary

In this chapter, you learned

- How to create recordsets to retrieve database records

- How to display database records dynamically on your web pages

- How to filter recordsets using parameters and show and hide regions based on conditions

- How to use the Application panel efficiently while building dynamic content

- How to create a connection to a database

- How to use the Bindings panel to store the dynamic variables

- How to use server behaviors and application objects to generate large blocks of ASP code

- How to use the built-in user authentication server behaviors to secure your web applications various pages

You used a wide variety of the server behaviors available in Dreamweaver MX 2004 to create a simple but effective content management system.

This chapter demonstrated some of Dreamweaver MX 2004's more powerful features—hopefully you are now fully equipped to start creating your own database applications.

CHAPTER 7

Code Reuse in Dreamweaver

MANY PEOPLE CHOOSE to use Dreamweaver instead of writing ASP in a text editor because of the way Dreamweaver can streamline your workflow. There are a number of ways you can use Dreamweaver MX 2004 to develop web applications and sites quickly. In this chapter, we will look at the following ways to streamline development:

- Using Dreamweaver templates to speed up development time

- Incorporating library items to manage small repeated elements

- How to develop using ASP Includes to save time and effort

- Incorporating snippets into your workflow

Dreamweaver Templates

The template features in Dreamweaver enable you to create a master copy of a layout, and set up editable and non-editable areas of it. A non-editable or **locked** region is one that stays the same on each page—for example the banner and logo at the top of each page. An editable region is one that contains content that is unique to each page. Once you have created a template, you can create new pages from it.

Another benefit of using templates is that when you create a document from a template but need to change something in a locked region, you can update the main template file and Dreamweaver will update all pages that have been created from that template.

Creating a Simple Template

The easiest way to find out how templates work is to use one. You can either create a new Dreamweaver template by selecting File ➤ New ➤ Template Page, or you can simply save a layout that you have created as a template. To do so, open your layout in Dreamweaver MX and select File ➤ Save As Template.

In the Save As Template dialog box, make sure that the site you are working in is selected in the first box. If you have any templates created for this site, they will appear in the Existing templates box. You can name your template in the Save As Template box, as shown in Figure 7-1.

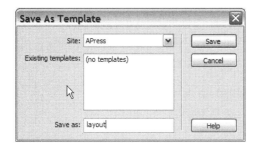

Figure 7-1. The Save As Template dialog box

The layout will be saved with a .dwt extension, indicating that it is a template file. If this is the first template you created for the site, a new folder named Templates will have been created in the root of the site and the template will be stored in this folder.

> **NOTE** *You should not rename or move the Templates folder because Dreamweaver will be unable to find your templates.*

Editable Regions

In Code view, you can see that some markup has been added to the head of the document.

```
<head>
<!-- TemplateBeginEditable name="doctitle" -->
<title>Untitled Document</title>
<!-- TemplateEndEditable --><meta http-equiv="Content-Type" content="text/html; ⤶
charset=iso-8859-1" />
<link href="../ch8/global.css" rel="stylesheet" type="text/css" />
<!-- TemplateBeginEditable name="head" --><!-- TemplateEndEditable -->
</head>
```

This markup shows the editable regions that Dreamweaver adds by default when creating a template. The first editable region on the page is for the title, and the second editable region is in the head, where to add JavaScript or CSS that is unique to certain pages. The editable region begins with the following comment:

```
<!-- TemplateBeginEditable name="doctitle" -->
```

And closes with this one.

```
<!-- TemplateEndEditable -->
```

All editable regions will follow this same pattern, except with a different name attribute.

Adding an Editable Region

The next step in creating a template is to add some editable regions of your own.

Switch back to Design view. You want to make the area of the page where you will be adding the content editable. The example we are using (see Figure 7-2) is a CSS layout: a div houses the main content. The same principle applies with a table-based layout, though; there is a main content area within a <td> in that case. To make the content inside editable, first select all the content in the layout.

Then select Insert ➤ Template Objects ➤ Editable Region.

The New Editable Region dialog box will appear, as shown in Figure 7-3. Enter a name for this editable region that will enable you to easily identify it, and click OK.

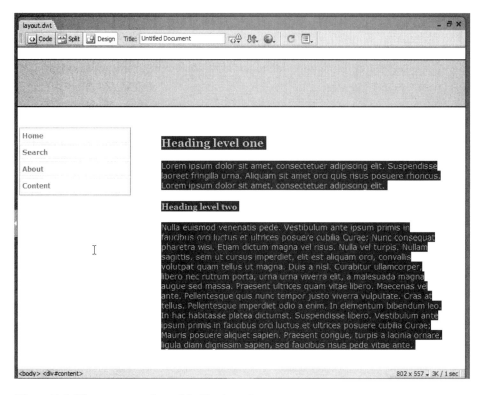

Figure 7-2. The content selected in Design view

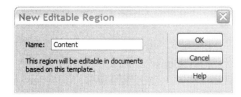

Figure 7-3. The New Editable Region dialog box

In Design view, you should now see your editable region highlighted. The name of the region appears in a small tab at the top, as shown in Figure 7-4.

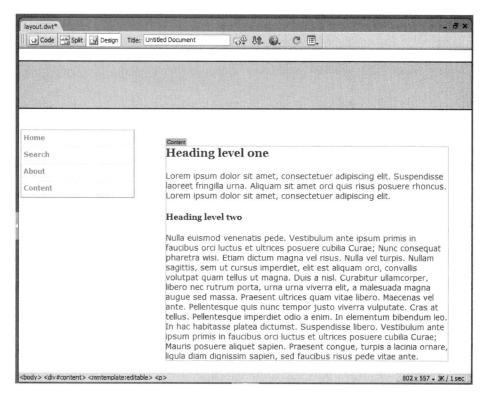

Figure 7-4.The editable region highlighted in Design view

Creating a New Page From a Template

Once you have created a page with at least one editable region in the body, you can create new pages from this template. To do so, select File ➤ New and click the Templates tab at the top of the New Document dialog box. In this tab, select the site in which you just saved your template, and in the second list, select your template. You should see a preview of the template appear in the right side of the dialog box, as shown in Figure 7-5.

Make sure that the Update page when template changes check box is selected and then click Create. A new untitled document will be created that will contain the elements that are in the template, as shown in Figure 7-6.

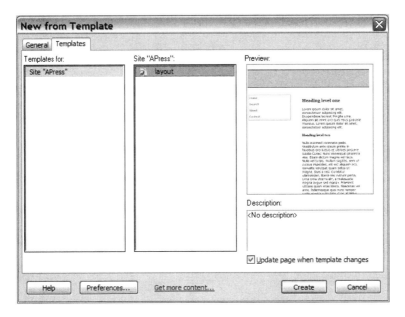

Figure 7-5. Preview of template

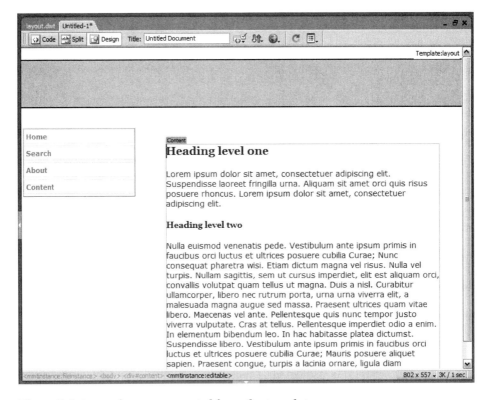

Figure 7-6. A new document created from the template

In Design view, the yellow border around the edge of the document indicates that this document has been created from a template. The name of the template is displayed in the top right corner of the document, as shown in Figure 7-6. Editable regions are highlighted in the same way that they were in the template itself. You cannot click outside the editable region of the document because these regions are non-editable.

Switch into Code view to see the effect the template has on this view (Figure 7-7). You will find that the code within the non-editable region cannot be altered.

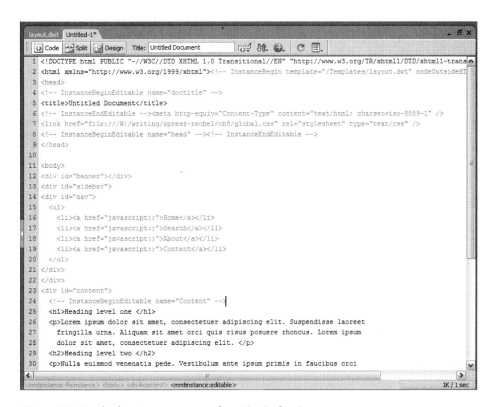

Figure 7-7. Locked regions are grayed out in Code view.

You can now save the document and add content to the editable region.

Updating Templates

The real power of templates is the ability to update documents on your site without having to open and edit each document individually. You created one page from the template but the process will work in exactly the same way if you had created 500 pages.

To demonstrate templates in action let's add an item to the menu—a common task but one that is tedious if you have a large site and need to alter every menu. After adding a new item to the menu, save the template.

When you save a template, Dreamweaver will ask if you want to update the pages based on this template, as shown in Figure 7-8.

Figure 7-8. The Update Template Files dialog box

Click Update to update the pages. If you are not ready to update yet, click Don't Update and Dreamweaver will just save the template for you and you can continue working on it. If the update is successful, Dreamweaver displays some information (shown in Figure 7-9). If for some reason it was unable to update a page, Dreamweaver gives you information about that as well so you can investigate further.

If you open the page that you created from the template, you will see that your changed content remains untouched but that the additional menu item has been added. If any pages linked to the template are open when the update runs, you will need to save them afterward.

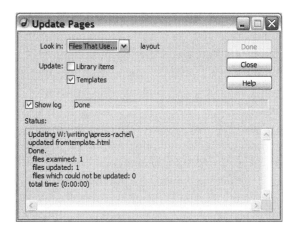

Figure 7-9. Information displayed after update

Removing Template Markup

Although templates are very useful for development, you might not want all the additional comment tags that the template requires visible on the live web site. Dreamweaver enables you to have the best of both worlds—a development version of the site that uses the templates for rapid development and management of the pages, and a live version that strips out that markup.

Select Modify ➤ Templates ➤ Export without Markup to display the dialog box shown in Figure 7-10.

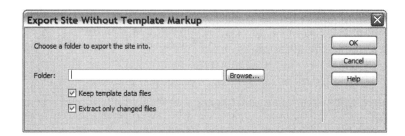

Figure 7-10. The Export Site Without Template Markup dialog box

In the dialog box that appears, select or create a new folder in which to put the template-free site. If you want to continue working on your development version that contains the templates, check Keep Template Data Files. Because this is a new export, it doesn't matter whether the Extract Only Changed Files check box is selected, however, in future if you select this check box, Dreamweaver will only export the files that you have changed.

Click OK and the site will be exported to the new folder. If you are uploading with Dreamweaver you will need to create a new site and upload from the exported version. In future development if you make any edits to the template version, you will need to remember to re-export the site before uploading from the template-free version.

Template Tips and Tricks

This was a very short introduction to templates; there is a lot more to template functionality. However, because this book concentrates on building dynamic web applications, the more advanced template functionality is not necessary and in fact just complicates matters. The following points are worth bearing in mind when working with templates.

Templates from Earlier Versions of Dreamweaver

Templates from Dreamweaver MX should be fully compatible with Dreamweaver MX 2004, however, templates created in earlier versions of Dreamweaver use a different syntax. If you open a site created in Dreamweaver 4 or earlier in MX 2004, it will convert your templates to use the new syntax. After this conversion, you will be unable to work with the site in Dreamweaver 4.

Highlighting and Template Code Coloring

If you don't like the default way that Dreamweaver indicates there is a template or editable region present, you can change it in the preferences. To change the default code coloring, select Edit ➤ Preferences ➤ Code Coloring. Then select HTML under Document Type and click the Edit Coloring Scheme button. In the Edit Coloring Scheme for HTML dialog box (shown in Figure 7-11), scroll down to the bottom of the list to templates and you will see a preview where you can change the code coloring.

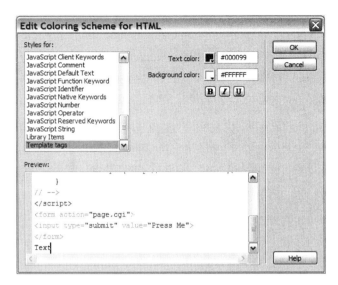

Figure 7-11. The Edit Coloring Scheme for HTML dialog box

To change the Design view highlighting select Edit ➤ Preferences ➤ Highlight-ing. In Preferences dialog box (shown in Figure 7-12) you can choose new colors for this highlighting.

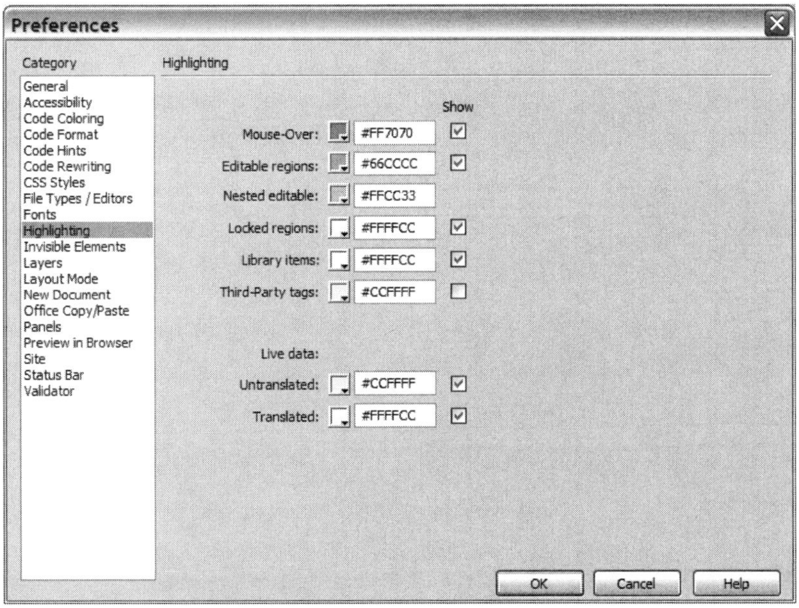

Figure 7-12. Change highlighting

Templates That Contain Dynamic Code

If you create a template that contains PHP, ASP, or other server-side code, you may notice that the extension of the template is .dwt.asp, .dwt.php, and so on. The reason for this is that although you do not need to upload your template files to the server many people do so, and if template files contain dynamic code they may also contain such information as paths to databases, and so on. This could constitute a security risk because a file with a .dwt extension would not be parsed by the server and this information could be viewed as plain text and used to compromise the site. By giving the template files an extension that is recognized as a document that should be parsed by the server, this risk is removed because any dynamic code will be parsed before the user sees it so connection information will be removed.

Library Items

A library item is similar to a template but instead of being an entire layout, it is a smaller fragment of a document. Like templates, these can be updated by changing and updating the library item itself, which will then replicate over the other pages of the site.

Library items can only be inserted into the body of the page, and if they rely on things that would be found in the head of a document (such as JavaScript or CSS) these things must already be present in the document before you insert the library item.

Library items specific to the site are stored in a Library folder (in the same way that templates are stored in the Templates folder) and can be found in Dreamweaver in the Assets panel (shown in Figure 7-13)—click the book icon to view them.

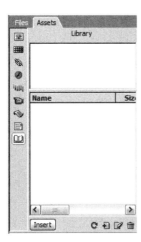

Figure 7-13. Library items in the Assets panel

Creating a Library Item

The easiest way to create a library item is to create your layout and when you are ready to start creating the new pages, decide whether any of the elements on the page would be best turned into library items. In the template that you created earlier, you created only one editable region, assuming that your navigation would be identical on all pages. However, in practice this may not be the case and you might want to have different navigation on different sections of the site—perhaps highlighting which section the user is in. To achieve this you can combine templates with library items.

Return to the template, and create an editable region that contains the menu by selecting the div#nav tag and inserting an editable region, as shown in Figure 7-14.

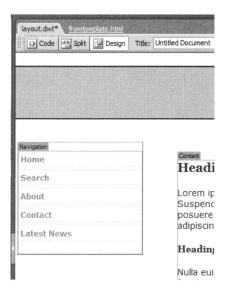

Figure 7-14. The navigation editable region

Select the div tag again so that the entire menu is selected. In the Assets panel, with library items open, click New Library Item. If you are working with a menu that uses CSS, by default Dreamweaver will display an alert telling you that the item will not look the same because the style information (which is in the external stylesheet) is not copied with it. This is fine because the external stylesheet will be attached to every page on which you will use this library item, so the information will be available for it. If you understand this point and don't want to keep seeing this message (shown in Figure 7-15), you can check the check box so it will not appear again.

Figure 7-15. The style information is not copied with the item.

After clearing this alert, the library item will appear in the Assets panel. Give it a name that will help you to locate the correct library item in the future. You will see that the library item appears in the upper half of the panel as a preview. It does not display the style information there so heavily styled items will look plain in the preview (as shown in Figure 7-16).

Figure 7-16. Library items in preview

If you now look at your library item in the template, it will be displayed with a yellow highlighting (as shown in Figure 7-17); this is to show that this item is now a library item and needs to be edited separately.

Figure 7-17. Library item inserted into Design view

Because you will be adding this library item independently of the template, you can delete it from the template and update any pages linked to this template.

Inserting a Library Item into Your Document

Now that you have created a library item, you can use it on your pages. Create a new document from this template and save it into your site. Place your mouse pointer into the navigation editable region and then open the Library pane of the Assets panel. Select the navigation library item and click Insert (you can also drag library items onto the page). The library item will appear on the page, it will be non-editable because you need to update the main library item to make any changes.

Editing Library Items

To edit a library item, select the item in the library items pane of the Assets panel and click Edit. The library item will open in Design view (shown in Figure 7-18) where you can edit it. Saving the item will update all instances of it in documents across the site.

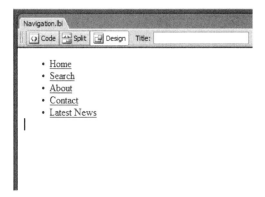

Figure 7-18. The library item in Design view

Because the item uses a stylesheet for its layout, it looks just like a list (which is what it is). If you want to add or remove a menu item, you will probably not have a problem—any changes to the style are done using the stylesheet.

Design Time Stylesheets

Design time stylesheets allow you to attach a stylesheet to a document that only applies while the site is in development in Dreamweaver. These stylesheets are not used on the live web site but are simply referenced by Dreamweaver when you are working in Design view.

To apply a Design time stylesheet to your library item, select Text ➤ CSS Styles ➤ Design-time, this will open the Design Time Style Sheets dialog box, as shown in Figure 7-19.

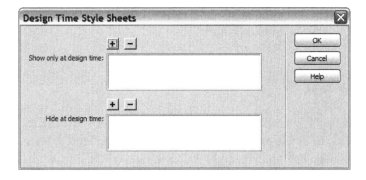

Figure 7-19. The Design Time Style Sheets dialog box

Click the plus sign above the Show only at Design Time box and browse for your stylesheet. Click OK and it will appear in the box. Click OK again. The styles will then be applied to your library item so you can work with it more easily.

> **TIP** *Design time stylesheets can also be very useful in documents that dynamically select the correct stylesheet using server side code, that have multiple stylesheets for different media types, or that use @import to hide stylesheets from Netscape 4 because they mean that you can work in Dreamweaver with the stylesheet applied.*

ASP Includes

If you have used SSI (Server Side Includes) before, the syntax of an ASP Include will be familiar to you. ASP does not contain all the SSI functionality, but it does allow you to use the #include directive. An Include is another file that you *include* in the document. This happens on the server so when the document is served to the browser, you will only see the html and not any indication of whether or not you used an Include.

A Basic Include

To show how Includes work, create a new HTML document in Dreamweaver, and add a few lines of text. Save this document as includes.asp.

Now create another new document, but this time select File ➤ New ➤ Other ➤ VBScript to get a blank document. Add the following to this document:

```
<p>Today's date is <%=Date()%></p>
```

Save the document as date.asp.

Return to includes.asp and switch to Code view. At the top of the document, after the opening body tag, add the following:

```
<!--#include file="date.asp"-->
```

Your document should now look something like this in Code view.

```
<!DOCTYPE html PUBLIC "-//W3C//DTD XHTML 1.0 Transitional//EN"
"http://www.w3.org/TR/xhtml1/DTD/xhtml1-transitional.dtd">
<html xmlns="http://www.w3.org/1999/xhtml">
<head>
```

```
<title>Chapter 8 - Includes</title>
<meta http-equiv="Content-Type" content="text/html; charset=iso-8859-1" />
</head>

<body>
<!--#include file="date.asp"-->
<p>Lorem ipsum dolor sit amet, consectetuer adipiscing elit. Morbi sollicitudin
  imperdiet nibh. Ut ante ante, placerat nec, pharetra ut, tincidunt a, magna.
  Duis ultricies mi nec leo. </p>
<p>Nam sit amet pede nec sapien bibendum venenatis. Suspendisse
    porttitor velit ut velit. Sed purus magna, fermentum eget, mattis eu, porttitor
    et, wisi. Aenean porttitor dolor et mauris. </p>
</body>
</html>
```

Save the document and view in your web browser, as shown in Figure 7-20.

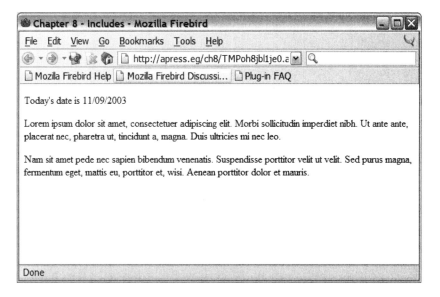

Figure 7-20. The Include is now displayed as part of the page.

You should see the contents of the included file in the document. There is nothing in the source that would indicate that this document has an Include in it because all that is sent to the browser is the completed page.

File or Virtual Includes

In the example just shown, you used the syntax

```
<!--#include file="date.asp"-->
```

Using `include file` means that the path needs to be relative to the current document. So if `date.asp` was stored in a directory named *includes*, you would add the Include like so

```
<!--#include file="includes/date.asp"-->
```

If you are working on a web site that is at the root of your server you might use root relative paths. To do so, you need to slightly change the Include syntax. To include the file with a root relative path you would need to use the following.

```
<!--#include virtual="/includes/date.asp"-->
```

Using Includes for Items That Appear on Every Page

A common use for Includes is to create files for headers and footers of documents so that any changes to these files only need to be made once. These typically include site navigation—a common place to need to add additional items. To "chop up" a layout in this manner, first open the layout in Dreamweaver and highlight the main content area, as shown in Figure 7-21.

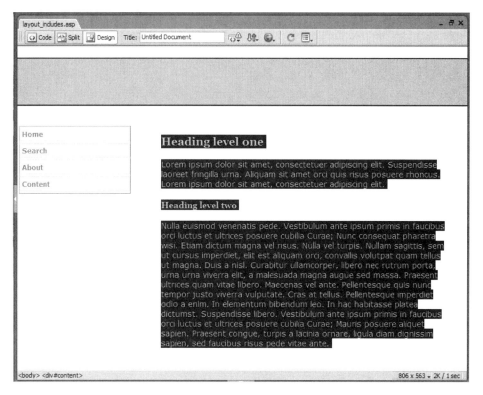

Figure 7-21. The content highlighted in Design view

Switch into Code view, where the content should still be highlighted. Everything above this section in this layout remains the same on all pages in the site. When you create a template of this layout, this whole area was in the non-editable region.

Click your mouse pointer just above the area that you selected, and select up to just underneath the title tag, as shown in Figure 7-22. As with templates, you want to ensure the title tag can be unique on every page so you do not want to include it in the Include.

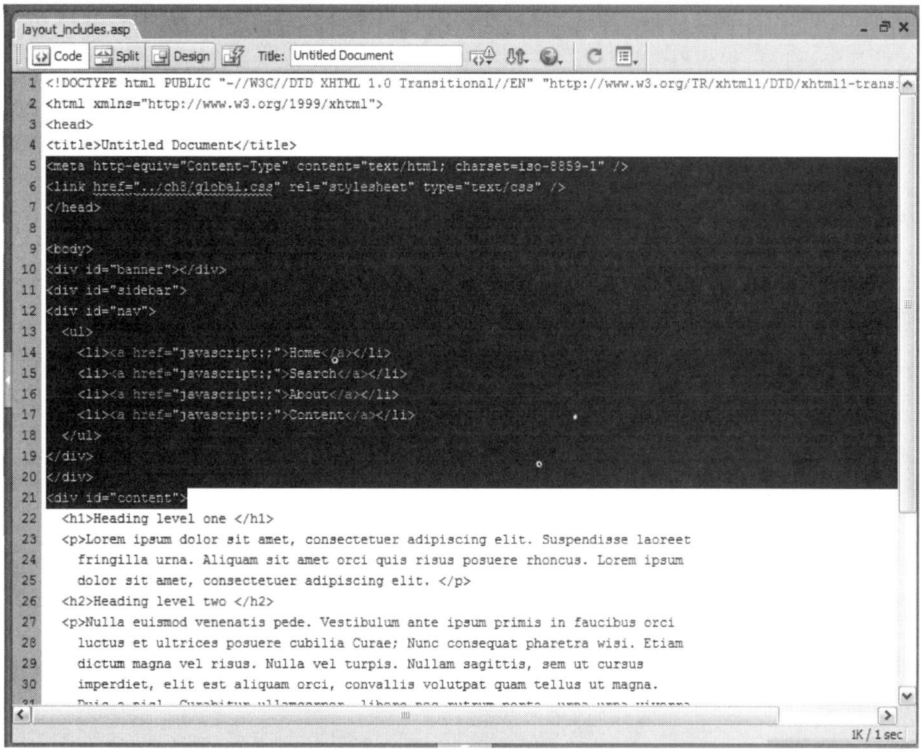

Figure 7-22. Copying the navigation markup in Code view

Copy this markup. Create a new, empty document and paste the selection into it. Save this document as top.asp.

Return to your layout document and delete the markup that you just selected. Now include top.asp into your document.

```
<!--#include file="top.asp"-->
```

Save your document and return to Design view. Although you can see the contents of the top.asp Include, you cannot edit it. That's because Dreamweaver is seeing the Include and including it, but it isn't actually part of this document.

You can repeat this process for the bottom of the document. Switch into Code view and select everything from just below your content, as shown in Figure 7-23.

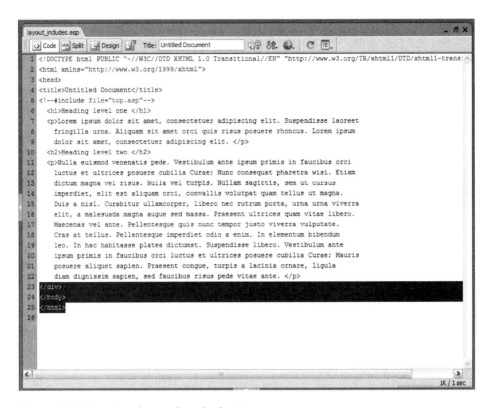

Figure 7-23. Copying the markup for bottom.asp

Save this as `bottom.asp` and link it in with.

```
<!--#include file="bottom.asp"-->
```

The only area on your page now editable with Dreamweaver should be the main content of the page. If you view your page in a browser, the markup should look no different to how it did before you created the Includes. This is because the page is reassembled on the server.

Templates vs. Includes

The choice depends on your site. Includes add extra processing to your site; however, if you are already using ASP, this really isn't going to make any noticeable difference to load time. You might feel that for a static site or a site with a very small amount of ASP, you don't want to add this extra load on the server, and in that case templates would be useful to you. The main problem with using templates to manage the site is that if you change a template and update the site you still have to re-upload every document on the site that is linked to the template, whereas with Includes you would only need to upload the one Include file.

Templates can also be used in *conjunction* with Includes. For example, if there were a team of people working on a web site, a good use of templates would be to lock down a section of a document that includes complicated Includes. Junior members of the team, when adding content, wouldn't need to worry about accidentally moving something in that section of the document because it would not be editable for them. When the site is ready to go onto the live server, the template markup can be removed but the working copy is kept in the templates to make team working easier.

You could save the sample layout just shown as a Dreamweaver template. If you turned the content area into an editable region as we did before, you end up with markup like this:

```
<!DOCTYPE html PUBLIC "-//W3C//DTD XHTML 1.0 Transitional//EN"
"http://www.w3.org/TR/xhtml1/DTD/xhtml1-transitional.dtd">
<html xmlns="http://www.w3.org/1999/xhtml">
<head>
<!-- TemplateBeginEditable name="doctitle" -->
<title>Untitled Document</title>
<!-- TemplateEndEditable --><!--#include file="../ch8/top.asp"-->
  <!-- TemplateBeginEditable name="main content" -->
  <h1>Heading level one </h1>
  <p>Lorem ipsum dolor sit amet, consectetuer adipiscing elit. Suspendisse laoreet
    fringilla urna. Aliquam sit amet orci quis risus posuere rhoncus. Lorem ipsum
    dolor sit amet, consectetuer adipiscing elit. </p>
  <h2>Heading level two </h2>
  <p>Nulla euismod venenatis pede. Vestibulum ante ipsum primis in faucibus orci
    luctus et ultrices posuere cubilia Curae</p>
  <!-- TemplateEndEditable -->
  <!--#include file="../ch8/bottom.asp"-->
```

You can see that the Include files are contained with the non-editable regions. This might seem to be a strange thing to do—after all using Includes means that the need for the template functionality isn't really there because we only need to update one file to make changes to all pages that include it. In addition to the benefits of combining Includes with templates when working with a team, there are other reasons why this can be a good way to work.

You might have noticed when looking at the template markup that Dreamweaver has changed the paths of the Include files. In the layout, the Include looked like this

```
<!--#include file="../ch8/top.asp"-->
```

However, because it is now in the template directory, Dreamweaver has correctly changed the paths to navigate out to the right directory and the Include now looks like

```
<!--#include file="../ch8/top.asp"-->
```

When you create a new file from this template, Dreamweaver changes the path to the Include so it will be correct to wherever the new page is saved.

During development, you may decide to add another Include. If you are using templates, you can simply add the markup for the new Include into the template and update your site, which means that the Include will be added to all the pages. Templates don't have to be seen as something permanent on your site; you can simply use them as a tool to speed up development, and then remove the markup before launch.

Displaying Includes Conditionally

One way that Includes are very useful in a dynamic site is to display data conditionally. A good example of this in practice is when you have a site in which members can log in, and then are given additional options on the site. Once a user has logged in, you are tracking them with a cookie. In this scenario, you may just have an entirely different set of pages that the users are redirected to, and if they go out of those pages onto the main site, they will see the login box again. However, it is more user-friendly to be able to replace the login box with their additional "members only" options or simply with a link to log out from the site.

The layout `ch8_02.asp` has a login box for members to sign in with their username and password, as shown in Figure 7-24.

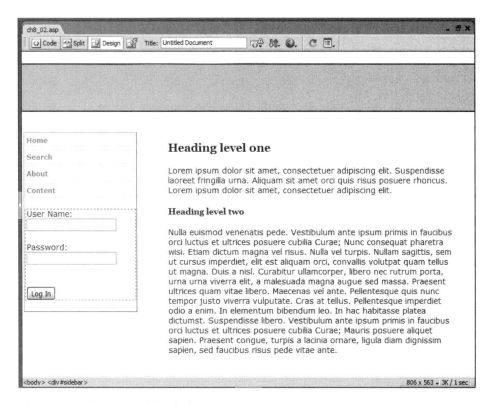

Figure 7-24. Layout with login box

You can make this login box an Include by selecting it and copying the markup to a new file named login.asp.

```
<div id="login">
<form method="post" action="">
<p>User Name:<br />
  <input name="username" id="username" type="text" class="text" />
</p>
<p>Password:<br />
  <input name="username" id="username" type="password" class="text" />
  <p>
  <p><input type="submit" name="btnSubmit" id="btnSubmit" value="Log In" />
</p>
</form>
</div>
```

You can then include this file in the document.

```
<!--#include file="login.asp"-->
```

This will simply display the login form as it was before. Now create a new empty file. This will again be an Include file so it needs no DOCTYPE, html, head, or body tags. You can place members' only navigation and log out links into this file. The following is the content of that Include:

```
<div id="membernav">
  <ul>
    <li><a href="javascript:;">Members News</a></li>
    <li><a href="javascript:;">My Details</a></li>
    <li><a href="javascript:;">Log Out</a></li>
  </ul>
</div>
```

Save it as membernav.asp.

The conditional statement that selects which Include to use is a simple if. . .else statement. Let's assume for simplicity that once you have done your security check, you identify the logged in user with a cookie named ckUsername that contains their username. So you simply need to check for the existence of this variable as shown in Figure 7-25.

```
<%if Request.Cookies("ckUsername")<> "" Then%>
<!--#include file="membernav.asp"-->
<%else%>
<!--#include file="login.asp"-->
<%end if%>
```

This code block simply checks that there is something in ckUsername and if there is, it assumes that it has a logged in user and displays the menu shown in Figure 7-26.

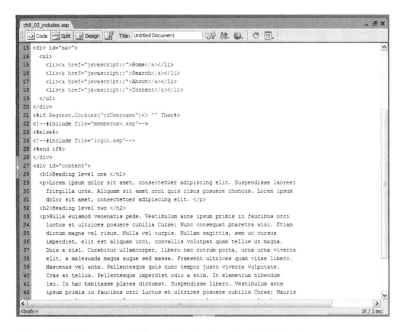

Figure 7-25. The conditional Include code in Code view

Figure 7-26. The layout showing the members' menu

If there is nothing in `ckUsername` or it does not exist, it will display the login box, as shown in Figure 7-27.

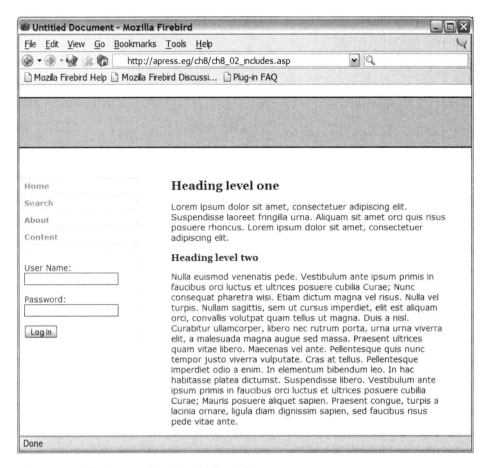

Figure 7-27. The layout showing the login box

A quick way to test if you have a login system up and running is to simply set the cookie at the top of the page.

```
<%Response.Cookies("ckUsername") = "foo"%>
```

Don't forget that you must set it to "" again to see the login box!

You might at this point be thinking that you could have simply created conditional regions on the page for these blocks instead of using Includes. However, if the member's menu is quite large and complex, it saves having all the markup on this page. Additionally, there doesn't need to be any ASP code in the Include, so if someone who has less experience with ASP is editing the site, he or she can more easily make changes to this section without having to worry about messing up the conditional statements. Also, many sites have different levels of membership or admin users who have special functions. You could change the `if. . .else` statement to check for user levels and display any number of different menus without adding two much clutter to the page itself.

You will need to make decisions about which of these techniques to use and where, and your decisions will be different for every site you work on because no two applications will be quite the same.

Snippets

You may often find yourself working on a document or script and realize that the thing you need to write, you have already done in another site. So you try and remember where it was, find it, and then copy and paste the relevant code into your new document. Snippets in Dreamweaver can help you centralize these useful pieces of code and save you from having to write things over and over again or from hunting around your hard drive looking for them.

Snippets in Dreamweaver are a different type of functionality than templates or library items. They simply allow you to insert prewritten pieces of code into your document. Once inserted, Dreamweaver does not manage this code or change it if you change the original snippet. Snippets are simply a convenient place to store useful code.

Snippets are not linked to one site—a snippet added while working on one site will be available for the next and so you can build up a very useful collection of standard pieces of code in the Snippets panel.

Snippets That Ship with Dreamweaver

To get started with snippets, look at the snippets that come preinstalled with Dreamweaver. Open the Snippets panel, which is part of the Code Panel group, as shown in Figure 7-28.

Figure 7-28. The Snippets panel

There is a lot of information stored in the Snippets panel, which is not always immediately obvious. The main part of the panel is a tree menu of all the installed snippets. You can expand these trees to view the snippets that they contain.

If you expand a tree and select a snippet, a preview of the snippet will appear in the top half of the Snippets panel. If the snippet can be rendered, the preview will display how the snippet will look in Design view, otherwise it will simply show some of the code.

You should be able to see the name of the snippet in the tree menu but there is also a description that you can view by using the scrollbar at the bottom of the panel or making the Panel slightly larger by dragging the borders, as shown in Figure 7-29.

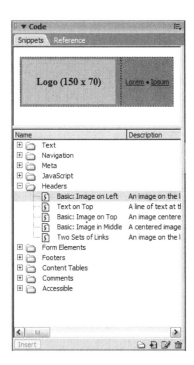

Figure 7-29. The Snippets panel

Inserting Snippets

Create a new document, expand the Navigation item in the Snippets panel, expand Breadcrumb, and select Angle bracket denotes path. Then click the Insert button at the bottom left of the panel.

The markup for the breadcrumb navigation is inserted into your document. You can now change and add to this in your document—the snippet itself will remain unchanged.

You can also insert a snippet by dragging the snippet from the Snippets panel to your document or by double-clicking the snippet in the Snippets panel.

Deleting Snippets

You will probably find that some of the snippets installed aren't useful to you so you'll want to delete them to tidy up the panel. To delete a snippet, select it in the Snippets panel and then click the Delete button, which is a garbage can icon in the bottom-right corner of the panel.

Dreamweaver will ask for confirmation before deleting the snippet.

Editing Snippets

You can also edit snippets. Select the snippet that you would like to edit in the
Snippets panel, and then click the Edit Snippet button as shown in Figure 7-30.
The snippet will appear in a dialog box and you can then edit the snippet. Changes
to the snippet will not affect any snippets of this code already added to documents.

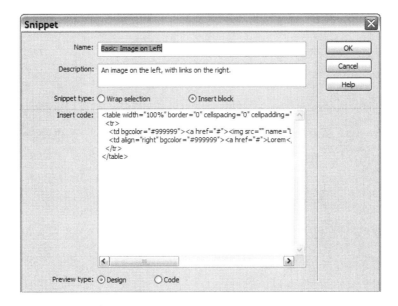

Figure 7-30. Editing a snippet

Rearranging the Snippets Panel

You can drag snippets and folders of snippets around in the Snippets panel and
create new folders by clicking the New Folder button on the bottom of the Snippets panel.

After deleting snippets that you know you will not use, it is worth spending
some time arranging the Snippets panel so that you will be able to find things
quickly. You can even rename folders by right clicking and editing the name, so
that you see at a glance what the contents are. It is worth spending some time
thinking of and applying a naming convention and organizational structure to
your snippets, particularly if you are going to share them with a team. If you end
up with hundreds of snippets in the panel, they will need to be well organized to
be useful.

Third-Party Snippets

You can download new, useful snippets from various third-party web sites. One of the best places to find snippets is the Snippets Exchange on the Dreamweaver FAQ web site at: `http://www.dwfaq.com/Snippets/default.asp`.

If the third-party snippet is available as a download, it will probably be in the format of an .mxp file, which is the file format Dreamweaver uses for its extension packages. After selecting a third-party snippet, download it. To install the snippet into Dreamweaver you will need to use the Extension Manager. With the Extension Manager launched, select File ➤ Install Extension and browse for the snippet.

After clicking Install, you will be prompted to agree to the licensing agreement, as shown in Figure 7-31, and then the snippet will be installed. After you restart your computer, you will be able to use and edit it in the same way as the pre-installed snippets.

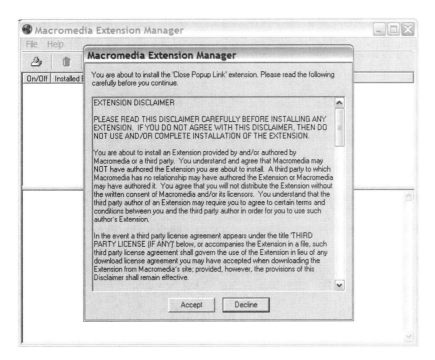

Figure 7-31. Installing an extension—the license agreement

Creating Your Own Snippets

There is another way to add the snippets from the Snippets Exchange. Snippets are helpfully displayed in text areas on their page in the same format that they should be added if you were to create the snippet yourself. Remember that snippets are simply blocks of useful code, so you can turn any useful code into a snippet by using the following method.

To create a snippet, click the New Snippet icon at the bottom of the Snippets panel. The Snippet dialog box opens with empty fields. Type the name of the snippet and add a description of the snippet—if you are copying the snippet from a third-party resource site, it might be a good idea to put in the URL of that site in case you want to go back there later. If it is something that you have used in another application, you could reference that in case you ever need to remember how you used a particular piece of code in context.

Select the snippet Type. If the snippet will usually be inserted after you have selected an element on the page, select Wrap Selection, as shown in Figure 7-32. If you select this option, you will be presented with two text boxes to complete: Insert Before and Insert After.

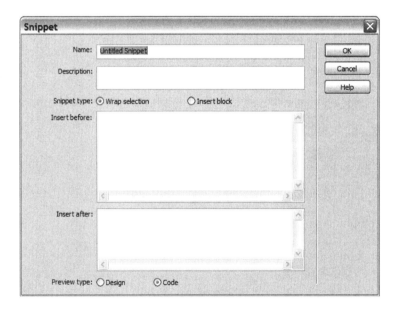

Figure 7-32. Creating a new snippet—Wrap selection

Insert Block is for snippets that place a section of code onto the page. If you select this type you will just get one text box to complete, as shown in Figure 7-33.

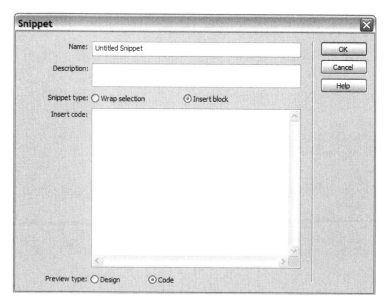

Figure 7-33. Creating a new snippet—Insert block

For this example, we use the snippet Close Popup Link, which inserts a link with the JavaScript necessary to close a popup window that was opened with JavaScript. This snippet will be best as a "Wrap Selection" type because we want to be able to type the text or insert the image that will be used as the link that closes the window and apply the snippet to add the close functionality.

After adding the title and description we need to select Wrap Selection and add the code that will go before the text or image that we selected in the Insert before text box.

```
<a href="javascript:;" onClick="self.close();return false">
```

Then we add the code that will be inserted after the selection into the Insert After box, as shown in Figure 7-34.

```
</a>
```

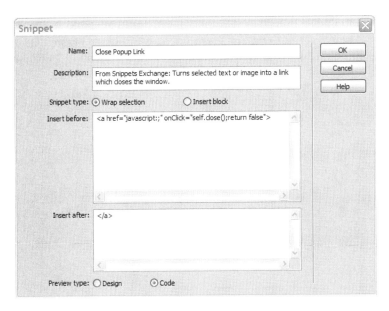

Figure 7-34. New snippet

The Preview Type radio buttons allow you to set the type of preview that should appear in the top half of the Snippets panel. For most snippets, leave Code selected. Click OK and your snippet is ready to use.

Summary

We covered a lot of ground in this chapter, and gave you a broad overview of the ways you can streamline your working practices when using Dreamweaver. You will probably not find that all these things are useful to you; however, it is worth spending some time creating good working practices because a good workflow helps you save time and get projects completed far more quickly. Having stream-lined practices becomes even more important if you are working in a team.

CHAPTER 8

Dreamweaver MX 2004 Extensions

ONE OF THE GREAT THINGS about Dreamweaver MX 2004 is its extensibility. The base program is an extremely powerful tool but adding your own functionality to it by building extensions is what really makes the program sing as well as dance.

Extensions can speed up and simplify the process of writing code. Dreamweaver MX comes with lots of ready-made extensions but if they don't fit your situation, you need to build your own extensions.

There are many developers who are producing some amazing extensions. There has been a growing market for commercial-quality extensions for some time now, and this can only be a good thing in terms of pushing back the boundaries of what is possible.

The following is a selection of the more prevalent types of extensions that you can create to add functionality to Dreamweaver MX:

- Behaviors

- Objects

- Commands

- Server behaviors

- Panels

In this chapter, you will look at some sources of downloadable extensions, both free and commercial, and you'll go through the installation process. You'll then build two simple server behaviors (SB). The first will make it easy to maintain the paragraph formatting that a lump of text-based data contains when retrieved from a database. It will also include some simple validation that will prevent the code from throwing an error on the web page. Then we'll see how to package an extension and make it ready for distribution. Finally, you'll build the second server behavior, which will make it easy to use web links that are stored in a database.

Finding Extensions

There are many sites that offer extensions for download and many of them are entirely free. The saying "you get what you pay for" doesn't apply in many cases when it comes to extensions. There are some fantastic extensions available that don't cost a penny! This chapter doesn't intend to offer an exhaustive list of extension locations; however, we will try to cover some of the more popular locations.

The first port of call when looking for extensions for Macromedia products should be the Macromedia exchanges. There is an exchange for each of their products but we'll concentrate on the Dreamweaver exchange, for obvious reasons.

Go to: `http://www.macromedia.com/exchange/dreamweaver` to get to the Dreamweaver exchange homepage. At the time of this writing, there are 905 extensions available through the exchange (although not all of them are made for Dreamweaver MX 2004). On the right of the exchange page is a list of the top ten extensions for Dreamweaver. Project Seven (`http://www.projectseven.com`) is featured prominently. They offer some fantastic extensions, from design packs to the best menu systems going. There is also a massive list of free extensions (mostly behaviors and objects) that cover a wide range of functionality.

There are several well-known extension developers in the Dreamweaver community and we will cover a few of them here, in no particular order.

- One of the best known is Massimo Foti. He has contributed an enormous amount of time and effort and made the lives of other developers easier by writing a huge collection of extensions. Go to `http://www.massimocorner.com`, click Dreamweaver, and then use the lower menu to navigate the extensions by category.

- Tom Muck developed some remarkable extensions too. We use his recordset navigation suite regularly. Go to `http://www.dwteam.com` or `http://www.basic-ultradev.com` for some of his free and commercial extensions.

- When Dreamweaver MX was about to be launched, Macromedia ran a competition for extension developers. One of the top ten finalists was Jaro von Flocken's fantastic Check Form extension. Go to `http://www.yaromat.com` and click the Extend Dreamweaver link. There are many extensions available here, including the Check Form extension.

- A collection of extension developers going under the banner of DWWork has created some really great productivity enhancers for Dreamweaver. Go to `http://www.dwwork.com` to check out the new and the old from these guys.

- If eCommerce is what you're after and you are coding in ASP VBScript or JavaScript, a couple of sites have the answer for you. Go to `http://www.thechocolatestore.com/ultradev/` for the UltraCart II extension and `http://charon.co.uk/` for the CharonCart extension.

- Another long-standing extender of Dreamweaver is Drew McLellan and his fever-based extensions. Go to `http://www.dreamweaverfever.com` and click the Extensions (or Grow) link.

- The zones are a great source for extensions, tutorials, discussions, and more related to Macromedia products. George Petrov and company produce some remarkable extensions. Go to `http://www.dmxzone.com` and click the Extensions link.

There are many more extension developers than can be listed in this small amount of space. The short list just provided are those that we feel should not be missed at any cost. The following sites also offer some great extensions and we highly recommend you visit them all:

- `http://www.z3roadster.net/dreamweaver/`

- `http://www.valleywebdesigns.com/vwd_Vdw.asp`

- `http://www.fourlevel.com/`

- `http://ultradev.buzzinet.co.uk/extensions/index.asp`

- `http://www.kaosweaver.com/`

- `http://www.dreamweaver-extensions.com/`

- `http://www.webassist.com`

- And last but not least...my own! `http://robgt.com/products`

Although this is a fairly long list, it is by no means exhaustive. Visits to some of these sites will yield more sites with yet more extensions. Get out there and explore—they are all there just waiting for you to find them.

Once you have found and downloaded extensions that you want to use, you need to install them.

Installing Extensions

When you installed Dreamweaver MX 2004, the Extension Manager was installed with it. This program manages the extensions for the suite of Macromedia Studio products.

1. To launch the Extension Manager (shown in Figure 8-1), you can either locate it in your operating system menus and run it from there, or if you already have Dreamweaver MX 2004 open, click the Commands menu and then select Manage Extensions.

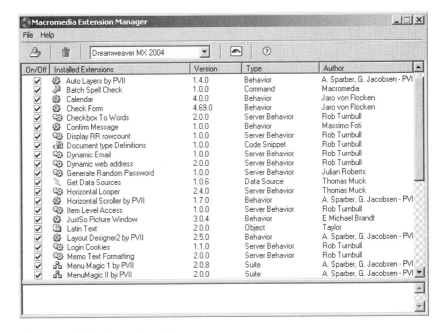

Figure 8-1. The Extension Manager

There are two main buttons on the Extension Manager interface (it's a simple program doing a complex job!). They are Install New Extension and Remove Extension. There is also a select list, which lists all the Macromedia products that are currently installed on your system for which the Extension Manager is managing the extensions.

2. If it isn't already selected, select Dreamweaver MX 2004 from the select list and then click the Install New Extension button to begin the installation process, as shown in Figure 8-2.

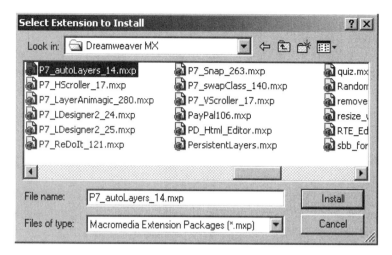

Figure 8-2. The Select Extension to Install dialog box

3. Locate the extension you want to install and click Install. You will be prompted to accept the license agreement and installation will then complete. If you do not accept the license agreement, the installation will abort.

> **NOTE** *If Dreamweaver MX 2004 was open at the time of installation, you will probably need to restart it before you can use the extension.*

In the Extension Manager, all the installed extensions are listed with a check box next to them. If you experience problems with Dreamweaver MX 2004 that you think might be extension related, you can disable an extension by clearing the check box for that extension. You would then restart Dreamweaver MX 2004 and check if the problem has gone away. If it has, you can uninstall that extension to stop the problem. Disabling extensions is useful for troubleshooting tasks, and also to reduce the overhead on the program as a whole. If you have a lot of extensions installed, Dreamweaver MX 2004 has more work to do and will slow down because of it.

4. To uninstall an extension, click it in the list of installed extensions and click the Uninstall Extension button. A confirmation box will pop up to ask you to confirm this action. Confirming it will uninstall the selected extension.

Importing Extensions

The Extension Manager that ships with Dreamweaver MX 2004 has a new feature that makes it easy to install all the Dreamweaver MX extensions into Dreamweaver MX 2004.

1.   From the File menu, select Import Extensions.

2.   Select the product to import the extensions from and then specify that product's installation location on your computer, as shown in Figure 8-3. Clicking OK begins the Import process.

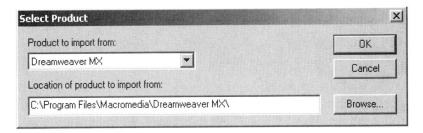

Figure 8-3. The completed Import Extensions dialog box

For every extension that gets imported in this manner, you will be asked to accept the license agreement. It doesn't tell you to which extension that license agreement pertains, which is unfortunate because the agreements are more or less identical.

You will be notified about any problems with the installation of any extensions, although, again, it doesn't tell you which extension. That said, it does give you the file name that is causing a problem, and you might be able to work out which extension it is from that. Knowing which extension is causing a problem is useful because once the import procedure is finished, you will want to remove the problem extensions. If possible, Dreamweaver will install an extension even if there is a problem with it, but it will be put into a Miscellaneous menu on the Commands menu. The import procedure will tell you that this happened, so if you cannot tell which extension caused this problem during the import procedure, you can find out by looking at that menu in Dreamweaver MX 2004.

Building an Extension (or Two)

The order in which you go about building an extension is not set in stone, but there is an obvious progression that will make your life far easier if followed. Step one is to write the final version of the code so you can test it to make sure it works exactly as intended. Step two is to build the extension. You will launch the **Server Behavior Builder** (SBB) and begin adding the code and the required parameters so that the SBB can build the extension interface, write the code necessary to run the SB interface, and insert the correct code into your document. Step three is to tweak the extension interface and write a help document.

For the purposes of this chapter, the only code you'll need to know is the code you will include in the server behavior itself; the rest of the code is written for you. However, if you are serious about writing extensions, or if you want to create some of the other extensions (behaviors or objects, for instance), you should arm yourself with a thorough knowledge of JavaScript.

The Anatomy of an Extension

It can take many component parts to make an extension. The first and most obvious part is the actual piece (or pieces) of code that provides the functionality that the extension provides. The next part is the interface that the user interacts with when using the extension. The not so obvious part is the code that works behind the scenes to make the other parts work successfully in the Dreamweaver MX 2004 environment. The average Dreamweaver MX 2004 user will very likely never directly encounter these files, yet they are very important from an extensions point of view.

The Extension Code

The first step is to write the code that comprises the extension's final output so that it can be tested and debugged to make sure that it will perform as expected.

The first extension you will write will maintain the paragraphs in text that is being displayed from a database. This doesn't happen automatically, so this extension fills a gap.

To do this, open a blank ASP/VBScript document and write the following code between the <body> tags:

```
<%
' Maintain paragraphs server behavior
varDynamicText = (RecordsetName.Fields.Item("ColumnName").Value)
IF varDynamicText <> "" AND NOT IsNULL(varDynamicText) THEN
  varReplaceWith = "</p><p>"
  Response.Write(Replace(varDynamicText,vbCRLF,varReplaceWith))
END IF
%>
```

The first line of code assigns the recordset content to a variable, which is then used in the rest of the code. The value in that variable is checked to see if it is non-empty and not null, and if it passes that test, the rest of the code is executed. You then set a value in a second variable that holds the html code with which you will replace the relevant parts of the incoming data. Finally, you perform the replacement and output the result to the page.

The reason you replace each line break with a closing paragraph tag and then an opening one (`</p> <p>`) is to take into account the fact that an initial paragraph format will have been applied to the dynamic text on the page. If you don't use paragraph formatting and would prefer to use `<br />` tags, you will be able to set that when applying the server behavior.

You can see that you are using two variables in your code, and when building an extension, a variable usually means that a parameter will be needed to fill that variable value. However, one of your variables gets the value from a recordset column, so you will need two parameters in your server behavior to cater for this single variable—one for the recordset name and one for the column name. The second variable will need only one parameter, which gives you a total of three parameters for this server behavior.

Now let's build the server behavior.

The Interface

One of the great things about building simple server behaviors like this one is that the SBB takes care of the code required to build the interface once you commit your server behavior code and the relevant parameters to it.

1. Click Server Behaviors ➤ + ➤ New Server Behavior. You will need to have a web page open in Dreamweaver MX 2004 to do this.

2. In the dialog box, set the name of the extension. We called ours Maintain paragraphs, as shown in Figure 8-4. It is an ASP VBScript extension so that select list can stay as it is.

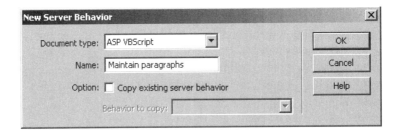

Figure 8-4. Naming your new server behavior

3. Click OK to move to the next stage. The main SBB window will appear, as shown in Figure 8-5.

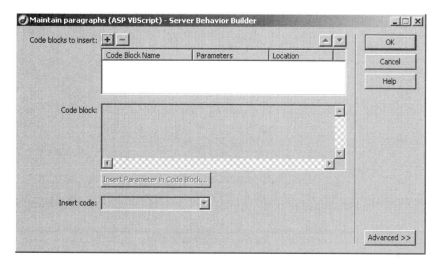

Figure 8-5. The main Server Behavior Builder window

4. Click the plus sign (+) button at the top of the window to open a dialog box in which you can change the name of the code block. The default name is fine so click OK and it will be added to the list.

5. Add your code to that code block. Go back to your web page on which you wrote your working code and copy it all, including the opening and closing ASP tags. Re-display the SBB and paste your code into the Code block window, replacing any content that was in there. Now you need to add your parameters to the code. These parameters will give your user interface the required form elements so that your code's variables will be populated with the users choice of values.

6. Select the RecordsetName text in the code and click the Insert Parameter in Code Block button.

7. The text you type here will be used on the server behavior interface form by default (you can change it later) so making it readable and friendly makes sense. Type **Recordset name** as the value for this parameter, as shown in Figure 8-6, and click OK.

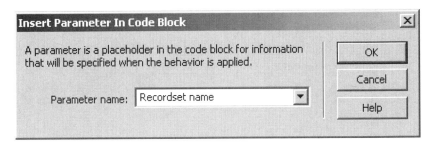

Figure 8-6. The Insert Parameter dialog box

The parameter is inserted into the code, and can be seen surrounded by @@ symbols.

8. Add the parameter for the `ColumnName` variable. Call it **Column name**.

9. Add the parameter for the varReplaceWith value. Select the `</p><p>` code and click the Insert Parameter in Code Block button. Call the parameter **Replace with**.

Your code in the Code block window should look like this:

```
<%
' Maintain paragraphs server behavior
varDynamicText = (@@Recordset name@@.Fields.Item("@@Column name@@").Value)
IF varDynamicText <> "" AND NOT IsNULL(varDynamicText) THEN
  varReplaceWith = "@@Replace with@@"
  Response.Write(Replace(varDynamicText,vbCRLF,varReplaceWith))
END IF
%>
```

Next, you need to decide where the code that your server behavior generates should be added. This type of server behavior is best suited to having its content inserted at the current location of the cursor, that is, the user places the mouse pointer on the page and then applies the server behavior to it. With that in mind you can set the SBB dialog box values appropriately.

10. Make sure the Insert code select list is set to Relative to the selection, and the Relative position select list is set to Replace the selection.

11. Click the Advanced >> button in the bottom of the dialog box. This allows you to set whether to show this server behavior in the Server Behaviors panel and how it should be identified.

12. Click the box next to Identifier and select Maintain paragraphs_block1 in the Code block to select list. The default server behavior title is fine, although you can change it. The parameters in your code block are used in the title but if you want to change their order or exclude one or more, edit them in this field.

    Your finished SBB dialog should look like Figure 8-7.

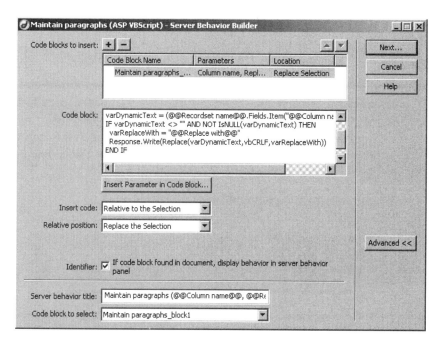

Figure 8-7. The completed Server Behavior Builder dialog box

13. Click Next to go to the final step in this building process.

14. Set the type of form elements that should be used for each of the three parameters you added to the code. You can also change their order to make a more logical progression for the user. The Recordset name parameter should be first, followed by the Column name, and then the Replace with parameter comes last, as shown in Figure 8-8.

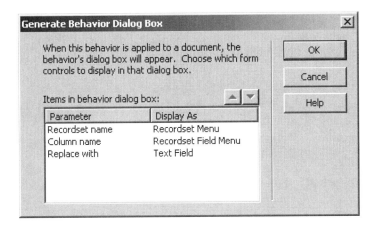

Figure 8-8. The Generate Behavior dialog box

15. Click the Recordset name parameter and use the sort arrows above the list to move it up to the top of the list. With Recordset name still selected, click the gray arrow in the Display as column and choose Recordset Menu from the list. Select the Column name parameter and set it to display as a Recordset Field Menu. The Replace with parameter can be left at its default setting of Text Field.

    The finished dialog should look like Figure 8-9.

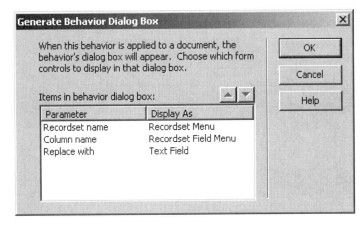

Figure 8-9. The Generate Behavior dialog box with items ordered

16. Click OK and the Server Behavior Builder will begin writing files and building your server behaviors' user interface. It will be automatically added to your Server Behaviors list without you needing to restart Dreamweaver MX 2004.

The server behavior in use looks like Figure 8-10.

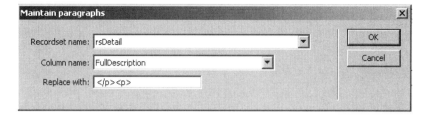

Figure 8-10. The server behavior in use

It's very basic and is missing a Help button. Changing the server behavior's .htm file that was automatically generated easily rectifies this.

17. If you are using one of the multi-user capable operating systems, (Windows XP, Windows 2000, Windows NT, or Macintosh OS X), you will have your own configuration folder separate from that of the program. This is to allow individual users to set up their own workspace, extensions, and preferences in a multi-user environment without disturbing anyone else's configurations. Assuming your computer's drive letter is C: your configuration folder can be found at the following location:

C:\Documents and Settings\<your login username here>\
Application Data\Macromedia\Dreamweaver MX 2004\
Configuration\serverbehaviors\ASP_Vbs

You might have to tell your operating system to show hidden files and folders in some cases, such as Windows 2000 and XP.

Having created your simple server behavior, you can see that Dreamweaver MX 2004 has created three files.

- `Maintain paragraphs.edml`

- `Maintain paragraphs.htm`

- `Maintain paragraphs_block1.edml`

The .edml files are XML files that store information about how Dreamweaver MX 2004 handles a server behavior. `Maintain paragraphs.htm` is the interface file that the user will see and use when applying this server behavior to a page. If you open this .htm page in Dreamweaver MX 2004, you can see the complexity of code that such a simple interface requires.

By default, the SBB does not add a Help button to the interface. It can't because no help file has been created yet, and there is currently no way of adding this information into the SBB anyway, so you must do it manually.

18. Scroll down through the code of this page to the bottom of the scripts section. At line 264, insert the following function just before the closing `</SCRIPT>` tag:

```
function displayHelp(){
    var varConfigFolder = dw.getUserConfigurationPath();
    var varHelpDocument = "ExtensionsHelp/maintainparagraphshelp.htm";
    dreamweaver.browseDocument(varConfigFolder + varHelpDocument);
}
```

This function, called `displayHelp`, is required to add the Help button to the server behavior interface. If you included the empty function, the button would be displayed but wouldn't do anything, which would be rather pointless.

The `displayHelp` function sets up two variables, one to find the root configuration folder, and one to pinpoint the path to the Help file. The third line runs the Dreamweaver MX 2004 `browseDocument` command, which uses the two variables combined to locate the help file and display it in a browser window.

Using this method means the Help document must be installed into the user's configuration folder when the extension is installed. We'll cover that in the section called "Writing the MXI File," later in this chapter.

If you want to host your Help files online, you would substitute the current path to the document with a fully qualified URL, such as this.

```
function displayHelp(){
dreamweaver.browseDocument("http://www.domain.com/maintainparagraphshelp.htm");
}
```

To have a Help file appear at all requires the existence of the file in the first place. We won't go into the details of creating a simple HTML page here; you all know how to write a few paragraphs of text onto a page! Please bear in mind, however, that if you are going to use any images in your Help documents, you need to use document relative paths.

Once you have created your help file, save it as `maintainparagraphshelp.htm` in the ExtensionsHelp folder in your configuration folder. If the folder does not exist, you should create it. Now when you click the Help button in your SB interface, you will be presented with a Help page. This isn't much use for your own extensions on your own computer but can be very useful when you are distributing extensions to other people who might not know how to use your server behavior or what it is supposed to do.

19. Tidy up the user interface elements to make them look more uniform. The select lists that were generated for you are quite wide and you can make them a little narrower. The width of the form elements is set using a style declaration so all you need to do is locate the style declarations and change them. We changed both select lists to 200px wide. We also changed the text field (which represents the Replace with value) to 100px wide. The last thing to do is add a default value to the Replace with text field so you don't have to type it in every time you use this server behavior. Go into Design view, select the Replace with text field and type **</p><p>** into the Init value field in the Properties inspector. If you want to use a different default value, type that in instead.

20. Save the file, restart Dreamweaver MX 2004 and use the server behavior to see your changes in effect.

    Notice the default value you specified for the Replace with field is there from the start and the Help button now appears under the OK and Cancel buttons, as shown in Figure 8-11.

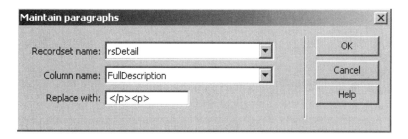

Figure 8-11. The Server Behavior dialog box with the Help button displayed

Distributing Extensions

If you plan on distributing your extensions for others to use, you will first need to package them in the correct format so that anyone can install them onto their computers using the Extension Manager.

These files need to be formatted as MXP files, which stands for Macromedia eXtension Package. Fortunately, you don't need to know how to build an MXP file; the Extension Manager takes care of that for you, but it needs to be given the right ingredients. Those ingredients come in the shape of an MXI file, which is covered next.

Writing the MXI File

The MXI (Macromedia eXtension Instruction) file is an XML file that describes all properties of the server behavior. Among these properties are the name and version number of the extension, the author's name, the products required to install the extension, the description of the extension, the instructions on where to locate it in the program after installation, a list of the files that are used in the SB, where those files should be stored on the user's computer when it is installed, and any configuration changes that need to be made to the installation of Dreamweaver MX 2004.

The basic structure of an MXI file looks like this.

```
<macromedia-extension
  name=""
  version="1.0.0"
  type="Server Behavior"
  requires-restart="true">
  <author name="" />
  <products>
    <product name="Dreamweaver" version="6" primary="true" required="true" />
  </products>
  <description>
  <![CDATA[
  This description will appear in the Extension Manager description window
  ]]>
  </description>
  <ui-access>
  <![CDATA[
  This user interface access data will also appear in the Extension Manager
description window
  ]]>
  </ui-access>
  <files>
    <file source="" destination="" />
  </files>
  <configuration-changes>
  </configuration-changes>
</macromedia-extension>
```

You could specify that the version number is 7 to limit the minimum software requirement to Dreamweaver MX 2004, but Dreamweaver MX uses the same structure as Dreamweaver MX 2004 so it makes sense to target the lower version to enable more people to use the extension.

To make packaging extensions easier, it is a good idea to create a staging area where you copy all the relevant files for an extension.

1. Create a folder in this location: C:\Extensions\maintain paragraphs.

2. Copy all your maintain paragraphs files into this folder. Now when you create your MXI file, you don't have to worry about path structure to locate your files—they are in the same folder as the MXI file!

3. With that in mind, you can populate this MXI structured document with the data relevant to your server behavior. Here's how it should look.

```
<macromedia-extension
 name="Maintain paragraphs"
version="1.0.0"
type="Server Behavior"
requires-restart="true">
<author name="Rob Turnbull" />
<products>
<product name="Dreamweaver" version="6" primary="true" required="true" />
</products>
<description>
<![CDATA[
This server behavior will maintain any paragraphs found in text retrieved
from a database when displayed on the web page.
]]>
</description>
<ui-access>
<![CDATA[
Access this Server Behavior by clicking
Server Behaviors ➤ + ➤ Maintain paragraphs
]]>
</ui-access>
<files>
<file source="Maintain paragraphs_block1.edml"
   destination="$dreamweaver/Configuration/serverbehaviors/ASP_Vbs/" />
<file source="Maintain paragraphs.htm"
  destination="$dreamweaver/Configuration/serverbehaviors/ASP_Vbs/" />
<file source="Maintain paragraphs.edml "
  destination="$dreamweaver/Configuration/serverbehaviors/ASP_Vbs/" />
<file source="Maintainparagraphshelp.htm "
  destination="$dreamweaver/Configuration/ExtensionsHelp/" />
</files>
<configuration-changes>
</configuration-changes>
</macromedia-extension>
```

Each <file> line should be one continuous line of code.

You can add line breaks to the text in the description area of the MXI by adding the relevant html tag, such as <br>, for example.

If you include images in your server behavior interface or in any documentation that you want to install on the users' system, you need to create a separate file source line for each image and ensure that it gets installed to the relevant directory in the configuration structure.

> **NOTE** *There are restrictions on the length of the names you can use for a server behavior and a slightly different length in the name of the MXI file. The server behavior's name can be no longer than 27 characters, but in the name of the MXI file, the limit is just 23 characters.*

4. That's the MXI file code written as you need it so name the file `maintainparagraphs.mxi` and save it into the same folder in which you copied all the extension files.

Now it's ready for packaging.

Packaging (from MXI to MXP)

Extensions are packaged in the MXP format so that they can be installed into any user's system.

There are two ways of starting the packaging process, the hard way (not *so* hard) is to open the Extension Manager and select File ➤ Package Extension. The easiest way is to double-click the MXI file that you just created.

Whichever way you choose, the first dialog box you'll see asks you to select the extension to package. Here you need to select the MXI file you just created as shown in Figure 8-12.

In the next dialog box, you will save the extension package. It will have already been given the MXP a file name so all you need to do is choose a location where to save it. You can change the name if you want but the default is fine in this case, as is the location (save it in the same place as the MXI that you started with). When you click Save, the extension package will be created and saved to the location you specified, as shown in Figure 8-13.

If everything goes as planned (and it usually does), you will see the message shown in Figure 8-14.

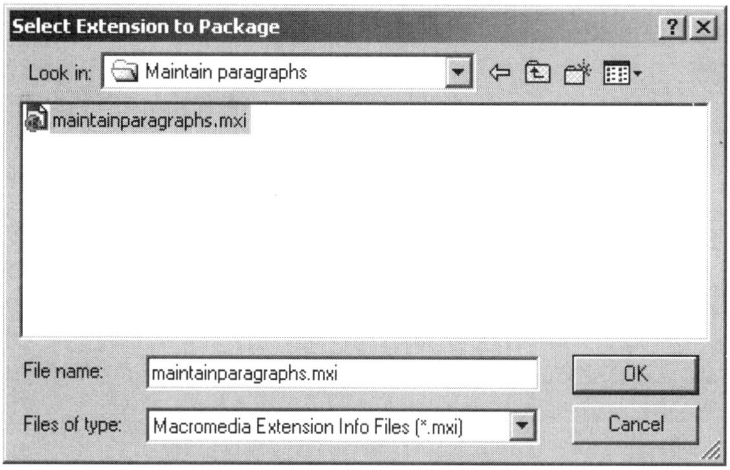

Figure 8-12. The Select Extension to Package dialog box

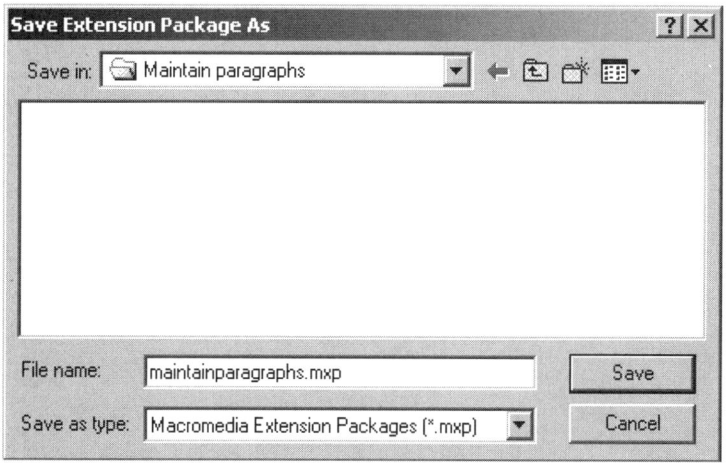

Figure 8-13. The Save Extension Package As dialog box

Figure 8-14. Extension created successfully

> **NOTE** *If you get an error at this stage, it is usually a problem with the length of the name you used for the extension. Again, names must be fewer than 27 characters in length. If you stick to fewer than 23 characters, you'll never have a naming problem (four fewer characters for the name of the file, excluding the file extension, .mxi).*

Congratulations, you have created your own distributable extension!

Distributing Your Extensions

Macromedia has strict guidelines when it comes to distributing your extensions through their Exchange. You can read all about it at the following page:
`http://www.macromedia.com/exchange/help/about_exchange.html#item-19`

Of course, you don't have to distribute your extensions through the Exchange. You can put them on your own web site for download, as many extension developers do. Or better yet, do both! The more exposure your extension receives, the more likely it is that people will find it and use it.

The Dynamic Web Address Server Behavior

Now you will build the second server behavior. This time around, we will be a little more succinct about the process. Of course, we'll give you the necessary code and instructions, but if you've read this far through this chapter, you'll already know how to do what we're telling you to do as you go along. It's really very easy!

The Code

This extension is intended to make it easy for the user to make a web address that is stored in a database and displayed on a page into a real link. To do this, you will need to know four things from the user.

- The name of the recordset

- The name of the column in the recordset with the web address in it

- The text the user would like to display on the page as the link

- The target that the link should use (same page, new page, and the like)

The code will also need to allow for web addresses that have been stored in the database without the required http:// prefix.

The code to cater for all these requirements is as follows:

```
<%
RobGT_www = (RecordsetName.Fields.Item("ColumnName").Value)
RobGT_Text = "Link Text"
RobGT_Target = "Target"
IF RobGT_www <> "" AND NOT IsNULL(RobGT_www) THEN
  IF LEFT(RobGT_www,7) <> "http://" THEN
    Response.Write("<a href='http://" & RobGT_www &_
"' target='" & RobGT_Target & "'>" & RobGT_Text & "</a>")
  ELSE
    Response.Write("<a href='" & RobGT_www &_
"' target='" & RobGT_Target & "'>" & RobGT_Text & "</a>")
  END IF
END IF
%>
```

We used our standard variable naming convention, which makes our variable names unique on the page and prevents any naming conflicts that might arise.

Building the Server Behavior

1. Now you have to get your code into the Server Behavior Builder. With a page open, click Server Behaviors ➤ + ➤ New Server Behavior to begin the creation process.

2. Type **Dynamic web address** as the name for this server behavior and leave ASP VBScript selected as the Document type. Click Next.

3. Add a code block and accept the default name for it. Then copy and paste your server behavior code into the Code Block window. Select the RecordsetName text and create a parameter called **Recordset name**. Select the ColumnName text and create a parameter called **www link column**. Select the Link Text text and create a parameter called **Link text**. Finally, select the Target text and create a parameter called **Target**.

The code block should look like this.

```
<%
RobGT_www = (@@Recordset name@@.Fields.Item("@@www link column@@").Value)
RobGT_Text = "@@Link text@@"
RobGT_Target = "@@Target@@"
IF RobGT_www <> "" AND NOT IsNULL(RobGT_www) THEN
  IF LEFT(RobGT_www,7) <> "http://" THEN
    Response.Write("<a href='http://" & RobGT_www &_
"' target='" & RobGT_Target & "'>" & RobGT_Text & "</a>")
  ELSE
    Response.Write("<a href='" & RobGT_www &_
"'  target='" & RobGT_Target & "'>" & RobGT_Text & "</a>")
  END IF
END IF
%>
```

4. Set the point of insertion for your code. Select Relative to the Selection in the Insert code select list, and Replace the Selection in the Relative position select list. Click the Advanced >> button to show the remaining options. Make sure the Identifier check box is selected. Then select the Dynamic web address_block1.

    Your finished dialog box should look like Figure 8-15.

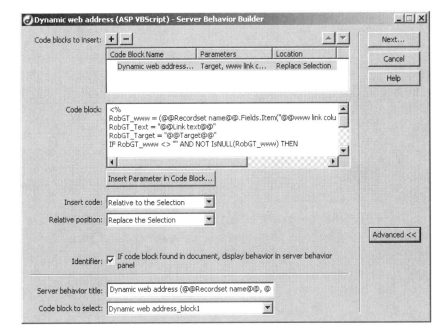

Figure 8-15. The completed Server Behavior Builder dialog box

5. Click Next to go to the final dialog box. Here you need to define which parameters should use which form elements. These should be set as follows, and in the following order:

   • The Recordset name should use a Recordset Menu

   • The www link column should use a Recordset Field Menu

   • The Link text should use a Text Field and Target should use a List Menu

   You use a list menu for Target because there are only four possible options that the user can enter and having them choose one from a list means that they can't enter an incorrect value (which would result in the finished code not working). You will finish the Target list off by editing the interface's .htm page shortly.

6. Use the sorting arrows above the parameter list to make sure the elements are in the correct order.

   Your finished dialog should look like Figure 8-16.

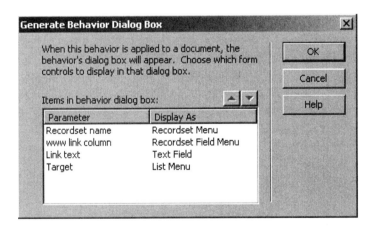

Figure 8-16. The Generate Behavior dialog box with items in order

7. Click OK to generate the server behavior.

Editing the Interface

1. Open the server behavior interface file (the .htm file), which you should be able to find in your user configuration folder. Ours is here:

   C:\Documents and Settings\<login username here>\
   Application Data\Macromedia\Dreamweaver MX 2004\
   Configuration\serverbehaviors\ASP_Vbs

2. With the file loaded in Dreamweaver MX 2004, click to select the Recordset name select list and go into Code view. Change its width to 200px and do the same for the www link column select list. Now set the width of the Link text text field to 150px and finally, set the Target select list to 150px too.

3. Switch back to Design view and select the Target list again. Click the List values button in the Properties inspector and add the following entries:

   - Self   _self

   - Blank   _blank

   - Top   _top

   - Parent   _parent

   Your completed list values dialog box should look like Figure 8-17.

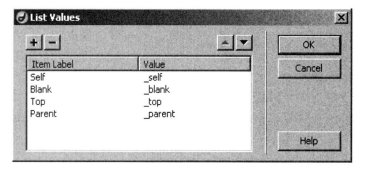

Figure 8-17. The completed List Values dialog box

4. Click OK to apply the values to the Target select list.

   Finally, you will add a default value to the Link text field.

5. Select the Link text field and in the Init val field of the Properties inspector, type "**& RobGT_www &**". Make sure to include the double quotation marks to ensure that the correct code is applied to the page. This code uses the variable name that contains the web address value.

> **NOTE** *If your variables have different names, obviously, you would need to use the variable name that you assigned.*

If you would prefer not to use the web address as the link text, type something else, such as **Visit our website** to have that text appear on the page instead of the web address.

Add the Help Button

Assuming that you have already created a simple .html document that shows the user how to use this server behavior, you need to link to that document. You do that by adding a little JavaScript code to the page that tells Dreamweaver MX 2004 to render a Help button on the interface, and where the help file is located. The code for this should be added to the ‹script› section of the interface document, just before the closing ‹/script› tag, which should be somewhere around line 283 in this file.

If your help document is called dynamicwwwhelp.htm, the code you need to add will look like this:

```
function displayHelp(){
  var varConfigFolder = dw.getUserConfigurationPath();
  var varHelpDocument = "ExtensionsHelp/dynamicwwwhelp.htm";
  dreamweaver.browseDocument(varConfigFolder + varHelpDocument);
}
```

Save and close the document. When you restart Dreamweaver MX 2004, your interface changes will take effect and the finished server behavior interface should look something like Figure 8-18 when in use.

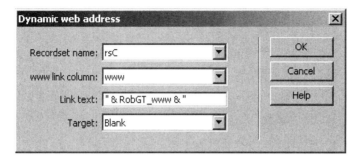

Figure 8-18. The Server Behavior dialog box in use

Summary

This chapter focused on extending the server-side capabilities of Dreamweaver MX 2004 by building two server behaviors. You built one server behavior that will help you easily maintain the paragraph formatting of text coming from a database, and another to display a web address that comes from a database.

Server behaviors are only one aspect of the extensibility of Dreamweaver MX 2004. There is plenty of room to add behaviors, commands, objects, and more.

Unfortunately, there isn't a builder mechanism like the SBB to help you build these other types of extensions; instead, you need to brush up on your JavaScript skills and write them by hand.

For a great learning resource, especially for building behaviors, commands, and objects, dive into Dreamweaver MX 2004's configuration folder and open some of the behaviors, commands, and objects that are there to see how they work.

CHAPTER 9

Debugging and Error Handling

As you worked through this book, you probably came across some error messages or encountered things that just don't quite work as expected. Dealing with error messages and bugs is just part of life as a web developer; however, as you gain experience, you will be better able to recognize the errors and know what to do when you see one. In this chapter, we explain some of the more common errors and bugs as well as touch on techniques for finding seemingly random bugs. You will explore:

- **ASP errors**: When your application causes an error that appears on the screen.

- **SQL errors**: When the error is a problem with your SQL, and how to test SQL using Access and SQL Server.

- **Bugs**: Techniques that makes locating bugs easier.

- **Resources**: Where to get help when everything else fails.

Errors

If an error message appears on the screen, you are lucky! Usually an error message will get you well on your way to understanding where the problem lies and how to fix it.

Viewing Error Messages

If you are using Internet Explorer and it is set to Show Friendly Error Messages, you won't see the real error message. To show the real error, open Internet Explorer and select Tools ➤ Internet Options ➤ Advanced. Then uncheck Show Friendly HTTP Error Messages, as shown in Figure 9-1.

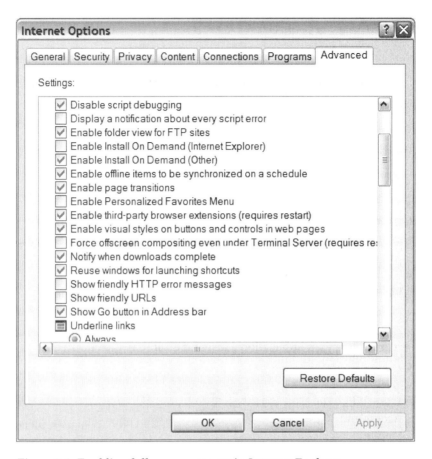

Figure 9-1. Enabling full error messages in Internet Explorer

ASP Errors—Script Errors

If you are using the Dreamweaver server behaviors and not writing or editing the code yourself, you may not see too many script errors. Script errors are due to a problem with something in your code, and you will usually find these fairly quickly because the page will generally not load until the error is corrected. We will cover the most common errors, particularly those that are difficult to understand if you haven't seen them before, and look at how to fix them. Check the end of this chapter for information on sites where you can get more help with any of these errors.

Subscript Out of Range

You will see the error shown in Figure 9-2 when working with an array.

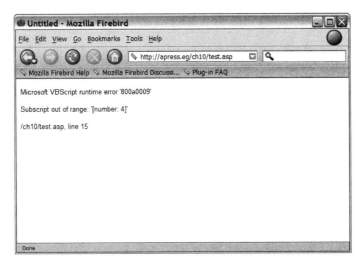

Figure 9-2. Subscript out of range

The range of an array is the number of elements in it. Therefore, if you have a one-dimensional array with four elements, myArray(0)—myArray(3), and then try to address myArray(4), you will get a subscript out of range error.

To fix this error you need to find out why your script is trying to address an array element that doesn't exist. It may be that you made a mistake in your script and are trying to access something that will never exist, however, you may get this message because under certain circumstances your array is smaller than you expect. In that case, you need to check the UBound of the array, which gives you its size before performing the action. For example, the following code gives a subscript out of range error:

```
<%
Dim myArray
myArray = array("item 1", "item 2", "item 3", "item 4")
response.write myArray(4)
%>
```

Check if there is another item in this array. If there is such an item, write the following:

```
<%
Dim myArray
myArray = array("item 1", "item 2", "item 3", "item 4")

if UBound(myArray) = 4 Then
    response.write myArray(4)
end if
%>
```

Type Mismatch

You will get a type mismatch error, as shown in Figure 9-3, if you compare two things that are of different types.

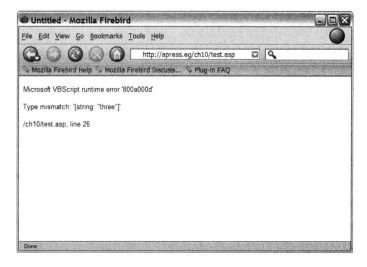

Figure 9-3. Type mismatch

For example, attempting to compare a string and an integer may cause a type mismatch error:

```
<%
Dim myInt, myString
myInt = 3
myString = "three"
if myInt + myString = 6 Then
    response.write "match!"
end if
%>
```

You can only compare things of the same type. If you are trying to compare two numeric values and are getting this error, then you can make sure that neither of them is identified as a string by turning it into an integer with the function CInt.

```
myInt = 3
CInt(myInt)
```

The code above will ensure that myInt is actually an integer for the comparison. Similarly, the function CStr will convert a variable into a string and CDate will convert to a date.

Variable Is Undefined

If you are developing with option Explicit (which we discuss later in this chapter), you will see the error message shown in Figure 9-4 if you have not defined a variable with dim.

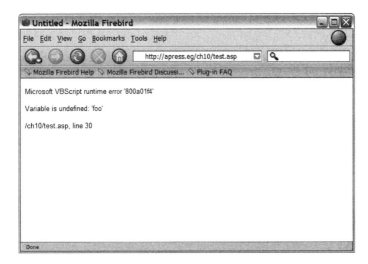

Figure 9-4. Variable is undefined.

The following will return this error:

```
<%
foo = "bar"
response.write foo
%>
```

To get rid of this error, define the variable foo using dim:

```
<%
Dim foo
foo = "bar"
response.write foo
%>
```

Expected Next/Loop/End/If

Figure 9-5 shows the error that you will get if you forget to close a loop statement.

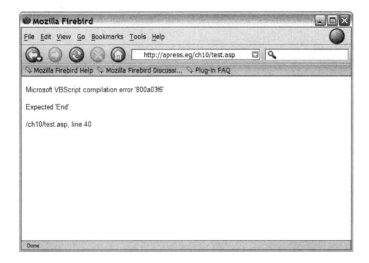

Figure 9-5. Expected "End"

These errors are usually due to forgetting to close a loop or If statement.

```
<%
if foo = "bar" then
    response.write "match"
%>
```

The code above will cause an error because there is no End If.

```
<%
if foo = "bar" then
    response.write "match"
End If
%>
```

Name Redefined

If you define a variable more than once, you will get the error shown in Figure 9-6.

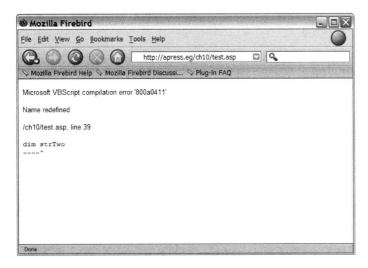

Figure 9-6. Name redefined

Often this is because you have already defined the variable in an Include file and then used it again on the page.

```
<%
dim strOne, strTwo
response.write strOne
dim strTwo
response.write strTwo
%>
```

Unterminated String Constant

The error shown in Figure 9-7 means you did not terminate a string with a quotation mark.

In a complex string with lots of variables, it can be easy to forget a closing quotation mark. The string My name is Rachel has not been terminated, so it gives the error message just shown. To fix the problem, put a quotation mark on the end.

```
<%
response.write "My name is Rachel
%>
```

Figure 9-7. Unterminated string constant

ODBC Errors

ODBC errors are a frequent occurrence when working with Dreamweaver, particularly if you are using an Access database as it is easy for the database to become locked because it is being accessed by Dreamweaver and then refuse to let you view the page in a web browser. The following errors are commonplace.

Operation Must Use an Updateable Query

The error shown in Figure 9-8 usually occurs because the permissions on your Access database file are preventing your application from writing to it.

The error will typically occur when you do an update or an insert. To correct the permissions, browse to your file in Windows Explorer. Right-click the .mdb file and select Properties. Then click the Security tab, as shown in Figure 9-9.

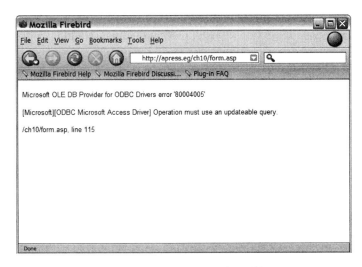

Figure 9-8. Operation must use an updateable query.

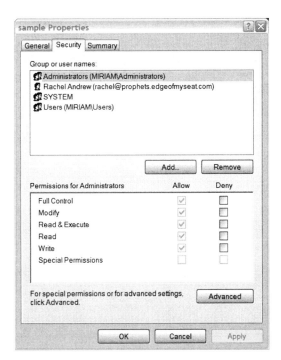

Figure 9-9. Security properties

The Internet Guest Account (IUSR) should be listed in the Group or user names box with Full Permissions checked. If it isn't listed, you need to add it. Click Add and in the Enter the object names to select box, type **IUSR**, as shown in Figure 9-10.

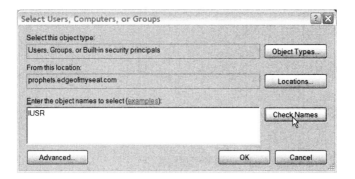

Figure 9-10. Select the IUSR user.

Now click the Check Names button to complete the entry.

Click OK and the IUSR account should appear. Give this account full permissions, as shown in Figure 9-11.

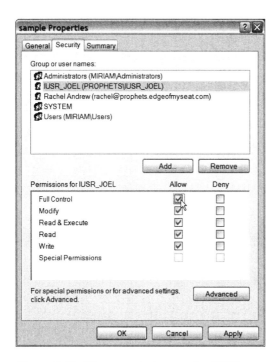

Figure 9-11. Give permissions to the IUSR user.

Other, less likely reasons for this error are that you are connected to the database via a DSN that is set to Read Only, or you are trying to update a database object that is not updateable. If you are simply trying to do an insert or update on a table, the latter is unlikely to be the cause.

Cannot Open File (Access)

The error shown in Figure 9-12 may appear within Dreamweaver when you are trying to use Live Data, or you may see it when you preview in a browser.

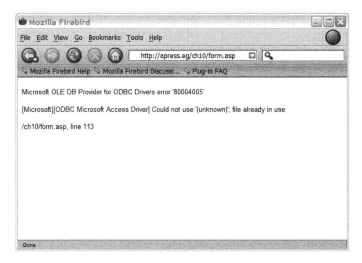

Figure 9-12. File already in use

There are a variety of things that can cause this error:

- **The database is open in Design view**: If the database is open in Design view, you will see this error because Access has locked the database to prevent it from being updated. Close Access, or switch to another view.

- **Permissions**: Check that the IUSR account has the correct permissions (as shown earlier); incorrect permissions can also cause this error.

SQL Errors

If you are using the Dreamweaver server behaviors, you are unlikely to see many SQL Errors, and the ones you do see are most likely errors caused by the expected variables not being passed to the script. If you are writing your own ASP code, you are likely to come across more errors—even if they are just due to typos they can sometimes be very tricky to diagnose.

Arguments Out of Acceptable Range

The error shown in Figure 9-13 will appear if you are trying to create a recordset.

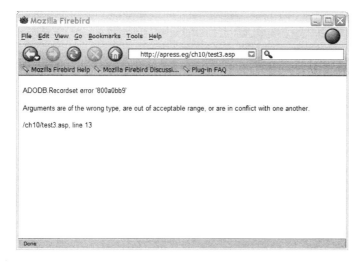

Figure 9-13. Arguments are of the wrong type.

A common reason for this error is that you have misspelled a variable in the connection.

Syntax Error in Insert Into Statement

The error shown in Figure 9-14 is commonly a result of the use of reserved words or an error in your SQL statement.

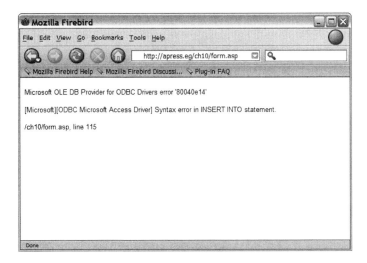

Figure 9-14. Syntax error in statement

Reserved words are those that have special meaning in SQL. For example, if you use a word that is used as field name, you will get an error. Words that are often used as field names include *date*, *money*, and *time*. The documentation for your database includes lists of these reserved words, but the easiest way to prevent this error is to prefix your field names with something so there is no chance you will use a field name word incorrectly. There are various prefix conventions, including the following:

- **Prefix all tables with tbl**: tblUsers

- **Prefix views/queries with v**: vUsers

- **Prefix field names within the table with the table name**: userFirstName

If you are sure that you haven't used any reserved words, check whether your SQL statement is complete. Is it using input that perhaps has been passed to the page? Later in this section we will discuss ways to track down errors that don't have an immediately obvious cause.

Date Type Mismatch

This error, shown in Figure 9-15, usually occurs on an insert or update because you are trying to insert data into a field that is not what the field expects.

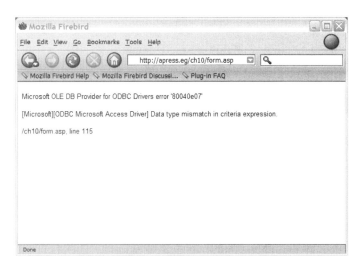

Figure 9-15. Data type mismatch in criteria expression

For example:

```
strSQL = "INSERT INTO tblUsers (username) VALUES (" & Rachel Andrew & ")"
```

The data Rachel Andrew is a string, and the field in the database is going to be some kind of text field, which means that the data must be enclosed in single quotes.

```
strSQL = "INSERT INTO tblUsers (username) VALUES ('" & Rachel Andrew & "')"
```

If you are using the Insert Record server behavior, check that you have selected the right kind of data. Click the down arrow to the right of the Submit as box. In the Form elements box, the data type appears in parentheses after the information about which form field is inserted into which database field, as shown in Figure 9-16. This ensures that Dreamweaver treats the data in the correct way when it adds the code for the insert or update.

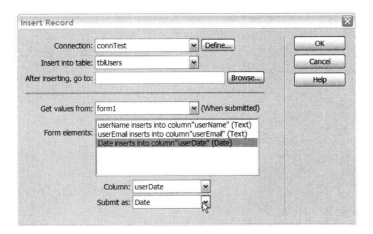

Figure 9-16. Checking the Insert Record dialog box

If you still get the error, another possibility is that username does not exist in the database. Check that you have spelled the field name correctly and that it exists.

Testing SQL

If none of the obvious problems apply and you still get a SQL error, you need to look a bit deeper to see where the problem is occurring.

On the Page

The first thing to check is whether your SQL string is correct once it has been parsed. Also check that any input variables area is getting into the string. If you have a form that submits to a script that does an insert or update and form variables are not picked up by the script, you will get an error.

The easiest way to check this is to print the SQL out to the page before it is executed. If you are writing your own ASP, simply comment out the execute statement and instead add

```
Response.write strSQL
```

strSQL is your SQL string.

If you are using the server behaviors, you will have to find the SQL string that Dreamweaver creates. If you look for the section in which the server behaviors actually do the action you should be able to find where the server behaviors are executed. An Insert Record server behavior looks like this:

```
If (Not MM_abortEdit) Then
    ' execute the insert
    Set MM_editCmd = Server.CreateObject("ADODB.Command")
    MM_editCmd.ActiveConnection = MM_editConnection
    MM_editCmd.CommandText = MM_editQuery
    MM_editCmd.Execute
    MM_editCmd.ActiveConnection.Close

    If (MM_editRedirectUrl <> "") Then
      Response.Redirect(MM_editRedirectUrl)
    End If
  End If
```

You can see that there is a comment in the code, execute the insert, that alerts you to the fact that that the insert occurs in this section. To write the SQL, comment out the following line by putting an apostrophe in front of it:

```
MM_editCmd.Execute
```

Then add the following:

```
Response.Write MM_editQuery
```

If your script redirects to another page after a successful insert, you will also want to comment out the following three lines so the script doesn't do the redirect:

```
If (MM_editRedirectUrl <> "") Then
    Response.Redirect(MM_editRedirectUrl)
    End If
```

If it redirects, you will not be able to see your printed out SQL string as you will be whisked to another page!

Now when you run your page, it won't try to do the `insert` or other action, it will simply display the SQL that it would have used, as shown in Figure 9-17.

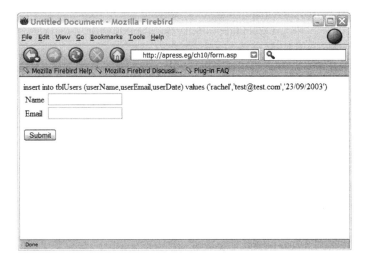

Figure 9-17. The SQL printed to the screen

Often just doing this is enough to see what the problem is. If all fields are required in the database and one is missing, you know that you need to find out why the data is not getting into the SQL. Perhaps you have named a field incorrectly or are not using validation to ensure that required fields are complete.

A common problem occurs when you post data that you are going to use to select a record from the database, such as when you create an edit record page. If you name the ID that you are posting differently to the ID that the page is expecting, you will end up trying to do a select with the following:

```
SELECT * FROm tblUsers WHERE userID =
```

With no ID after the equal sign (=), you will get an error because no record can be selected. Displaying this on the screen will show you that the ID is empty. You can check that the ID is being sent and that it matches what is expected on the page.

Access

If you can't see anything wrong with the SQL as parsed, you should test it from within the database to make sure it is returning the results that you want. You can test SQL from within Access by creating a Query using the SQL view.

1. Open the Access database.

2. In the panel, select Queries and double-click Create Query in Design View.

3. Close the Show Table dialog box, and you should see a Select Query window, as shown in Figure 9-18.

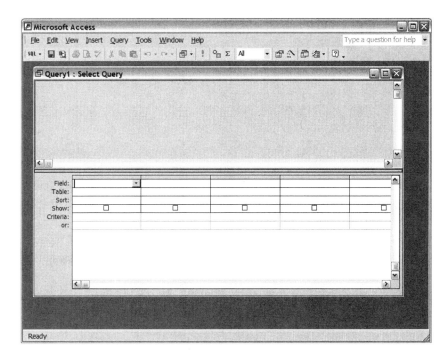

Figure 9-18. The Design view

4. Click the SQL menu, and click SQL View, as shown in Figure 9-19.

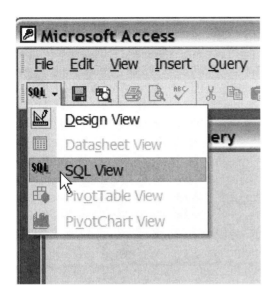

Figure 9-19. Select SQL view.

Use the blank box with `select` prefilled to test your Queries.

> **CAUTION** *Remember that anything you do in this box will affect your database, so* `inserts` *or* `updates` *tested here will happen in the database.*

You can paste the SQL `Response.Write` into this box to see whether it is returning the data that you expect. Sometimes the script fails because the database isn't returning the data that you expect, so checking it here gives you an easy way to see what is coming back. After pasting your SQL into the box, click the exclamation mark (!) icon to run the query. If you are testing a select query, Access returns the data from that query in Datasheet view—to go back to your SQL, use the menu again, as shown in Figure 9-20.

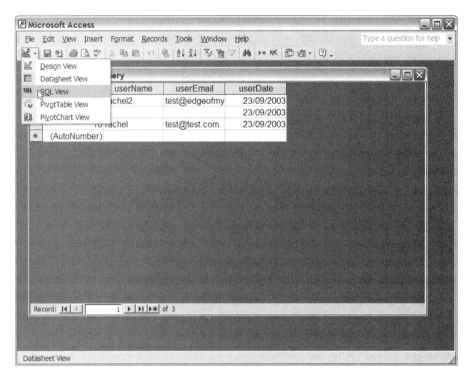

Figure 9-20. Returning to the SQL after running the query

If you run a query that will affect your data, Access will warn you of what it is about to do, as shown in Figure 9-21.

Figure 9-21. Warning in Access

If Access returns an error, edit your query until it returns the data or does the action that you were expecting. If the data returned is not what you expected, it is generally easier to edit and test the query in Access than it is to do it on the page. Once you are finished testing, you can copy the new query back into your script and replace the hard-coded variables with your dynamic ones. When you close the query, Access prompts you to save it. You do not need to save queries that are just for test purposes so click No.

SQL Server—Query Analyzer

The SQL Server tools include Query Analyzer, which is just for testing queries, You can also use Query Analyzer instead of Enterprise Manager for managing your database if you are comfortable with SQL. If you have the SQL Server tools installed, open Query Analyzer (shown in Figure 9-22), which gets installed in the same location as Enterprise Manager.

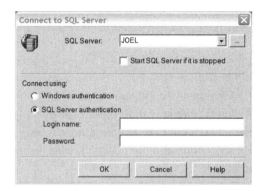

Figure 9-22. Connect to SQL server.

To log into your database, give Query Analyzer your login information. Once logged in, select the database that you are working with using the drop-down menu of available databases on the Menu bar. In Query Analyzer, the main screen includes the box where you enter your queries and view the results. In the left panel, all of the databases available to you are displayed, and you can expand them in order to see table and column names, as shown in Figure 9-23.

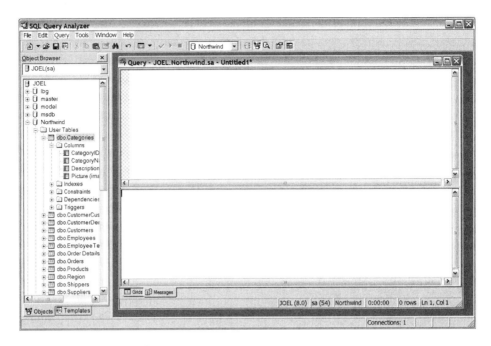

Figure 9-23. Query Analyzer

To test a query, simply paste it into the top half of the Query box. As with Access, any queries that you run here will be run against your database; however, in SQL Server you can also test that a query is formed correctly before running it on your database. To test a query, paste it into the box and then click the blue check mark on the toolbar, shown in Figure 9-24.

If the query is syntactically correct, in the bottom half of the box you will see the message "The command(s) completed successfully". If there was an error, you will see some information about that error instead.

To run the query on the database, click the green arrow. A report on what has been done will appear in the bottom of the panel, as shown in Figure 9-25, or if you have done a select, the data will appear.

As with Access you can continue testing until your query behaves as you expect before transferring it back to the page.

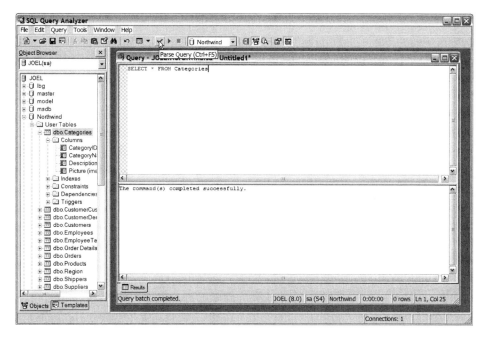

Figure 9-24. Running a SQL command

Figure 9-25. A select *statement returns data.*

Bugs

A bug is anything that doesn't behave the way you expect it to. Your email script sending out duplicate emails when you only want to send one is a bug, a login page that gives access to people who don't have the correct passwords is a bug, an error message that only appears under certain circumstances is a bug. Bugs that don't break the application or error consistently can be very difficult to track down. Fixing these bugs is usually the easy part—finding out where they are and why they are occurring is the real challenge!

Re-Creating the Problem

The first thing you need to be able to do to fix a bug is to make it happen again. This is not always as easy as it sounds. When users report a bug, often the only data they can provide is along the lines of "it broke," "…all of a sudden," and "I can't remember exactly what I was doing but…."

All you know is that something somewhere isn't working properly. Getting useful information from your users is an art in itself. If you can speak to the person who fields these support requests (who may be your client), you might be able to give him or her some understanding of the questions to ask in order to get useful information.

User Input

Probably the most common reason that something breaks after it has been released to the users or to the client is user input. Often users enter random data into form fields. If you are stumped by a problem, try to find out what the user was trying to input at the time and try it yourself. Things that frequently happen include:

- **Users enter data of the wrong type**: As we discussed earlier, if the script expects an integer, or a database table expects a numeric data type and the user enters something other that what is expected, you will get an error. To avoid this you need to validate the user input and return a message explaining what needs to go into that field. It is always a good idea to also add some JavaScript validation as well, however, don't rely on this because users turn JavaScript off or may be using browsers that do not have JavaScript support.

- **Users enter data larger than your database field expects**: If you expect a user to enter only a few words and then you type an essay, you will get an error if the database field is not large enough to contain the data. Again, validation of user input can prevent this.

Working Through the Process

If you know an error is happening somewhere but you're not quite sure where, you can step through the application, displaying information to the screen, and checking the database as you go, step by step, until you find the point at which it breaks. If there are different paths that you can take through the process, make a note of which ones you have covered.

As you take each step, check that any changes to the database happen as expected by manually checking the database. Check that any variables that need to be returned and passed to the next script are getting returned. If for some reason a variable that is meant to go to a hidden form field doesn't make it there, your update won't work. You can spend a long time looking at the update script before you realize that the problem occurs earlier.

In this situation you can obviously view source and check the hidden field. Another thing to do is to write the variables at the top of the page so that you can see at a glance what you have. Anything from a form sent by the `post` method will be accessible with the following:

```
Response.write Request.Form("your_variable")
```

Anything in the `QueryString` is accessible with

```
Response.Write Request.QueryString("your_variable")
```

If you just want to see what is being sent in a form `post` simply write

```
Response.Write Request.Form
```

Another way to isolate the problem in a complex script is to comment out sections until you find the point at which the error occurs. You can also simplify the problem by commenting out sections that you know are working so that you only need to concentrate on the problematic part.

You could also set up a test case in isolation from the rest of the script. This will help you determine whether the problem is with this section or with its interaction with the rest of the script. If you ask for help on a mailing list, send the test case instead of the whole problem—people will be more likely to help you if they don't have to wade through hundreds of lines of code!

By stepping through the application logically you should be able to discover at which point things stop being correct. When you are up against a seemingly mysterious error it can be incredibly frustrating—the best advice if all logic fails is to take a break—get away from the code for a little while and then come back and work through it step by step.

Coding to Avoid Bugs

There are various techniques that you can use that will help prevent bugs in the first place and that make finding them when they do occur far easier.

Comment Your Code

It may sound obvious, but it's easy to forget! Commenting your ASP code will make your life much easier when you need to debug the script. Although it seems like you can recite the code in your sleep when you are working on an application, after a couple of months you'll never remember what each part does.

Use Option Explicit

To use Option Explicit, as shown on line 2 of Figure 9-26, open your ASP page and underneath the language declaration type

```
Option Explicit
```

```
1  <%@LANGUAGE="VBSCRIPT" CODEPAGE="1252"%>
2  <%Option Explicit%>
3  <!--#include virtual="/Connections/connTest.asp" -->
4  <%
5  Dim rsUsers
6  Dim rsUsers_numRows
7
8  Set rsUsers = Server.CreateObject("ADODB.Recordset")
9  rsUsers.ActiveConnection = MM_connTest_STRING
10 rsUsers.Source = "SELECT * FROM tblUsers"
11 rsUsers.CursorType = 0
12 rsUsers.CursorLocation = 2
13 rsUsers.LockType = 1
14 rsUsers.Open()
15
16 rsUsers_numRows = 0
17 %>
18 <!DOCTYPE html PUBLIC "-//W3C//DTD XHTML 1.0 Transitional//EN" "http://www.w3.org/T1
19 <html xmlns="http://www.w3.org/1999/xhtml">
```

Figure 9-26. Option Explicit added to the ASP code

This tells the ASP engine that you are going to explicitly declare all your variables. You declare variables by using dim. If you do not declare a variable, the page will return an error.

Declaring your variables is a good thing. First, it makes debugging easier. In the following example, we are not using Option Explicit; we are simply writing out the contents of the variable to the screen:

```
<%
Dim myName
myName = "Rachel"
response.write "My name is " & mName
%>
```

However, we misspelled the variable—we typed mName instead of myName. The result of this is that the variable doesn't appear on the screen (as shown in Figure 9-27).

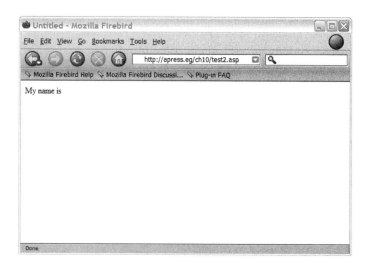

Figure 9-27. The partial string in a browser

If you had Option Explicit turned on, though, when you tried to run the page, you would have received an error message that the variable mName is undefined on line 13, as shown in Figure 9-28.

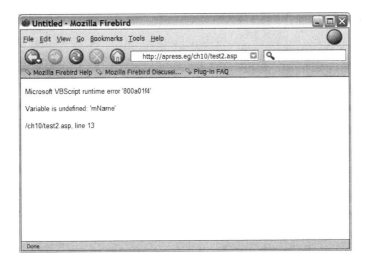

Figure 9-28. Variable is undefined

You know you don't have a variable called mName, so when you look at line 13, the typo is obvious. In this simple example you would probably spot your mistake fairly quickly, but if you were working on a script of several hundred lines, just figuring out that you made a typing mistake when entering the variable could take a long time.

The other reason why you should use Option Explicit is because explicitly declaring your variables increases the speed at which your page loads. If you declare your variables at the top of the page, the ASP engine can go through, find them, and allocate memory to them all in one pass. It doesn't need to wait until you use the variable to allocate memory to it and so resources are better used, which can result in faster load times.

Naming Variables

You will save yourself a lot of stress when you come back to an application if you use sensible names for variables. For example, if you write the username to a variable a,

```
a = Request.QueryString("userName")
```

this might seem like a good idea at the time, but when you have a problem with the application, perhaps six months after the last you looked at it, will you remember that a = username?

Use a variable name that reflects what the variable contains.

```
strUsername = Request.QueryString("userName")
```

This will save you a lot of grief later on.

Additionally, use a standard prefix before the sensible name to identify the type of data being stored. Prefixing an integer with i and a string with str is common practice but it doesn't so much matter what convention you use, as long as you stick to it. Identifying in the variable name what the variable is makes it much easier to spot a problem (such as when you are trying to compare a string with an integer and so on).

Including Repeated Elements in Variables

In your script you might use data from a form post or recordset more than once on the page. You could write out the data each time as

```
Response.Write Request.QueryString("userName")
```

or

```
Response.Write rsUsers("userName")
```

However, if you write that data into a variable, you don't have to keep going back to the request or recordset object to retrieve the data each time, and it makes for less typing and less chance of typing errors.

```
strName = Request.QueryString("userName")
```

or

```
strName = rsUsers("userName")
```

Now you simply use strName in your code whenever you need to write out the name.

```
Response.Write strName
```

Display Errors on the Screen

You may come across on error resume next in ASP Scripts, although Dreamweaver does not insert this. Using on error resume next means that the ASP engine will attempt to continue even if it comes across an error that would otherwise halt the script and error to the screen.

This can be very useful in production code because users are less likely to see errors, however, if it is used during development it can make it all but impossible to locate the error because the application continues on regardless and the final state of the application may be very far removed from the point at which the error occurred. If a script you are working with is being problematic and is using on error resume next, comment it out and run the script again—you may well find that the error is easy to spot once the error is displayed on the screen.

Where to Get Help

Eventually you will come up against something that you can't solve easily, something for which even isolating location of the problem doesn't help. However, you can console yourself with the thought that you are unlikely to be the only ASP developer in the world that has seen this and search the web for answers.

Web Resources

Although the 4 Guys from Rolla web site appears at first glance to be very ASP.NET-centric, this is one of the best resources for ASP. There are lots of articles about how to do specific tasks, some good generic scripts, and advice for all levels of ASP developers from the beginner to the very experienced.

http://www.4guysfromrolla.com/

Search the Microsoft Developer Network for technical information about error messages and other problems. It can be very difficult to navigate but it is well indexed by Google so a search for the problem using Google may well turn up the correct article here!

http://msdn.microsoft.com/

Search the Dreamweaver tech notes if you are getting error messages when using the Dreamweaver server behaviors.

http://www.macromedia.com/support/dreamweaver/more_issues.html

SQL Team is the best place to search if you have errors and problems relating to SQL Server databases.

```
http://www.sqlteam.com/
```

Don't forget Google! Type your error message in quotes into the Google search box and see what is returned. Many of the sites just listed are quite hard to search, but Google will often return the relevant article quicker than if you had searched the site directly.

```
http://www.google.com
```

Newsgroups and Forums

If you have searched and are unable to work out the problem yourself, try posting to a relevant newsgroup or forum. You are more likely to get useful answers if you

- Search the newsgroup first. Someone may have already asked your question and the answer is already posted.

- Use a subject line that explains your problem briefly. Don't just say "Help!"

- Explain your problem clearly. State the steps that you have taken and what you have tried already.

- Be polite—don't get stressed out with people if they try to help and it doesn't work. If the answer helps you, say thank you. It will also help other people searching the group for the same problem if they can see what solved it for you.

Here are a few options:

`http://groups.google.com`: You can search across lots of groups by using Google, a good first place to start and can help you to find relevant groups to post to.

`http://webforums.macromedia.com/dreamweaver/`: The Macromedia Dreamweaver forums These can also be accessed via a newsreader by going to `news://forums.macromedia.com`.

`News://news.microsoft.com:microsoft.public.inetserver.asp.general`: This is the Microsoft ASP newsgroup, it is also accessible via Google groups.

Summary

In this chapter, you looked at some of the common errors that you may encounter and we discussed how to deal with some of these specific errors. We also discussed how to isolate errors and develop using best practices to see fewer errors. Finally you saw how to help ensure that those errors that crop up are easy to fix.

CHAPTER 10

Final Case Study

IN THIS CHAPTER you will take the techniques you learned in this book and apply them in a real-world situation. You will create a compact yet functional web application that will contain the following elements:

- **Dynamic content pages**: Including a home page with dynamic content as well as list and detail pages

- **User Authentication**: Including login facilities and access restriction for pages and parts of pages

- **User Registration**: Enabling new users to sign up, and existing users to edit their membership details

- **Contact Form**: Sending email from a form to the site owner or administrator

- **Administration pages**: Enabling the site administrator to manage users and site content

Once you have mastered the techniques used in this chapter you should be ready to take them out into the real world and apply them to the applications you are building. As a good number of the techniques used have already been covered at some point during the book—don't be afraid to flip back and forth, reminding yourself as necessary.

Setting Up the Site

The first step in starting any project with Dreamweaver is to set up a site. This helps Dreamweaver to keep track of file paths, and helps you to keep your project in one, tightly contained bundle.

Configuring a Dreamweaver Site

1. In the Files panel, click Manage Sites ➤ New ➤ Site. The Site Definition Wizard appears, as shown in Figure 10-1. At this point you can chose between Basic and Advanced mode. For the purposes of this exercise, flip over into Advanced using the tab at the top of the window.

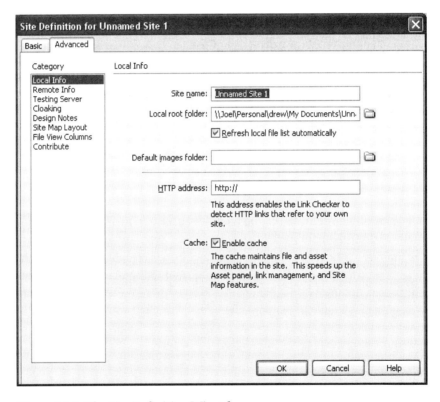

Figure 10-1. The Site Definition Wizard

As you can see, this is now pretty much a blank canvas for all your settings. From the top down, the following are typical settings to configure the site to work with your local web server. If you are working with a dedicated web server on your network, you'll need to take account of this in your own settings. (Speak to the person who runs your network if you're unsure of any settings. If that's you, best of luck!)

- **Site name**: Case Study

- **Local root folder**: C:\Inetpub\wwwroot\

- **HTTP address**: `http://localhost/`

2. Move to the Testing Server category and pick the following settings to let Dreamweaver know how you're going to be testing your work:

- **Server model**: ASP VBScript

- **Access**: Local/Network

- **Testing server folder**: C:\Inetpub\wwwroot\

- **URL prefix**: `http://localhost/`

3. Click OK to confirm your changes, and complete your configuration of the site you'll be using for this chapter. Next, you'll configure the local web server so that it's ready to serve up the files.

Setting Up the Web Server

Once your site is configured in Dreamweaver, you need to check your web server settings to make sure that both it and Dreamweaver are singing from the same song sheet.

1. Open the Internet Information Services manager. Right-click Default Website (or whichever site you are using) and choose Properties.

2. In the Home Directory tab, make sure that the Local Path matches the location you gave Dreamweaver as the path to your files. (In Figure 10-2, you can see that our files are stored on the F drive. This is because we're working with a networked web server. If you're working locally, this path will usually be C:\Inetpub\wwwroot. Once you're happy with your settings, click OK and exit the IIS Manager.

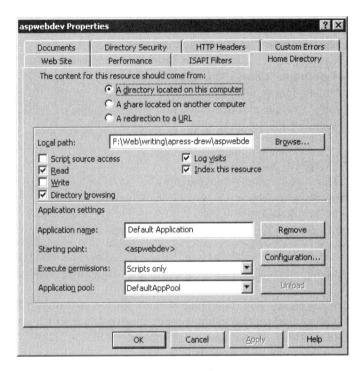

Figure 10-2. The Home Directory tab

Testing Your Setup

Before you go any further, it's a good idea to test that everything is working as you expect. Checking this now will prevent any confusion later when your own fallible code is involved!

1. Switch back to Dreamweaver and create a new ASP VBScript page. Save it in the root of your new site as default.asp. In Code view, enter the following code between the body tags:

```
<h1>Hello World!</h1>
<%=ScriptEngine & ScriptEngineMajorVersion & "." &
ScriptEngineMinorVersion%>
```

This short snippet of ASP simply writes the name and version of the scripting engine that your web server is using. It's an easy and useful way to check that your page is working as an ASP page.

2. Switch into Design view and enable Live Data View from the Document toolbar. If all goes well, you'll get no errors, and a page that looks a little like Figure 10-3.

Figure 10-3. Live Data View of default.asp

3. This should indicate that everything is working correctly, but as a final test, browse to your web site in a browser and check that the page is displayed well there too.

Building the Page Framework

Now that the site is working, it's time to build the folder structure that you will be using and create the necessary framework files to support your application. For this project, you'll use server-side Includes to provide the general page framework. This will help keep individual pages free from code clutter.

1. Create a new folder in the root of your site called **Includes**.

2. Create a new basic HTML page (not an ASP page) and save it as header.asp in the Includes folder. In Code view, delete the closing body and html tags and resave the page. This will form the uniform header for your site.

3. After the opening body tag, use the Insert Div Tag object from the Layout category of the Insert bar to insert three new div tags. Assign them the following IDs:

    *   **navigation**: This will hold the navigation menu for the site.

    *   **login**: This will be the container for a login box.

    *   **content**: This will hold the main content for each page.

        ```
        <div id="navigation"></div>
        <div id="login"></div>
        <div id="content"></div>
        ```

4. Delete the last closing div tag to leave the content div open, and then resave.

5. Create another new page, this time saving it as footer.asp. In Code view, delete everything *except* the closing body and html tags. Add a closing div tag as the first line of the file to close the content div tag you opened in the header. Resave the page to form the site's footer Include.

6. Delete the original default.asp page you used to test your configuration. Create a new ASP page and save it as default.asp. In Code view, modify the file to replace the opening and closing HTML segments with your new Include files.

    ```
    <%@LANGUAGE="VBSCRIPT" CODEPAGE="1252"%>
    <!--#include virtual="/includes/header.asp"-->
    Page content goes here
    <!--#include virtual="/includes/footer.asp"-->
    ```

The line marked "Page content goes here" sits between the body tags when the page is put together by the web server, so naturally this is where the HTML will go.

7. Test the new default page in your browser and check that everything works as expected. If you switch to Design view in Dreamweaver, you'll notice that the contents of the header and footer Include are processed by Dreamweaver to piece your page together as it will look when built by the web server. This is very useful indeed.

8. The site will need a number of supporting files such as images, JavaScript files, and probably most importantly, CSS files. Create a new folder at the root of your site called **assets** to contain these files. Organize your files within this folder however you like.

9. Create a new CSS document and save it into the assets folder as main.css. Return to the header Include, locate the CSS Styles panel in the Design panel group, and use the Attach Style Sheet button to attach main.css, as shown in Figure 10-4.

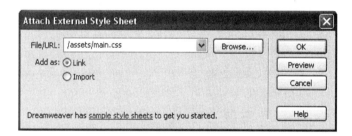

Figure 10-4. Attaching an external style sheet

10. Make sure that the file path starts with a slash (/) rather than a dot-dot-slash (../) so that the CSS file is referenced in relation to the root of the site rather than relative to any particular page. Save header.asp.

11. Open the CSS file and define any basic styles you like. Include a generic class for styling errors.

```
.error{
        font-weight: bold;
        color: #990000;
        background-color: #FFFFEE;
}
```

12. Use the style sheet to position the navigation, login, and content div tags to create a rough page layout. Here's the CSS we used to get the elements roughly in the right place:

```
body{
            margin: 0;
            padding: 0;
}

#login{
            position: absolute;
            top: 100px;
            left: 30px;
            width: 200px;
}

#navigation{
            position: absolute;
            top: 320px;
            left: 30px;
            width: 200px;
}

#content{
            position: relative;
            margin-left: 260px;
            margin-top: 100px;
}
```

13. Once you're done with your style sheet, save all your open files.

Creating a Database

The next important step is setting up the database that the web application will use to store its data.

Create a new database by using whichever database software you prefer. Because this is an ASP project, we'll use the most obvious choice—Microsoft SQL Server 2000—but you could use Microsoft Data Engine (MSDE), Microsoft Access, or even something like MySQL.

Defining Tables

1. Create a table of users. There are three types of user who will use this web application. The first is simply anonymous web visitors. You do not need to worry about this group as far as database design goes because they never log in. The second group is the general authenticated users. These are the users who hold accounts and have login details but are not site administrators. The final group is the site administrators themselves. To address the multiple groups, add a field to the users table indicating the group to which a user belongs, as shown in Table 10-1. One user can belong to one group.

Table 10-1. Users

Field	Data Type	Description
userId	int	The primary key field. Set this to auto-increment. (In SQL Server, set the Identity property to Yes.)
userName	varchar(50)	The username used to login.
userPassword	varchar(50)	The user's password (unencrypted).
userEmail	varchar(100)	The user's email address.
userFname	varchar(50)	The user's first name.
userSname	varchar(50)	The user's surname.
userAccessLevel	char(3)	USR or ADM to indicate site user or site administrator. Default value is USR.

For a real-world application, you may want to collect more user details than shown here. However, you should be able to discern how more fields can be easily added.

2. Save this table as **tblUsers**. Open the table and add two test users. Give one ADM access level, and the other USR.

3. Create a second table to store basic content for the site. Name it **tblArticles** and give it a nice, generic article structure, as outlined in Table 10-2.

Table 10-2. Articles

Field	Data Type	Description
articleId	int	The primary key field. Set this to auto-increment.
articleTitle	varchar(100)	Title or headline.
articleTeaser	varchar(255)	Teaser or lead-in paragraph.
articleBody	text	The full text of the article.
articleDate	datetime	The date the article was published. Default value is getDate().

You may want to enter a few rows of test data to help when using this table later on.

Setting Up a DSN

Once your simple database is set up, you need to create a mechanism by which to connect to it. We will use a DSN. If you'd prefer to use a different method of connecting to your database, now would be a good point to refer back to earlier in this book where we discuss the different methods of connecting to a database. You can choose whichever method suits your needs the best. For a DSN, use the ODBC Control Panel to set up a DSN on the web server to point to your database. We'll call ours dsnCaseStudy.

Defining a Connection

In order for it to be able to connect to our database, you need to tell Dreamweaver which DSN it can use. This is done by defining a connection.

1. Back in Dreamweaver, locate the Databases panel in the Application panel group. Click the plus sign (+) icon and choose Data Source Name (DSN).

2. Enter the details of your DSN as shown in Figure 10-5 and click Test.

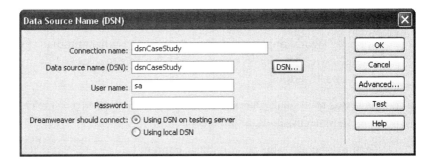

Figure 10-5. The Data Source Name dialog box

Dreamweaver confirms that the connection is fully operational, as shown in Figure 10-6.

Figure 10-6. Connection made successfully

A Note About Connection Include Paths

Dreamweaver automatically places an Include statement in each page to link it to the Connections Include. This is usually very helpful, but in certain circumstances it can cause your page not to load. This is the case particularly with IIS servers that have security settings locked down tightly and don't like you to use **parent paths**. The Dreamweaver Include statement looks something like this.

```
<!-- #include file="../Connections/dsnCaseStudy.asp" -->
```

If this is the case, modify the statement to use the virtual Include type, and to start with a leading slash.

```
<!-- #include virtual="/Connections/dsnCaseStudy.asp" -->
```

This should clear up most Include file problems.

Creating a Login Module

Now you will build a login module. A large part of this project depends on a user's access rights, so it's important to be able to log in and out of the site to test that it is working.

1. Open the header Include, and in the login div create a typical login form.

```
<form action="" method="post" name="loginform" id="loginform">
  <p>
    <label for="username">Username: </label><input name="username"↵
  type="text" id="username" />
  </p>
  <p>
    <label for="password">Password: </label><input name="password" ↵
type="password" id="password" />
  </p>
  <p>
    <input name="remember" type="checkbox" id="remember" value="true" /> ↵
<label for="remember">Remember details</label>
  </p>
  <p>
    <input type="submit" name="Submit" value="Log in" />
  </p>
</form>
```

2. Locate the Server Behaviors panel in the Application panel group and apply the Authentication/Log In User server behavior.

3. Map the form fields to the fields in your database table, matching username, password, and access level fields appropriately, as shown in Figure 10-7. Apply the server behavior. At this point you may need to check that Dreamweaver hasn't inserted an additional @language directive at the top of the page. If it has, remove it. You'll need to watch out for this as you go along—you can only have one @language directive per page.

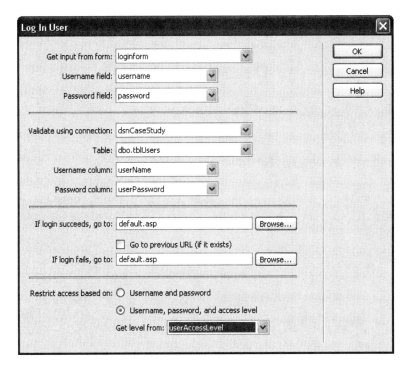

Figure 10-7. Mapping the form fields to the fields

Error Messages

Users don't get their login details correct every time they log in. It's important to offer users a reasonable level of feedback so that they know what's gone wrong. To do this, you need to know when a failed login attempt has been made. Re-inspect the Log In User server behavior and add a ?login=fail query string to the end of the URL for the failure page. Then, in an appropriate place on your login form (maybe above the submit button), include the following test:

```
<% if request.QueryString("login") = "fail" then %>
          <p class="error">Username or Password incorrect, please try again.</p>
<% end if %>
```

Display Logic

1. Of course, you don't want to display the login form once the user is
    already logged in. Therefore, switch into Code view and insert the follow-
    ing conditional statement around your login form:

    ```
    <% if session("MM_Username") = "" then %>
              <!-- login form here -->
    <% else %>
              <p>Log out</p>
    <% end if %>
    ```

    This logic basically says if there is no value held for the user's username,
    display the login form, otherwise display a Log out link.

2. Select the Log out text and apply the User Authentication/Log Out User
    server behavior as shown in Figure 10-8.

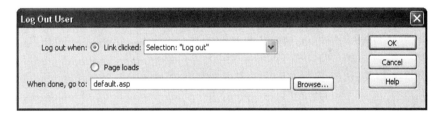

Figure 10-8. Applying the User Authentication/Log Out User server behavior

Storing Login Details Using a Cookie

Sometimes it's helpful to offer users an option to store their login details so that
the next time they return to the site they can simply click "log in" without the need
to re-enter their details. The login form you built has a check box set up for this,
but you need to add the appropriate ASP to make it function.

In the ASP block at the top of the header Include, add the following to store login details in a cookie:

```
' *** Store login details in a cookie
if Request.Form("username") <> "" and Request.Form("remember") = "true" then
        Response.Cookies("username") = Request.Form("username")
        Response.Cookies("username").Expires = dateadd("yyyy", 1, now)

        Response.Cookies("password") = Request.Form("password")
        Response.Cookies("password").Expires = dateadd("yyyy", 1, now)
end if
```

This will set a cookie when the user attempts a login and checks the box to remember details. The cookie will persist for a year, but that value can be configured by altering the Expires property.

Assembling the Admin Pages

Any site that uses a database to manage user and content needs a method of administrating that data. For a web application, it makes sense to use the same technologies to power our admin pages as for our front-end site.

1. Create a folder called **admin** and within it place the following placeholder files. Note that you don't need a page to add users because users for this site will register themselves.

    • user_view.asp

    • user_edit.asp

    • user_delete.asp

    • article_view.asp

    • article_add.asp

    • article_edit.asp

    • article_delete.asp

2. Each of these pages needs to have its access restricted to users with an access level of ADM. This is done with the User Authentication/Restrict Access To Page server behavior, shown in Figure 10-9. Apply this server behavior to each and every page in the admin section.

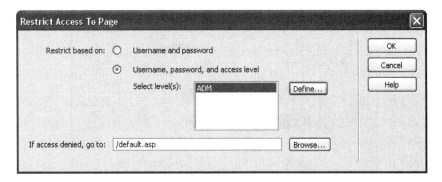

Figure 10-9. Applying the User Authentication/Restrict Access To Page server behavior

The application of this server behavior will result in users being redirected back to the home page if they do not have a value of ADM in the access level field.

3. Link all the pages into the site's main navigation, but place a conditional block around them so that they only appear if the user is an admin user.

```
<div id="navigation">
<% if Session("MM_UserAuthorization") = "ADM" then %>
        <p>
          <a href="/admin/user_view.asp">Manage Users</a>
        </p>
        <p>
          <a href="/admin/article_add.asp">Add New Article</a><br />
          <a href="/admin/article_view.asp">Manage Articles</a>
        </p>
<% end if %>
</div>
```

User Management

The user management will hinge on a list page displaying all the users—user_view.asp. For each user there will be a link to edit their details or to delete them from the database altogether.

1. Create a basic recordset containing all the users, sorted alphabetically by username, as shown in Figure 10-10. It's not common to display passwords in plain text, so for this page, leave the userPassword field unselected.

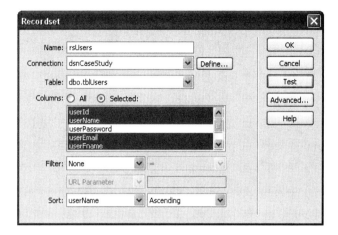

Figure 10-10. Creating a recordset

2. Insert a table, two rows by six columns, with a header row at the top, as shown in Figure 10-11. This will contain our list of users, with the Edit and Delete links.

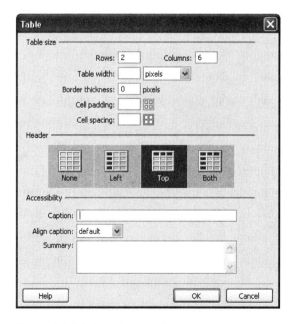

Figure 10-11. Creating a table

3. Insert the recordset fields into this table, and create a Repeat Region for all the data on the bottom row of the table, as shown in Figure 10-12.

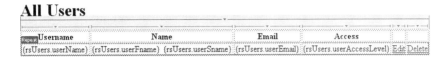

Figure 10-12. Creating a Repeat Region

4. Insert Edit and Delete links, with the user ID as a query string parameter.

    ```
    <a href="user_edit.asp?id=<%=(rsUsers.Fields.Item("userId").Value)%>">Edit</a>
    <a href="user_delete.asp?id=<%=(rsUsers.Fields.Item("userId").Value)%>">Delete</a>
    ```

5. Save your changes and preview the page in a browser to make sure it works. With any luck your two users (one admin, one regular user) will show up the in list.

Editing User Records

1. Open the user edit page. Create a recordset to bring back a user's record based on the value of the ID query string parameter, as shown in Figure 10-13.

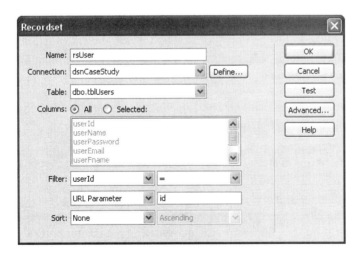

Figure 10-13. Creating a recordset

2. From the Application category of the Insert bar, choose the Record Update Form Wizard, as shown in Figure 10-14. Be sure to modify the labels to user-friendly names and select the appropriate display type. All your fields should submit as text. Remember not to include the userId field because this is a table ID and cannot be updated. If you leave it in, the database will return an error when you try to update.

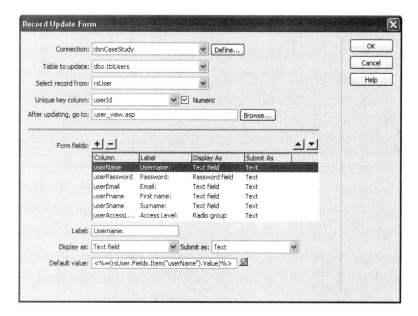

Figure 10-14. The Record Update Form Wizard

3. Click OK to insert the Record Update Form, and save the page. Check that the form is working as you expect by trying it out in the browser.

Deleting User Records

For the purposes of this exercise, you're going to create a junk user record in the users table so you can test the delete without messing up the data.

1. Open the user delete page and create a recordset just as on the edit page. Again it should be filtered on the query string parameter of ID against the user ID. Insert text on the page similar to **Are you sure you wish to delete this user?**, and then insert a form with a submit button.

2. From the Application category of the Insert bar, click Delete Record to display the Delete Record dialog box, as shown in Figure 10-15.

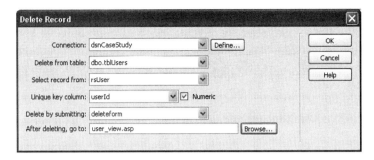

Figure 10-15. The Delete Record dialog box

3. Click OK and save your page. In the browser, check that the delete function is working by deleting the junk user you created.

Content Management

You manage articles almost the same way you manage users. You are essentially dealing with the same functionality, but with different data. Therefore, we will cover how to create the page to insert new articles here, but leave the list, edit, and delete pages up to you. You can follow the same directions given for user administration.

Adding a New Article

1. Open the `article_add.asp` page. From the Application category of the Insert bar, choose the Record Insertion Form Wizard, shown in Figure 10-16.

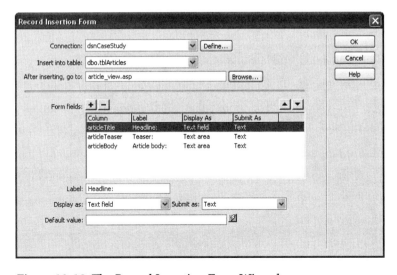

Figure 10-16. The Record Insertion Form Wizard

2. Choose your connection and table, and then browse for the article listing page to go to after the form has been submitted. In the Form Fields section, give each field a suitable label. Remember that `articleId` and `articleDate` are automatically filled in so you don't need to include them here.

3. Click OK, save the page, and check that it functions in a browser.

List, Edit, Delete

Again, the list, edit, and delete pages for articles are exactly the same as the ones you created for users. As a learning exercise, attempt to construct these pages by remembering what you learned so far in this chapter and the rest of the book. If you can't remember, refer back to the explanation of the user management pages and try again.

Constructing the Home Page

The purpose of the content management system and the articles is so you can display up-to-date news and articles on the site's home page. To that end, you need to devise a mechanism for displaying the articles.

Adding News Items

1. Create a recordset, selecting the articles in reverse date order, so that the newest appear at the top, as shown in Figure 10-17. For the home page, select only the headline, teaser, and date. The full article will only be available to logged in users.

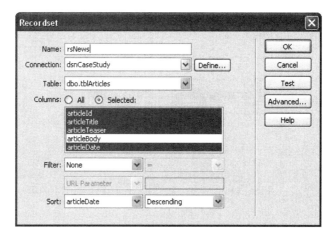

Figure 10-17. Creating a recordset

2. Using the Bindings panel, place the recordset data onto the page. After the teaser, create a More >> link to a page called `article_view.asp`, passing the article ID as a query string parameter called `id`, as shown in Figure 10-18. Then apply a Repeat Region to show the top ten articles.

News

Here's what's new on the site

Figure 10-18. The More >> link

3. Save the page and test it in a browser. Then open the article view page and create a recordset filtering on the article ID from the query string, as shown in Figure 10-19.

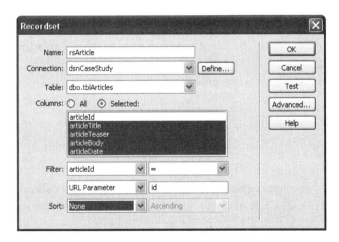

Figure 10-19. Creating a recordset

4. Insert the recordset fields into the page from the Bindings panel. This will enable users to click through from the More >> links on the home page to view the complete articles. However, you only want to allow logged in

users to access the complete articles, so you need to apply the User Authentication/Restrict Access To Page server behavior to allow both regular users and administrative users, as shown in Figure 10-20.

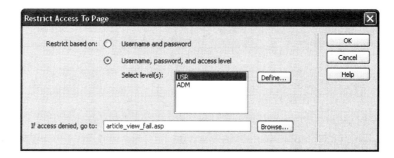

Figure 10-20. Applying the User Authentication/Restrict Access To Page server behavior

5. Create `article_view_fail.asp` as an error page, displaying a message instructing users to register and log in before reading the full articles. This page requires no particular functionality, just a simple and polite error message.

User Registration

The last major task in your application is user sign up. It's important to enable users to register themselves on the site, and not to have to rely on an administrator to perform this task.

In the root of the site, create two new files.

- `register.asp`

- `register_edit.asp`

The first of the two requires no access restriction, but the latter should only be available to logged in users, because you need to know which user you are going to be editing!

Registration

1. Open your new registration page. Instead of using the Record Insertion Form Wizard for this operation, you will create your own form. The important difference is that you need to include two password fields. These will be used for validation.

2. Insert a table of six rows and two columns. Set out the registration form using logical names for the fields. Don't forget the two password fields. Name one `password`, and the other `password_confirm`, as shown in Figure 10-21.

Register

Username:	
Password:	
Confirm:	
Email address:	
First name:	
Surname:	
	Register

Figure 10-21. The completed registration form

Of course, you now need a method of checking that the two passwords entered by the user match. For this you'll use Jaro von Flocken's Check Form behavior, which you can download from `http://www.yaromat.com/`.

3. Select your form, and from the Behaviors panel in the Tag Inspector panel group, apply Yaromat/Check Form, as shown in Figure 10-22. Select the registration form and go through each field making it required. For the email field, check the option to validate it as an email address.

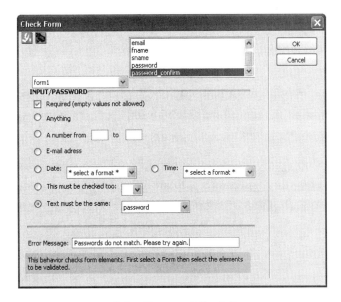

Figure 10-22. Applying Yaromat/Check Form

4. When you get to the `password_confirm` field, check Text must be the same and select the password field. Enter a custom error message explaining that the passwords don't match for when the user gets it wrong.

5. Apply the Insert Record server behavior, as shown in Figure 10-23.

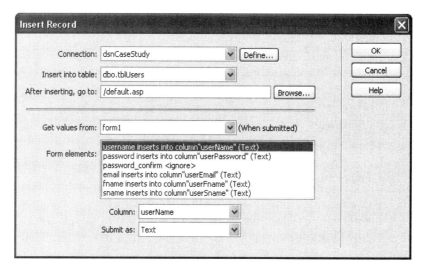

Figure 10-23. Applying the Insert Record server behavior

6. Test your registration form in a browser to make sure it's working as you expect. The last step is to add a link into the navigation Include so that the page can be accessed.

Editing User Details

Once users are signed up, it's helpful to enable them to edit their own details. You can do this using exactly the same form as used when the user registered, but with different server behaviors applied.

1. Open both the registration page and the registration edit page, and copy and paste the form from one to the other. Then create a recordset filtering the username on a session variable called `MM_Username`, as shown in Figure 10-24.

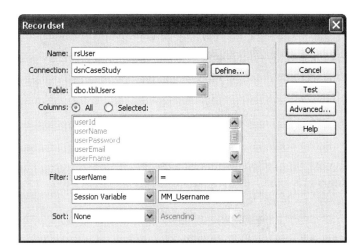

Figure 10-24. Creating a recordset

2. Bind the data from your recordset to the form fields so the user has the existing data as a starting point for his or her editing. Insert a hidden field called userId and bind the user ID to it. Then apply the Update Record server behavior to the form, as shown in Figure 10-25.

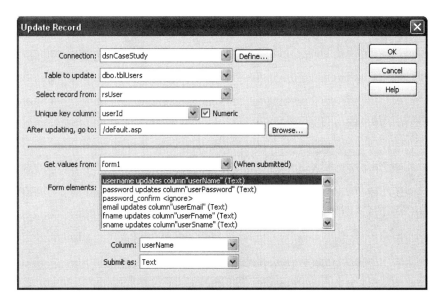

Figure 10-25. Applying the Update Record server behavior

3. Click OK, save your page, and test it out in a browser. Edit the navigation Include to link to the page.

Contact Form

The last piece of functionality you need to add is the contact form. It's sometimes helpful to give users a form to contact a site or company. This enables them to send an email directly from the contact page without needing to start their email client. It also offers the opportunity for the site to specify the information it wants to gather.

1. Create a new page called contact.asp and add a simple contact form, including name, email address, and message. Set the form to submit to contact.asp, as shown in Figure 10-26.

Contact us

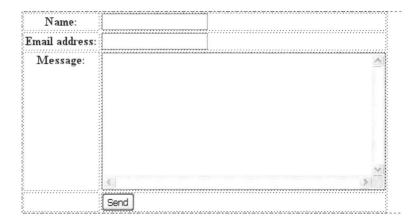

Figure 10-26. The contact form

2. Switch to Code view, and in the top of the page, enter the following:

```
<%
if len(request.form) > 0 then
Dim ObjMail
Set ObjMail = Server.CreateObject("CDO.Message")
objMail.From = request.form("name") & " <" & request.form("email") & ">"
objMail.To = "your.email@here.com"
objMail.Subject = "Contact from Your Website"
objMail.TextBody = request.form("message")
objMail.Send
Set objMail = Nothing
end if
%>
```

The code just shown detects that the form has been submitted and sends an email to the address in line five. This leaves you with issuing the user a thank you message. Wrap this conditional statement around your contact form.

```
<% if len(request.form) = 0 then %>
        <!-- your contact form goes here -->
<% else %>
        <p>Thank you for contacting us. Someone will be in touch
shortly.</p>
<% end if %>
```

Summary

In this chapter, you took the techniques you learned throughout various chapters in the book and applied them to a small but functional web application. You built a common site framework, an administration site, and front-end pages for users of different access levels. You should now be able to build web applications of your own based on these principles. Don't be afraid to re-read at any point if something is eluding you. All the best developers work with a stack of well-thumbed books on their desks.

Index

Numbers and symbols

4 Guys from Rolla
website address for, 376
& (ampersand)
concatenating variables with, 131–132
using to pass multiple name/value
pairs, 156
* (asterisk)
using to designate selection of all
columns, 195
= (equal sign)
assignment operator, 137–138
. (period)
denoting a class in a stylesheet with,
73
+ (plus sign)
using in place of ampersand (&), 132
+ (plus sign) button
clicking to add a variable to an SQL
statement, 253
(pound sign)
denoting an id in a stylesheet with, 73
use of for Access date values, 206
' (single quote)
use of for SQL Server date values, 206
_ (underscore) character
using in object and property names,
179
<!-- --> delimiters
for commenting code, 130
<% %> delimiters
for ASP script code, 124–125
<%= %>
writing data to a page with, 129–130

A

Access. *See* Microsoft Access 2000
accessibility
advantages of setting for people with
disabilities and all users, 91–92
Dreamweaver MX and, 89–113
importance of adding to web site
design, 91–92
innovative technology used by, 92
new national requirements for web
pages, 91
overview, 90–99
preferences options, 99–100

accessibility guidelines and standards
developed by W3C, 95–99
prioritized checkpoints, 95–97
recent adoption of, 89
Accessibility pane
in Preferences dialog box, 36–37
accessibility reference
included in Dreamweaver MX 2004,
110
Accessibility Reports tool
for validating web pages, 108–110
accesskey attribute
function of, 102
Add Book insert form
viewing in a browser, 269
Address bar
maximum length of characters
allowed in, 151
admin pages
assembling in the case study, 392–398
creating placeholder files for, 392
restricting access to in case study, 393
Advanced Recordset Builder
building more complex recordsets in,
214–217
vs. Simple Recordset Builder, 214
Advanced Recordset dialog box
after setting up SQL statement, 254
Database Items window in, 214–215
defining what CategoryID should
equal in, 215–216
example of completed, 217
Align property
setting for tables, 283
Allow Multiple Consecutive Spaces check
box
importance of leaving unchecked in
Preferences dialog box, 36
alt attribute
for spacer images with no content,
101
alternative (alt) text
general limitation for, 101
importance of in web pages for users
with disabilities, 94
ampersand (&)
concatenating variables with, 131–132
using to pass multiple name/value
pairs, 156

ASPToday is a unique solutions library for professional ASP Developers, giving quick and convenient access to a constantly growing library of **over 1000 practical and relevant articles and case studies**. We aim to publish a completely original professionally written and reviewed article every working day of the year. Consequently our resource is completely without parallel in the industry. Thousands of web developers use and recommend this site for real solutions, keeping up to date with new technologies, or simply increasing their knowledge.

Exciting Site Features!

Find it FAST!
Powerful full-text search engine so you can find exactly the solution you need.

Printer-friendly!
Print articles for a bound archive and quick desk reference.

Working Sample Code Solutions!
Many articles include complete downloadable sample code ready to adapt for your own projects.

ASPToday covers a broad range of topics including:

► ASP.NET 1.x and 2.0   ► Security
► ADO.NET and SQL   ► Site Design
► XML   ► Site Admin
► Web Services   ► SMTP and Mail
► E-Commerce   ► Classic ASP and ADO

                           and much, much more…

To receive a FREE two-month subscription to ASPToday, visit **www.asptoday.com/subscribe.aspx** and answer the question about this book!